A Programmer's Introduction to Computer Systems

Hardware and Software

A Programmer's Introduction to Computer Systems

Hardware and Software

John Graham and Roger Loader

Lecturers in the Department of Computer Science
Systems Architecture Group
University of Reading

McGRAW-HILL BOOK COMPANY

London · New York · St Louis · San Francisco · Auckland · Bogotá · Guatemala
Hamburg · Lisbon · Madrid · Mexico · Montreal · New Delhi
Panama · Paris · San Juan · São Paulo · Singapore · Sydney · Tokyo · Toronto

Published by
McGRAW-HILL Book Company (UK) Limited
MAIDENHEAD · BERKSHIRE · ENGLAND

British Library Cataloguing in Publication Data
Graham, John
    A programmer's introduction to computer
    systems.
    1. Computer systems
    I. Title   II. Loader, Roger
    004

    ISBN 0-07-084192-6

Library of Congress Cataloging-in-Publication Data
Graham, John (John M.)
    A programmer's introduction to computer systems: hardware and software/
John Graham and Roger Loader.
    p. cm.
    Bibliography: p.
    Includes index.
    ISBN 0-07-084192-6
    1. Electronic digital computers.   2. Computer software.
I. Loader, Roger. II. Title.
QA76.5.G6574 1989
004--dc19

1 2 3   AP   8 9

Printed and bound in Great Britain by Alden Press Ltd, Oxford

CONTENTS

Preface   ix

Abbreviations   xi

1. Computers and computer systems   1

    1.1   Hardware   2
    1.2   Computer system   7
    1.3   Computer system complex   9
    1.4   Division of memory between system and user   12
    1.5   Summary and overview   14

2. Representation and coding of information   15

    2.1   Encoding of letters and digits   15
    2.2   Representation of numbers to a base   17
    2.3   Representation of characters   20
    2.4   Conversion of decimal to binary, octal, hexadecimal   24
    2.5   Addition and subtraction in binary, octal, hexadecimal   25
    2.6   Representation of integers   27
    2.7   Representation of real numbers   33

3. Parallel communications – computer bus   39

    3.1   Information exchange – sample computer problem   39
    3.2   Computer bus mechanics   42
    3.3   Instruction fetch sequence and computer bus   44
    3.4   Formal control and timing of bus activities   48

4. Serial communications – local and wide area   59

    4.1   Information exchange – sample computer problem   59
    4.2   Computer networks   65

4.3 Public data network – wide area   74
4.4 Local area network – Ethernet   75
4.5 Local area network – Cambridge Ring   77

5. Computer Peripherals   80

5.1 The printing process   80
5.2 Overview of the computer production of human-readable
     information   82
5.3 Impact printers   83
5.4 Laser printer – a non-impact printer   86
5.5 Visual display unit (VDU)   87
5.6 Graphics devices   94
5.7 Magnetic disk   99
5.8 Magnetic tape   103
5.9 Conclusions   108

6. Assembler programming – elementary constructs   110

6.1 Memory   111
6.2 Processor   112
6.3 Assembler programming   119
6.4 Generation of assembler from a Pascal design   122

7. Assembler programming – advanced constructs   140

7.1 Arrays   140
7.2 Records   144
7.3 Procedures   146
7.4 Functions   155
7.5 Conclusions   157

8. Introduction to operating systems   161

8.1 Typical user interaction   161
8.2 Operating system view   161
8.3 User task representation   163
8.4 Interrupts and processes   166
8.5 Process representation   168
8.6 Dispatcher (low-level scheduler)   170
8.7 Scheduler   171
8.8 File handler   173

Bibliography   177

Appendix   178

  1 Summary of the simple register machine (SRM)   178
  2 Summary of the Motorola 68000 and high-level language
     templates   184
  3 Summary of the Intel 8086 and high-level language templates   198

Index   212

Preface

This book has been written as an introductory first-year text. The reader will find it helpful to have some experience of a high-level language such as Pascal and to have used an operating system like Unix. Some minimum acquaintance with mathematical and scientific notation is also required. It concentrates on what a programmer needs to know in order to begin to understand complex computer systems. However an attempt is always made to offer as simple a model as possible to explain the real-world events.

Although the hardware and actual machine-code instructions are described, they are always shown in a high-level language context if possible. Thus while it is admitted that assembler or machine code may be the final definition of a computer, these are approached from a high-level language standpoint through the use of program templates. The central exposition of the main features of an instruction set is through a model machine, the *simple register machine*, that has been specially designed for this purpose (defined in Appendix 1). This machine has been successfully used in teaching for several years and has been realized via an assembler–emulator system programmed in Pascal. Although the model machine has not been developed as a reduced instruction set computer (RISC), its simple features bring it closer to this than the architecture of many commercial microprocessors. The application of program templates to particular microprocessors is covered in appendices.

The material given in this book should enable the programmer to profit from more specialist books on computer hardware, peripherals, communications and operating systems. It should also be possible to make use of the manufacturer's specifications of microprocessors or other computers. Finally it should provide vital background information for anyone attempting to program, or understand, systems problems expressed in systems programming languages such as Modula 2 or language 'C'.

Our thanks go to all our colleagues in the Department of Computer Science, and especially to Anne Aust for her indispensable typographic assistance.

Various manufacturers have, upon request, kindly sent us photographs of their equipment. We are happy to acknowledge especially Digital Equipment

Co. Ltd and Hewlett-Packard Ltd, whose illustrations we have gratefully incorporated in the text.

Abbreviations

ACIA	asynchronous communications interface adaptor
ASCII	American Standards Committee for Information Interchange
b	byte
BCD	binary coded decimal
bps	bits per second
CC	condition code (see SRM)
CCITT	Consultative Committee of the International Telegraph and Telephone
CRT	cathode ray tube
DCE	data circuit-terminating equipment
DMA	direct memory access
DTE	data terminal equipment
hcf	highest common factor
HDLC	high-level data link control
IEEE	American Institute of Electrical and Electronic Engineers
ISO	International Standards Organization
LAN	local area network
OS	operating system
OSI	reference model for Open Systems Interconnection
PAD	packet assembler–disassembler
PC	program counter (see SRM)
R	register (see SRM)
RS-232-C	American Electrical Industries Association standard VDU
SR	status register (see SRM)
SRM	simple register machine (as defined in Appendix 1)
UART	universal asynchronous receiver transmitter
VDU	visual display unit

1
Computers and computer systems

Anyone who has used a high-level language (HLL) such as Pascal, in conjunction with an operating system like Unix, will be familiar with the precision with which statements and commands need to be formulated. Computer systems are in general very fussy about fine detail, and to get the system to do what the user requires needs a concentration of effort not only on the difficult part of the problem, but also on trivial matters such as punctuation. This stress on detail in both HLL and operating system (OS), gives the user an image of computing that may seem fixed, immutable and well defined; however, the system offered to the user is the product of a number of hardware and software designers who have attempted to reconcile a whole series of competing requirements, to produce a general-purpose system that will be found helpful by a reasonably large group of people. In this book the many layers of software and hardware will be peeled away, to get beyond the details and show overall how the designers have combined hardware and software to produce a complete computer system.

Some knowledge of how the computer works and performs is vital for a systems programmer, not only in understanding how an existing system might work but also in designing any future one. The hardware of a computer system consists of the processor, memory, disk, terminal and anything that can be touched, however constructed. The processor on the other hand obeys instructions, and it is these sequences of instructions or programs that constitute the software of the machine. The operating system itself consists of a large set of different programs that allow the ordinary user to take advantage of the high computing speed and storage capability offered by the hardware of the machine. The common software tools made available to the user include: compilers for high-level languages, editors, loaders, run-time systems, filing systems and a host of other facilities to help with getting work completed on a computer.

1.1   Hardware

Most electronic computers are unimpressive in appearance. Large machines, sometimes referred to as *mainframes*, are frequently accommodated in a series of specially designed racks that look like steel cupboards or filing cabinets. These are linked together by cables that are most easily placed under a false floor. A requirement for cleanliness, that is a lack of dust particles combined with the need to dissipate large amounts of heat from the cabinets normally means that large machines have to be placed in special air-conditioned rooms (Fig. 1.1). Visiting such rooms gives very little useful information about what a computer is or how it works. *Minicomputers* are also built into racking systems and although there may be fewer cabinets than with a main frame, their function is equally well disguised. Even *microcomputers* placed on a desk top, despite being easy to see and touch, still reveal nothing of how they work internally (Fig. 1.5(b)). What is required is a model of how a simple computer works that can be applied to mainframe, mini- and microcomputer alike.

The hardware of the computer consists of all the components from which it is assembled. Within an enclosure is held a racking system that allows for the mounting of widely different elements. These vary from power supplies to printed circuit boards to complete disk units. When assembled and plugged together in the right way, it is these components that enable the computer to carry out its various feats of arithmetic, logic and storage. Once more it is worth stressing that although all these components, including the integrated circuits or chips that contain the processing power of the machine, can be handled and inspected, this will not give any direct insight into how it works. Most computers can be thought of as consisting of a few logically distinct groups of components. The processor contains the main arithmetic/logic unit, which is used to transform data input to the computer by addition, subtraction and other well-defined operations (Fig. 1.2).

The *control* unit coordinates the sequencing of events that cause the machine to obey a program instruction. The repeated action of the processor is to fetch an instruction held in the *memory*, identify it and obey it. Because this action is repeated over a million times a second, a special register known as the *program counter* is reserved to point to the next instruction in the store. Any program merely consists of a sequence of such instruction accesses. Intermediary arithmetic values may be held in the processor in special *registers* that give very rapid access to the information. It usually takes much longer to send data to or from the main memory. Even so, the principle of keeping both program instructions and data in the main memory of the computer is central to its working. Normally both these quantities are held within the same linear store, which has a structure like a large one-dimensional array. It is nonetheless vital that system software should keep track of the division between instructions and data, since if the processor was to try and obey data as though it was program, random results would be achieved. The program counter is used to index or address the relevant memory cells, to give orderly access to program and data as required.

Figure 1.1 Large computer in an air-conditioned room (Courtesy of Hewlett-Packard Ltd)

In order to understand the main features of a computer, it is very helpful to have a concrete simple model of how it works. This will now be rehearsed in slightly more detail than previously. Figure 1.3 shows the memory and processor of a typical computer.

It is imagined that a sequence of program instructions have been placed in memory beginning at location 65 536 (often written as 64K, since K (for kilo) denotes 1024 in computing parlance). It consists of some simple assignments to the variable A, which is held as data at a higher memory location. The data location can be thought of as a box, which is large enough to contain an integer value. The program counter (PC) is a special register used to point to or address the memory location containing the next program instruction. Obeying the instruction in memory, shown in Fig. 1.3, can be described in a number of steps:

1. Processor fetches instruction from
   memory location indicated by PC: [64K   ]
2. Processor inspects current instruction,
   decodes it, and tells arithmetic unit to
   take appropiate action A: [0]
3. Processor increments PC:
   and repeats from step 1.   [64K + 1]

Clearly this sequence goes on fetching and obeying sequential instructions indefinitely. In practice it is vital that the instructions allow tests of values to be

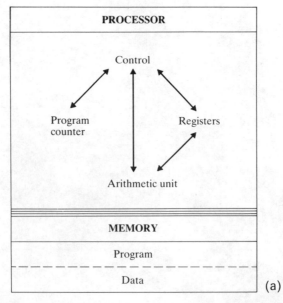

Figure 1.2 (a) Central part of a typical computer; (b) components of a computer on a printed circuit board (Courtesy of Hewlett-Packard Ltd)

Figure 1.2 (continued)

(b)

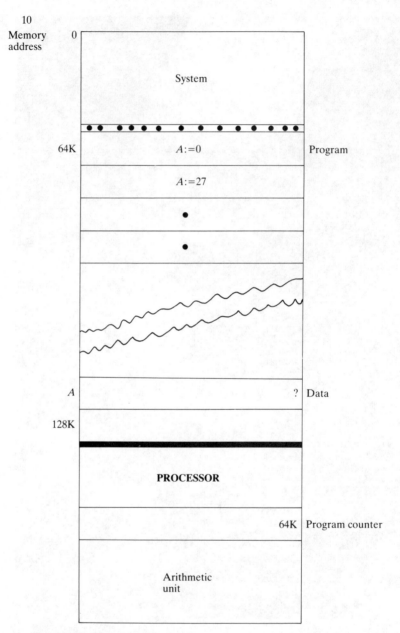

Figure 1.3   Memory with simple program for execution by processor

made, such as whether $A > 0$, and a choice of action to be taken. One sequence of instructions is obeyed if $A > 0$, and another if this is not true. It is these very simple operations that the computer is repeatedly and rapidly executing day after day.

1.2 Computer system

So far the hardware of the central part of the computer has been described, but the ability of the processor to rapidly transform data is only of use if fresh information can be input to the computer and results returned to the outside world. Devices that are suitable to fulfil this input/output function are termed *peripherals* because, whatever their nature, they are outside the central processing element of the machine. Hence a minimal useful computer system consists of processor, memory and computer terminal for the transfer of information. Figure 1.4 shows a typical multi-access system. Here the model processor works at 1 million instructions per second and has a memory big enough to store 1 million characters or bytes of information. These speeds and capacities are all given in round numbers to give the right order of magnitude for comparison. Another system might for example be able to obey 10 million instructions/s with a memory of 10 million bytes. To the central processor are connected a number

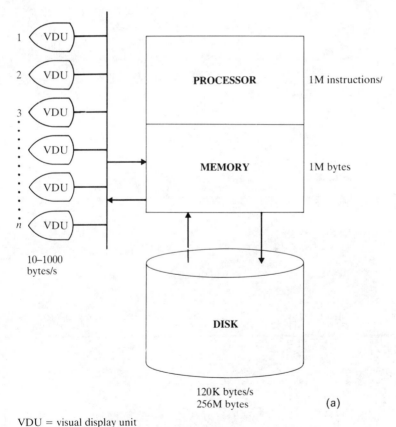

VDU = visual display unit

Figure 1.4 (a) Multi-access terminal computer system; (b) several terminals connected to a computer (Courtesy of Digital Equipment Co Ltd)

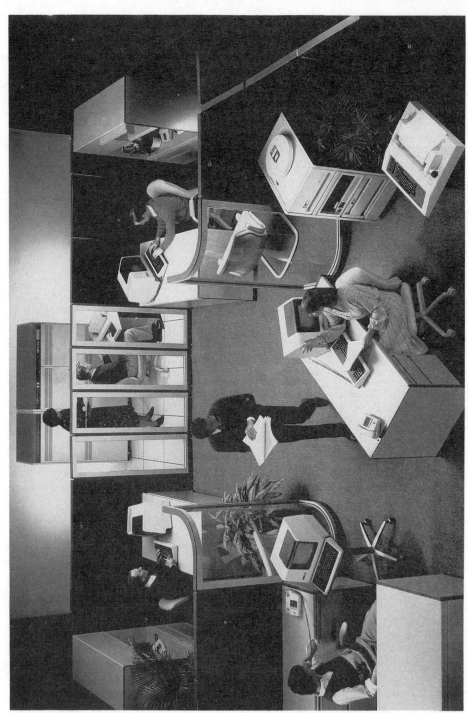

Figure 1.4 (continued)

(b)

of visual display units (VDU), with electronic keyboard and television screen to display 24 lines of 80 characters of textual information. Many terminals are connected to the computer so that several people can use the machine at the same time (multiaccess). It is possible for the processor and memory to be shared out in this way partly because of the slow working of the terminals. 10 bytes/s is usually more than adequate for anyone typing information into the computer, while 1000 bytes/s output is still quite slow when the processor is able to obey 1 million instructions/s. Hence it is normally possible for the processor to switch its attention from one user to the next, each person still having the impression that they have the whole of the computer to themselves.

Another vital element of the system is some sort of backing store. This is needed to extend the size of the main memory, which may be large enough to deal with a single problem for a user, but is far too small to deal with the information base accumulated to deal with the many problems of multiple users. Hence most systems have at least one disk store attached to them. In the model system of Fig. 1.4, 256 million bytes can be stored permanently on the disk. Its electromagnetic surfaces allow data to be written and then read back by request some time later. The speed of transfer, about 120 000 bytes/s, is slow when compared with the processor, but very fast when compared with a terminal working at best at 1000 bytes/s. Hence, like the processor and the memory, the disk capacity can be shared out between a number of users apparently at the same time.

A multiaccess system provides one model of a computer system. However, another equally valid model is that of a single-user system, where a processor with memory and disk is completely taken over by one person. These *personal computers*, or more sophisticated workstations, still have the same variety of peripherals to manage and hence require sophisticated software to help users solve their problems. Indeed with operating systems such as Unix, precisely the same operating system code can be used, both in a single user and a multiaccess context. For a single-user system a sophisticated graphics window manager may allow the control of multiple tasks. Figure 1.5 gives an idea of the type of dialogue that might be involved.

Each of the sub-windows allows the user to start, interact and control a different task or process. The clock is updated by one process, another compiles a high-level language program for the user, and in the foreground task the user is editing another program text. If a problem is sufficiently complex, it may be that several windows are devoted to helping with different aspects of it. But however different these tasks may appear from the user's point of view, the operating system will look on them as much like the multiple tasks created by a multiaccess system. Thus from a systems organization viewpoint, a sophisticated single-user system poses very similar problems to a multiaccess system.

1.3 Computer system complex

The computer systems described so far, whether used for multi-access or single-user access, are essentially isolated systems. However, in most large organizations there are a number of different computers, and there is a need to access them from the same terminal or to pass information from one computer to another. Figure 1.6 shows a computer complex linked together by a variety of means.

Two fast local area networks, Ethernet and the Cambridge Ring, are shown, allowing fast communications up to 10 million bits/s. It will be noted that most of the computers are linked to only one of the networks; in the ideal world they would all be joined to the same network in a similar way. Terminal connections can also be made to one or other of the networks, but both Ethernet and the Cambridge Ring are frequently restricted to linking computers together in the same building or within a few hundred metres. Hence on Fig. 1.6, the mainframe computer is shown to be made available via a packet switch network through

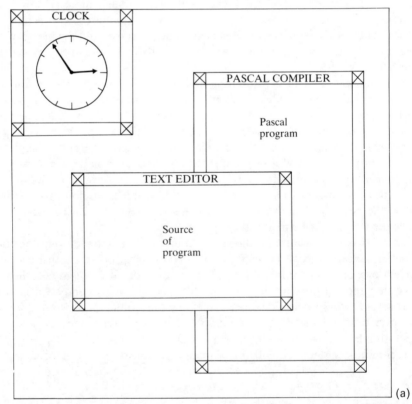

Figure 1.5 (a) Typical window manager software for a single-user system; (b) window manager with multiple tasks in an office environment (Courtesy of Hewlett-Packard Ltd)

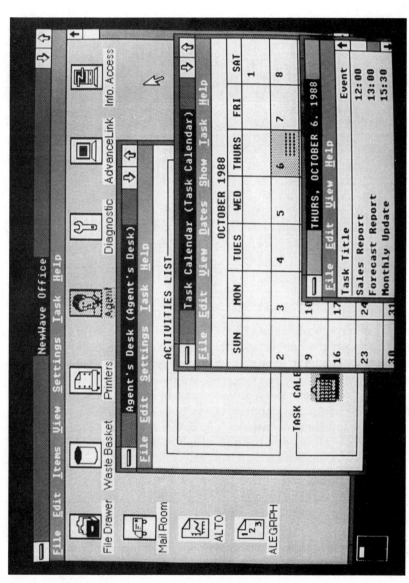

Figure 1.5 (continued)

(b)

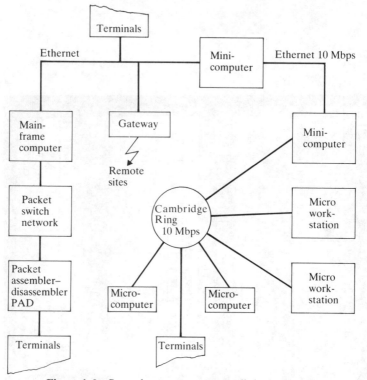

Figure 1.6   Several computer systems linked together

a packet assembler–disassembler (PAD). This then means that terminals can access the computer through a single telephone link between the PAD and the computer, thus potentially giving much longer distance communications of several kilometres. Finally a gateway is shown that provides communications with other remote computers, in a different town or even in a different country. The basis of these computer communications, both local and wide area, will be considered more fully in later chapters. For now it is sufficient to note that the communication of information is just as vital as its transformation by computers.

1.4   Division of memory between system and user

Although a firm model has been given of the processor obeying a single program at any one time, it is also essential that the computer system is able to change from one program to another. Thus a whole series of programs are loaded into the memory of the computer, waiting to be obeyed. Figure 1.7 shows a typical memory layout that allows the processor to switch rapidly from one program to another.

The operating system normally takes charge of all the peripherals, so that they can be equitably shared out between the different programs that may be competing for them. Even the humble terminal, which may appear to be entirely within the user's grasp, is in reality completely serviced by the system on behalf of the user. To this end, the system has special handling programs that deal with the differences between the various devices. For line printers they will make sure that complete user documents are printed sequentially, before the device would be available for another user. The disk, on the other hand, needs to be accessed by a number of users at approximately the same time. The handler needs to be especially careful to interleave reads and writes of information, to try and share

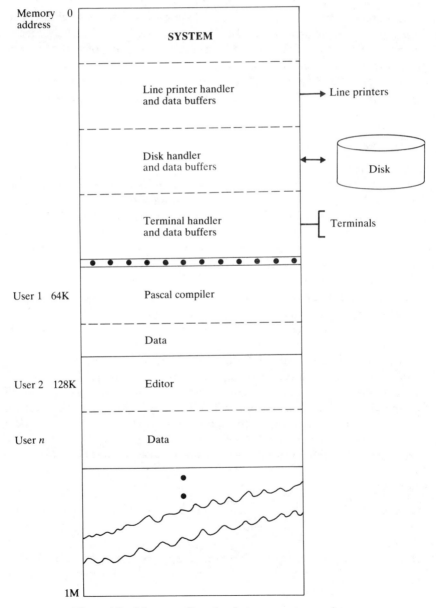

Figure 1.7   Memory allocation between system and users

out the capacity of the disk amongst the users. The terminal handler again needs to try and keep all users active, by transferring information as rapidly as possible. In all cases the handlers will be moving data in and out of memory, and to help with this process they will buffer variable amounts of information in system memory to try and even out extremes of input–output activity.

In addition to these many system tasks, there are also a number of separate areas reserved for users. It is imagined in Fig. 1.7 that user 1 is making use of the Pascal compiler, and user 2 is editing a program. The system needs to try and keep each user active by devoting appropriate resources to them. Each user can have his own separate area of memory, but the processor has to be switched from one program to another. Thus by obeying some instructions for each user in turn, it may be possible to make sufficient progress with each program that everyone is satisfied. At any rate, it is the task of the operating system to take on this complex organization, and to be as efficient as possible in sharing out the resources available.

1.5   Summary and overview

This introductory chapter has established a simple model of how the hardware of a computer functions and of the tasks which are frequently assigned to the software of the operating system. It is now necessary to analyse each of these elements in more detail. As a preliminary to that, Chapter 2 establishes the representation and coding of information on computers. Chapter 3 builds up how information is manipulated within the computer, while Chapter 4 is concerned to see how information is communicated over local and wide area networks. Chapter 5 further investigates how information can be represented in printed and displayed form, as well as stored on a variety of computer peripherals. Chapter 6 and 7 return again to a detailed examination of the processor, this time from a programming point of view. Here, in order to describe the many low-level instructions, a model machine, the *simple register machine* (SRM), is used extensively. It is formally defined in Appendix 1. The dominant theme in describing machine architecture is the way in which high-level languages are supported through a detailed specification of machine instructions. Having established how the machine works, and how it may be programmed in detail, Chapter 8 returns once again to the central tasks that the operating system performs, to give the user a high-level view of the computer system hardware and software much more in tune with the problems he wishes to solve.

Exercises

1. Draw a diagram that shows the main elements of the largest single computer to which you have access. Identify the speeds and capacities of all the main elements.
2. Draw a box diagram representing all the computers on a complex site known to you. Identify them and show how they are linked together, noting the speed of the communications employed.

2
Representation and coding of information

In order to convey or manipulate information in any way, a suitable representation needs to be found. From a computing point of view, the main distinction to be drawn is whether the information is analogue or digital. Analogue information can be thought of as continuous; for example the sound of someone's voice or a piece of music produces a complex wave form that varies continuously with time. Digital information on the other hand is typified by discrete steps or changes; for example a turnstyle counting people proceeds from one number to another by a series of well-defined discrete steps. Digital computers are built round the idea of representing all information by a finite set of states. In practice this is not only applied to numbers, where there is an obvious correlation between a number and discrete state, but also to analogue data. Here the analogue waveform will be represented by a discrete series of numbers that approximate the continuous waveform. Hence prime concern is with the digital representation of data, and digital models, despite the fact that the real world remains obstinately continuous in its variation.

2.1 Encoding of letters and digits

Words and numbers are commonly used to represent information. They require the specification of a discrete set of valid symbols. Each one of these, known as letter or digit, is distinctly different from any other member of the set. Words or numbers can then be identified, by being placed adjacently on lines from left to right with blank spaces indicating the separation of a discrete word or number. Reading is the acquired skill of recognizing the groupings of words and building up complete sentences from sequences of words from left to right across the page. Most message systems rely heavily on these simple conventions in order to convey information. Morse code, for example, allows the exchange of an infinite range of information by a series of short or long signals. These might typically be expressed by a bell that sounds at the other end of a wire, or by a light that is switched on and off. Morse retains the normal conventions of representing information by a sequence of digits and letters, and it is necessary only to invent a fresh encoding for them to adapt it for a new medium.

2.1.1 MORSE CODE

The achievement of Samuel Morse was a milestone in communications history not just because of his coding scheme, but also because he set up a telegraph line between Washington and Baltimore that by 1844 was exchanging messages between the two. Essentially the letters and digits are coded by a sequence of short or long signs, conventionally represented on paper by dots and dashes. Figure 2.1 shows a selection of Morse codes for some familiar symbols.

The coding adopted for the digits provides a sequence that relates to the value of the digit. Zero has five dashes, one a single dot followed by four dashes, two has two dots and so on through the series. This is easy to understand for digits, but it is not followed for letters. For the alphabet the time or effort to encode the letter was taken into account. Hence the letter E, by far the most common in English, has been given the minimum encoding, namely a single dot. The rest of the letters are encoded in declining order of their frequency of occurrence. Special symbols such as question mark and comma are also included to allow the message to use the full conventions of written English. In addition, further symbols have been generated to deal with some of the problems of the new medium. Once a symbol has been sent it is difficult to correct it, hence an error symbol can be transmitted to cancel the last symbol. As well as the usual pauses between words and punctuation, it is also vital to be able to recognize the beginning and end of messages. Hence there are two unique symbols to *start* and *stop* transmission.

For successful transmission and reception of a message using Morse, there

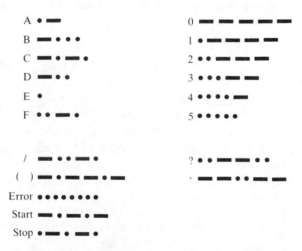

Figure 2.1 Morse code for selected symbols

needs to be a well-defined mapping or encoding of the symbols as described. However, the system also relies on the presence of two trained operators to complete the transaction. The speed at which they work is determined by their ability to distinguish between a sequence of dots and dashes. This gives an upper bound to the rate of message exchange. Other factors are important in practice, such as the fact that the timing of the operator may not be perfect, but it may still be possible for the receiver to make sense of the word because of his general understanding of spelling and language. Equally, the medium itself will not perfectly reproduce the dots and dashes: especially over long distances, some may become indistinguishable. Hence errors are introduced to the system, but because there are human beings involved in the message encoding and decoding it may be possible to correct them immediately. However, if the received message has too many errors in it, there will be no alternative but to request its retransmission. This process will of course affect the rate at which messages can be successfully exchanged over the media. These additional factors, noted for Morse code exchanges, are equally vital when the details of computer communications are examined.

2.2 Representation of numbers to a base

In current technology most digital computers operate on information held in a very simple form. Characters, numbers, instructions are all held as binary numbers. That is, they use a number system with a base of 2, as opposed to the more familiar decimal system with base 10. In the binary system there are only two different digits, one and zero, hence its claim to be the simplest possible system. This simplicity makes it very convenient for electronic manipulation, as the circuitry needs only to be able to distinguish between two states. Thus the design tolerance and possible error correction are very much easier than with a 10-state system, for example. However, when it comes to representing numbers of any size, it is very difficult for human beings to distinguish between long sequences of 1s and 0s. Hence it is necessary to be able to translate from binary to more convenient bases, such as hexadecimal (base 16), octal (base 8) and of course decimal.

2.2.1 BINARY, OCTAL AND HEXADECIMAL EQUIVALENCE

In order to establish the principles of the different number bases used, the first four binary digits are tabled with their equivalents in Fig. 2.2. The binary numbers, as decimal, rely on positional significance.

msb			lsb
1	0	1	1

The least significant bit, as it is called, is written on the right-hand side and each digit to the left represents the next highest power in the base, ending with the most significant bit as the last digit position on the left.

Binary	Hexadecimal	Octal	Decimal
0000	0	0	0
0001	1	1	1
0010	2	2	2
0011	3	3	3
0100	4	4	4
0101	5	5	5
0110	6	6	6
0111	7	7	7
1000	8	10	8
1001	9	11	9
1010	A	12	10
1011	B	13	11
1100	C	14	12
1101	D	15	13
1110	E	16	14
1111	F	17	15

Figure 2.2   Binary, octal and hexadecimal conversion table

On Fig. 2.2 zero is represented by four zeros, because the numbers examined will take up four binary digit positions. It is usual, when writing binary numbers, to retain leading zeros to show the magnitude of the number, while in decimal notation these are normally omitted. Hence binary one is represented as:

$$0001$$

rather than a single one. In order to represent two, the next most significant digit position is needed:

$$0010$$

while decimal three again requires the least significant bit:

$$0011$$

Notice that all odd numbers have the least significant bit set to 1. For larger numbers the next binary digit position will be required, and it can be seen that these form a simple series when mapped back into decimal:

Decimal equivalent: 8   4   2   1

Binary digit: | 1 | 0 | 1 | 0 |

Each time a binary digit position becomes more significant the decimal equivalent is doubled, hence 1,2,4,8 ... Using the equivalents the above four-bit number can be written as

$$(8 + 0 + 2 + 0)_{10}$$

which of course gives the answer decimal 10.

The hexadecimal column of Fig. 2.2 is very easy to explain for the numbers 0–9, as it is exactly the same as the decimal representation. However, thereafter base 16 is still able to represent larger numbers in a single digit position. Hence new single digits need to be invented to represent decimal 10–15. In practice nothing new was invented, but the first few letters (capital A to F) were re-used to represent the required digits. Hence

$$10_{10} \equiv A_{16}$$

and so on, as shown in Fig. 2.2. Octal representation has the first seven digits in common with decimal; thereafter it has to utilize a second octal digit that allows it to get up to the equivalent of decimal 15.

Most computers use a fixed number of bits to represent integers. Using binary, 2^n integers can be held, where n is a count of the number of bits allocated to store the integer. For example:

Bits		Integers
4	2^4	16
8	2^8	256
16	2^{16}	65 536

2.2.2 BITS, BYTES, WORDS

The representation of four bits in hexadecimal and octal has been explored in an informal way to try and explain some of the differences between the number bases. However, the normal minimum item of information is a byte of 8 bits. Various larger groupings may also be referred to, for example:

$$\text{byte} = 8 \text{ bits}$$
$$\text{word} = 2 \text{ bytes or } 16 \text{ bits}$$
$$\text{longword} = 4 \text{ bytes or } 32 \text{ bits}$$

However, after the byte, there is no uniformity in naming convention; the length of words, halfwords, doublewords or longwords varies from one computer to another. The only common denominator is the byte and it is to byte conversion that attention will now be paid. Figure 2.3 shows 8 bits with the hexadecimal and octal digit positions indicated with their decimal equivalents.

The example takes the binary string 10101010 and shows how this can produce the equivalent numbers in other bases by simple addition. The decimal number is produced by reading off the decimal equivalent given in the topmost columns of Fig. 2.3(a), in every position a binary one occurs. All the numbers shown in brackets beneath should be summed to produce 170_{10}. The conversion between binary and hexadecimal is easier. Since $2^4 = 16$, it is only necessary to partition the string into successive groups of four. Each group can then be converted independently. This will be true for any 2^n base, and is explored more fully later. The hexadecimal digit divisions are shown directly on Fig. 2.3(b) as the numbers 4 and 4, because four bits make up each hexadecimal digit. In order

Decimal equivalent:	128	64	32	16	8	4	2	1
Binary:	1	0	1	0	1	0	1	0

(a)

Hexadecimal equivalent:	8	4	2	1	8	4	2	1
Binary:	1	0	1	0	1	0	1	0
Hexadecimal digits:	4				4			

(b)

Octal equivalent:	2	1	4	2	1	4	2	1
Binary:	1	0	1	0	1	0	1	0
Octal digits:	2		3			3		

(c)

Figure 2.3 Hexadecimal and octal digits derived from an 8-bit byte:
(a) decimal $(128 + 0 + 32 + 0 + 8 + 0 + 2 + 0) = 170_{10}$;
(b) hexadecimal $(8 + 0 + 2 + 0)(8 + 0 + 2 + 0) = AA_{16}$;
(c) octal $(2 + 0)(4 + 0 + 1)(0 + 2 + 0) = 252_8$

to derive the actual hexadecimal digit required, the decimal numbers in the top row must be selected wherever a binary one occurs, and summed in two groups of four as shown in brackets beneath the diagram, which produces the result AA_{16}. Finally the octal digit divisions are shown on Fig. 2.3(c) starting from the left as 2,3,3; thus producing a somewhat awkward mapping for a single byte. However the procedure is similar, this time taking the decimal equivalent given in the top row. Starting from the right, the first three binary digits give the least significant octal digit, the next three binary digits give the second octal digit and the final two binary digits the final octal digit. These groups are summed separately as before and give the answer 252_8. Using this method the decimal, hexadecimal and octal equivalents of any eight-bit binary number can be derived directly from Fig. 2.3. For larger binary numbers other methods will be described later.

2.3   Representation of characters

While it is true that everything within a digital computer is held in binary, it is also true that all information can be coded using the characters of the alphabet and the digits 0 to 9. For example, every VDU sends and receives the bit pattern given by the ASCII (American Standard Code for Information Interchange) character code. Thus in the field of communications ASCII can claim to be the Morse code of computers. Figure 2.4 shows the encoding for letters, digits, punctuation and various special controls.

Dec.	ASCII Char.	Code msb lsb		Hex.	Dec.	ASCII Char.	Code msb lsb		Hex
48	0	011	0000	30	96	'	110	0000	60
49	1	011	0001	31	97	a	110	001	61
50	2	011	0010	32	98	b	110	0010	62
51	3	011	0011	33	99	c	110	0011	63
52	4	011	0100	34	100	d	110	0100	64
53	5	011	0101	35	101	e	110	0101	65
54	6	011	0110	36	102	f	110	0110	66
55	7	011	0111	37	103	g	110	0111	67
56	8	011	1000	38	104	h	110	1000	68
57	9	011	1001	39	105	i	110	1001	69
58	:	011	1010	3A	106	j	110	1010	6A
59	;	011	1011	3B	107	k	110	1011	6B
60	<	011	1100	3C	108	l	110	1100	6C
61	=	011	1101	3D	109	m	110	1101	6D
62	>	011	1110	3E	110	n	110	1110	6E
63	?	011	1111	3F	111	o	110	1111	6F
64	@	100	0000	40	112	p	111	0000	70
65	A	100	0001	41	113	q	111	0001	71
66	B	100	0010	42	114	r	111	0010	72
67	C	100	0011	43	115	s	111	0011	73
68	D	100	0100	44	116	t	111	0100	74
69	E	100	0101	45	117	u	111	0101	75
70	F	100	0110	46	118	v	111	0110	76
71	G	100	0111	47	119	w	111	0111	77
72	H	100	1000	48	120	x	111	1000	78
73	I	100	1001	49	121	y	111	1001	79
74	J	100	1010	4A	122	z	111	1010	7A
75	K	100	1011	4B	123	{	111	1011	7B
76	L	100	1100	4C	124	|	111	1100	7C
77	M	100	1101	4D	125	}	111	1101	7D
78	N	100	1110	4E	126	~	111	1110	7E
79	O	100	1111	4F	127	DEL	111	1111	7F
80	P	101	0000	50					
81	Q	101	0001	51					
82	R	101	0010	52					
83	S	101	0011	53					
84	T	101	0100	54					
85	U	101	0101	55					
86	V	101	0110	56					
87	W	101	0111	57					
88	X	101	1000	58					
89	Y	101	1001	59					
90	Z	101	1010	5A					
91	[	101	1011	5B					
92	\	101	1100	5C					
93	]	101	1101	5D					
94	↑	101	1110	5E					
95	–	101	1111	5F					

Figure 2.4   ASCII encoding system

Dec.	ASCII Char.	Code msb lsb	Hex.	Comments.	
0	NUL	000 0000	00	Control – @	Null
1	SOH	000 0001	01	Control – A	Start of h(
2	STX	000 0010	02	Control – B	Start of te
3	ETX	000 0011	03	Control – C	End of tex
4	EOT	000 0100	04	Control – D	End of tra
5	ENQ	000 0101	05	Control – E	Enquiry
6	ACK	000 0110	06	Control – F	Acknowle(
7	BEL	000 0111	07	Control – G	Bell (audib
8	BS	000 1000	08		Back spac(
9	HT	000 1001	09		Horizontal
10	LF	000 1010	0A		Line feed
11	VT	000 1011	0B		Vertical ta
12	FF	000 1100	0C		Form feed
13	CR	000 1101	0D		Carriage re
14	SO	000 1110	0E	Control – N	Shift out
15	SI	000 1111	0F	Control – O	Shift in
16	DLE	001 0000	10	Control – P	Data link (
17	DC1	001 0001	11	Control – Q	Device con
18	DC2	001 0010	12	Control – R	Device con
19	DC3	001 0011	13	Control – S	Device con
20	DC4	001 0100	14	Control – T	Device con
21	NAK	001 0101	15	Control – U	Negative a(
22	SYN	001 0110	16	Control – V	Synchrono(
23	ETB	001 0111	17	Control – W	End of trar
24	CAN	001 1000	18	Control – X	Cancel
25	EM	001 1001	19	Control – Y	End of me(
26	SUB	001 1010	1A	Control – Z	Substitute
27	ESC	001 1011	1B	Control – [	Escape
28	FS	001 1100	1C	Control – \	File separat
29	GS	001 1101	1D	Control –]	Group sepa
30	RS	001 1110	1E	Control – ↑	Record sep;
31	US	001 1111	1F	Control – __	Unit separa
32	SP	010 0000	20		Space
33	!	010 0001	21		
34	"	010 0010	22		
35	#	010 0011	23		
36	$	010 0100	24		
37	%	010 0101	25		
38	&	010 0110	26		
39	‘	010 0111	27		
40	(	010 1000	28		
41	)	010 1001	29		
42	*	010 1010	2A		
43	+	010 1011	2B		
44	,	010 1100	2C		
45	-	010 1101	2D		
46	.	010 1110	2E		
47	/	010 1111	2F		

A further example which gives a slightly longer series:

Binary	Octal	Hexadecimal
$270 \div 2 = 135r0$	$270 \div 8 = 33r6$	$270 \div 16 = 16rE$
$135 \div 2 = 67r1$	$33 \div 8 = 4r1$	$16 \div 16 = 1r0$
$67 \div 2 = 33r1$	$4 \div 8 = 0r4$	$1 \div 16 = 0r1$
$33 \div 2 = 16r1$		
$16 \div 2 = 8r0$	$= 416_8$	$= 10E_{16}$
$8 \div 2 = 4r0$		
$4 \div 2 = 2r0$		
$2 \div 2 = 1r0$		
$1 \div 2 = 0r1$		

$$= 100001110_2$$

The conversion from a number to the base b to a decimal number is achieved by multiplying out the polynomial representation. This is shown in the following examples:

binary 101

$$(1 \times 2^2) + (0 \times 2^1) + (1 \times 2^0)$$
$$= 4 + 0 + 1 = 5_{10}$$

octal 101

$$(1 \times 8^2) + (0 \times 8^1) + (1 \times 8^0)$$
$$= 64 + 0 + 1 = 65_{10}$$

hexadecimal 101

$$(1 \times 16^2) + (0 \times 16^1) + (1 \times 16^0)$$
$$= 256 + 0 + 1 = 257_{10}$$

The number systems described all rely on this positional significance, and this is fundamental in the methods adopted to convert from one number base to another. This is necessary because most digital computers work in binary, but most people are normally using the decimal system.

2.5   Addition and subtraction in binary, octal, hexadecimal

Addition and subtraction in binary, octal and hexadecimal are very useful for understanding and checking the operation of the computer arithmetic unit. The addition of single digits in decimal or any other base may produce a carry digit. Similarly subtraction may involve the use of a borrow digit. The rules governing these operations can be summarized algorithmically. For addition, given two digits x and y to the base b, the *sum* and *carry* digits can be calculated in the following way:

$$sum := x + y$$
$$\textbf{if } sum >= b$$
$$\textbf{then}$$
$$\quad sum := sum - b$$
$$\quad carry := 1$$
$$\textbf{else}$$
$$\quad carry := 0$$

Subtracting y from x, the *difference* and *borrow* digits can be calculated in the following way:

$$\textbf{if } x < y$$
$$\textbf{then}$$
$$\quad difference := b + x - y$$
$$\quad borrow := 1$$
$$\textbf{else}$$
$$\quad difference := x - y$$
$$\quad borrow := 0$$

The binary operations are sufficiently compact to be summarized in tabular form:

Binary addition table

$$0 + 0 = 0$$
$$0 + 1 = 1$$
$$1 + 0 = 1$$
$$1 + 1 = 0 \text{ carry } 1$$

Binary subtraction table

$$0 - 0 = 0$$
$$1 - 0 = 1$$
$$1 - 1 = 0$$
$$0 - 1 = 1 \text{ borrow } 1$$

For multiple-digit numbers the preceding rules need to be applied digit by digit from the least significant end, including *carry* or *borrow* as appropriate. When *carry* is involved the digit sum must add the three elements $x + y + carry$ as pairs of digits. Similarly for a *borrow* the next digit subtraction has the form $x - (y + borrow)$.

Examples of addition for the three related bases binary, octal and hexadecimal are given below:

$binary_2$	$octal_8$	$hexadecimal_{16}$	
11010101	325	D 5	note D = 13_{10}
+ 1101	+ 15	+ D	
11100010	342	E 2	
111 1	1	1	

The existence of a carry is shown explicitly below the sum according to the usual conventions of positional significance. The given binary addition table can be applied to each binary digit sum, twice in the case where carry is involved. The octal digit addition can be performed using the algorithmic rules given earlier, i.e. if the result is greater than or equal to the base 8, subtract 8 to give the result digit and generate a carry. An example of this is the addition of the least significant digits in the octal addition given above. Hexadecimal addition is complicated by the existence of the digits A to F. The most convenient way of coping with this problem is to mentally convert the letter to its two-digit decimal equivalent, and then apply the rule as before, i.e. using conventional decimal addition. The result needs to be converted back to hexadecimal notation and the relevant digit recorded. The hexadecimal sum above illustrates this.

Examples of subtraction for the three related bases, binary, octal and hexadecimal, are given below:

$binary_2$	$octal_8$	$hexadecimal_{16}$
2		16
11010101	325	D 5
− Ø1101	− 15	−Ø D
1		1
11001000	310	C 8

When subtracting y from x, the *difference* and *borrow* digits can be calculated according to the algorithm shown previously. In the above examples, when a borrow is needed, the base b value is written above the current x digit, thus faciliating the calculation $b + x - y$. The *borrow* is added to the next most significant y value, thus setting up the next digit subtraction of the form: $x - (y + borrow)$. In the examples this is shown by crossing through the y value and placing the new digit beneath. For the hexadecimal subtraction it is assumed that the working can be most conveniently shown in decimal, though as before the results need to be converted back to hexadecimal notation.

2.6 Representation of integers

The use of binary to represent a decimal number has already been established. However, decimal integers are normally signed quantities. On a computer the number of digits available to represent an integer is usually fixed. If three decimal digits are chosen a total of 1000 integers, 0..999, could be represented. The addition of a sign, either + or −, would give equal numbers of positive and negative integers. This *signed magnitude* representation could be used on a computer, but there are advantages if the digits themselves can be used to indicate the sign of the number. In practice, the most common way of representing integers on a computer uses a *complementary* number system which has this property. The basis of this will be illustrated using three decimal digits. Once more, 1000 integers can be represented, but it is required that roughly equal numbers of positive and negative integers can be distinguished without the inclusion of a further symbol. The complementary system solves this problem by mapping the positive range $0..+499$ and the negative range $-1..-500$ onto the original $0..999$ as follows:

$$0..+499 \quad \text{to} \quad 000..499$$

$$-1..-500 \quad \text{to} \quad 999..500$$

This gives approximately 500 integers in each of the ordered sets of positive and negative integers, the relationship is illustrated in the following:

Tens complement

500	501	...	996	997	998	999	000	001	002	003	004	...	499
-500	-499	...	-4	-3	-2	-1	0	$+1$	$+2$	$+3$	$+4$	...	$+499$

Signed magnitude decimal

The positive signed magnitude integers given below the line are in step and identical with the tens complement given above the line. This is not the case with the negative integers and this may at first sight seem contradictory. However, the mapping of 999 to -1, 998 to -2 and so on, has an important consequence. In signed magnitude the addition of numbers on either side and equidistant from zero, n to $-n$, gives the answer zero. The addition of 999 to 001 in tens complement gives 000 with a carry. Thus ignoring the carry, complementary representation produces the same zero result, without the need to manipulate a separate sign.

Although tens complement has been illustrated, the normal representation for integers used on a machine is twos complement, as this relates directly to binary. As an example four binary digits are shown represented in twos complement and signed magnitude. With the desire to hold approximately the same number of positive and negative integers this gives a range of $+7$ to -8, following the conventions adopted previously:

Twos complement

1000	...	1100	1101	1110	1111	0000	0001	0010	0011	0100	...	0111
-8	...	-4	-3	-2	-1	0	$+1$	$+2$	$+3$	$+4$	...	$+7$

Signed magnitude decimal

Twos complement has similar properties to those already noted for tens complement. In particular numbers either side and equidistant from zero produce a zero sum (ignoring carry), thus allowing the representation of positive and negative numbers without the manipulation of a separate sign. In twos complement the most significant bit conveniently acts as an implicit sign, with zero indicating a positive and one a negative integer.

2.6.1   TENS COMPLEMENT CONVERSION AND SUBTRACTION

For positive integers, as explained in the previous section, apart from the omission of the sign, tens complement stays in step and identical to signed magnitude. Thus conversion between the two is trivial. Given a negative integer the tens complement of it may be formed by subtracting each digit of the number from the base minus one $(10 - 1 = 9)$, and adding one to the least significant digit. As an example returning to a three-digit decimal representation, the conversion of -87 and -323 is illustrated to show how negative numbers are treated:

Conversion:

$$
\begin{array}{r}
999 \\
- 87 \\
\hline
912 \\
+ 1 \\
\hline
913 \\
\end{array}
\qquad
\begin{array}{r}
999 \\
- 23 \\
\hline
676 \\
+ 1 \\
\hline
677 \\
\end{array}
$$

So -87 is 913 tens complement and -323 is 677 tens complement.

If the subtraction of two integers is symbolized by $x - y$, x can be called the *minuend* and y the *subtrahend*. In a complementary notation subtraction can be achieved through the use of addition, by rewriting the subtraction as $x + (-y)$. This implies that the first operation is the negation of y. Thus to carry out subtraction, add the tens complement of the subtrahend to the minuend and discard the final carry. For example to carry out $x - y$, with $x = 89$ and $y = 87$ using a three-digit complement:

Subtraction

	Normal	*Tens complement*
Minuend	89	89 maps to 089
− subtrahend	87	−87 913
	$\overline{2}$	$\overline{002}$
		1

Drop carry

Hence the conversion to complementary number representation allows subtraction to be achieved by addition. It is left as an exercise to the reader to verify the subtraction of a negative subtrahend using the method given above.

2.6.2   TWOS COMPLEMENT CONVERSION AND SUBTRACTION

The twos complement of a binary number is formed by subtracting each digit of the number from the base minus one $(2 - 1 = 1)$, and adding one to the least significant digit. For example:

Conversion

$$
\begin{array}{ll}
01101 & 10110 \\
\rightarrow 10010 & \rightarrow 01001 \\
+\quad\ 1 & +\quad\ 1 \\
\hline
10011 & 01010
\end{array}
$$

The operations carried out in binary conversion are very simple, $1 \rightarrow 0$ and $0 \rightarrow 1$, with one added to the least significant bit.

To carry out subtraction, add the twos complement of the subtrahend to the minuend and discard the final carry. An example follows:

Subtraction

	Normal	*Twos complement*		
	0	*Conversion*		*Subtraction*
Minuend	11011			
−subtrahend	10100	11011	11011	11011
	00111	10100 $\rightarrow$	01011	+01100
			+$\quad$ 1	00111
			01100	1
				drop carry

2.6.3 SIZE OF NUMBER REPRESENTED

In a machine using binary, the magnitude of a number is controlled by the number of bits n that are allocated to its representation. In general this allows a total of 2^n integers to be held. If twos complement representation is chosen with n bits, what is the range of numbers that can be held? Bearing in mind that equal numbers of positive and negative integers are normally required, each set will be approximately

$$2^n \times 0.5 \qquad \text{where } n \text{ is the number of bits.}$$

Although eight bits would be too small for a real machine, it is useful to adopt this for illustrative purposes and examine how this representation would be applied:

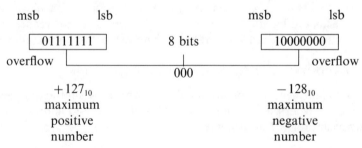

Note that with this format it is possible to hold a negative number one larger than the biggest positive integer. If one is added to the biggest positive integer: $1 + 01111111$, instead of an even larger number being produced, it reverts to the largest negative number instead. Clearly in any normal arithmetic schema, this result is anomalous. Hence this *overflow* condition needs to be detected within the machine and appropriate action taken. Such special arithmetic conditions are detected by the processor and the result held within a special register frequently known as the condition code. Although eight bits would be an unrealistically small number of bits to allocate to hold an integer on a real machine, the number varies widely from one computer to another, ranging from 16 to 64 bits or even more.

For a simple 16-bit machine, such as the simple register machine used in this book, a twos complement integer is represented by one 16-bit word. Thus the maximum positive integer is

$$2^{15} - 1 \quad 32\,767_{10} \quad \text{or} \quad 7\text{FFF}_{16}$$

The smallest negative integer is

$$2^{15} - 32\,768_{10} \quad \text{or} \quad 8000_{16}$$

A word with all bits set to one, FFFF_{16} represents -1 in the complementary system.

2.6.4 CONDITION CODE

In most computers the result of obeying each arithmetic instruction is continuously monitored by the processor. A special register is normally devoted to a simplified logical summary of the possible results, recording for example that a result was greater than zero. For the simple register machine a four-bit *condition code* is used to monitor results:

condition code: $\boxed{C\mid V\mid N\mid Z}$

$C = 1$ if carry has occurred,
$V = 1$ if overflow has occurred,
$N = 1$ if result was negative,
$Z = 1$ if result was zero.

For fixed-length arithmetic operations involving two integers x and y, which deliver a result r, the rules governing the setting of the N and Z bits of the condition code are simple. The negative case:

$$N = 1 \quad \text{if } r \text{ is negative.}$$

This is the equivalent of a copy of the most significant bit of r. Rule for the zero case:

$$Z = 1 \quad \text{if } r \text{ is zero.}$$

The setting of the carry (C) and overflow (V) bits is more complex: they depend on the signs of x, y and r, as well as the nature of the operation performed. With the add operation

$$r := x + y,$$

overflow on fixed length quantities can occur, if adding x and y of the same sign generates a *result* of the opposite sign. In algorithmic terms this can be expressed as:

> **if** $(x > 0$ **and** $y > 0$ **and** $r < 0)$
> **or** $(x < 0$ **and** $y < 0$ **and** $r >= 0)$
>
> **then**
>   *overflow* := 1
> **else**
>   *overflow* := 0;

Carry is generated if a positive *result* is obtained from the addition of x and y with different signs. If both x and y are negative, a carry always follows after addition. In algorithmic form:

> **if** $(x > 0$ **and** $y < 0$ **and** $r > 0)$
> **or** $(x < 0$ **and** $y > 0$ **and** $r > 0)$
> **or** $(x < 0$ **and** $y < 0)$
>
> **then**
>   *carry* := 1
> **else**
>   *carry* := 0;

Note that the last sub-condition $x < 0$ *and* $y < 0$, includes the case where overflow may be set as well. If $r \geq 0$ overflow will occur.

The rules governing subtraction

$$r := x - y$$

are a simple modification of those already given for addition. This can be seen by rewriting $x - y$ as $x + (-y)$. Thus the algorithmic formulations given for addition need only be modified by simultaneously replacing

$$y > 0 \quad \text{by} \quad y < 0$$

$$\text{and } y < 0 \quad \text{by} \quad y > 0.$$

After arithmetic operations, a check on the condition code (CC) would reveal if overflow had occurred, thus allowing appropriate action to be taken. Another common use for the CC is in making decisions. The high-level languages tests, such as $a > b$ or $a < b$, all rely on detecting the relevant setting of the condition code given above. This is explored in greater detail in Chapter 6.

2.7 Representation of real numbers

So far, only integers have been considered for direct representation on the machine. However, they are often rather restrictive in use because the number of bits allocated to them is small, and it is not possible to hold fractional numbers directly. For many calculations in the real world, the range of numbers will be large and cannot be constrained to deal only with whole numbers. A solution to both these problems is to hold real numbers directly. These can be held in two parts, one contains the digits which are to be operated on arithmetic- ally, and the other contains a smaller number that gives the magnitude of the main number. This method, known as *floating point*, is sufficiently widespread on computers that special integrated circuits are available to perform high-speed arithmetic using this format. The format relies on the fact that any real number A can be represented as

$$A = m \times 2^e$$

where m is the *mantissa* and e is the *exponent*. The mantissa gives the main digits of the number and is said to be *standardized* if the following conditions are satisfied:

1. if $A > 0$ then $1 \leqslant m < 2$
2. if $A = 0$ then $m = 0$
3. if $A < 0$ then $-2 < m \leqslant -1$

Real numbers are usually held within these constraints. For example:

25.6 is expressed as 1.6×2^4
-1.6 is expressed as -1.6×2^0
0.05 is expressed as 1.6×2^{-5}
Note that except for zero mantissa all standard numbers start
with an integer one. Thus the mantissa can be expressed as:
mantissa $= 1. \langle$fractional part$\rangle$.

Floating-point numbers are held in a variety of different layouts on different machines. Figure 2.5 shows two formats adopted by the IEEE *Standard for binary floating-point arithmetic*.

In this account the 32-bit format is adopted, where only the fractional part of the mantissa is stored explicitly:

31	30	27	22	19	15	11	7	3	0
S			F_1	F_2	F_3	F_4	F_5	F_6	

exponent $\longleftarrow$ fraction $\longrightarrow$

where

S is the sign bit
if $A > 0$ then $S = 0$,
         $A = 0$ then $S = 0$,
         $A < 0$ then $S = 1$

```
31  30                    22              0
  S  8-bit exponent  23-bit fraction  Single real
```

```
63  62                    51              0
  S  11-bit exponent  52-bit fraction  Double real
```

S = sign of fraction

Figure 2.5   32- and 64-bit IEEE floating-point numbers

The exponent is 8 bits long and the fraction is 23 bits. The allocation of four bytes to represent the floating-point number will of course determine its accuracy and magnitude.

2.7.1   FLOATING-POINT MANTISSA

The mantissa holds the main digits of the number to a finite accuracy. With the 4 bytes as allocated previously, it is restricted to six hexadecimal digits F_1–F_6 or 23 bits b_1–b_{23}.

$$hexadecimal\ m\ =\ (0.F_1F_2F_3F_4F_5F_6)_{16}$$

$$m\ =\ (F_1 \times 16^{-1} + F_2 \times 16^{-2} + \cdots F_6 \times 16^{-6}$$

$$and\ binary\ m\ =\ (0.b_1b_2b_3\cdots b_{23})_2$$

$$=\ b_1 \times 2^{-1} + b_2 \times 2^{-2} + \cdots + b_{23} \times 2^{-23}$$

Decimal notation is normally used for calculations, so a common requirement is to convert a decimal mantissa

$$(0.d_1d_2d_3\ldots)_{10}$$

$$to\ (0.F_1F_2F_3\ldots)_{16}$$

This can be considered in general terms by conversion to an arbitrary base r:

$$0.d_1d_2d_3..\ \ \rightarrow\ \ p_1r^{-1} + p_2r^{-2} + \ldots$$

A simple algorithm for the conversion can now be given where

$$IP\ \text{is an integer and}$$
$$DF\ \text{is a decimal fraction}$$

```
DF := 0 . d₁d₂d₃ ...
repeat
    IP := integer part of (DF × r)
    DF := fractional part of (DF × r)
    write ln (IP)
until (DF = 0) or required accuracy obtained
```

It is rare for DF to be zero, as the decimal fraction is unlikely to be exactly represented in the new base r.

The above algorithm can be applied to some conversion examples. Those in Fig. 2.6 are unusual because an exact mantissa is rapidly produced. A more typical example is given in Fig. 2.7. The last three digits in the conversion of Fig. 2.7 will recur indefinitely. But the fractional part has a finite size of only 23 bits. This can be solved either by arbitrary truncation after the 23rd bit or by a rounding scheme. For rounding, if the 24th bit was one then increment the 23rd

DF	$DF \times r$	IP	New DF
0.625	1.250	1	0.25
0.25	0.5	0	0.5
0.5	1.0	1	0
$0.625 \equiv (0.101)_2$			

(a)

DF	$DF \times r$	IP	New DF
0.0325	0.5	0	0.5
0.5	8.0	8	0
$0.0325 \equiv (0.08)_{16}$			

(b)

Figure 2.6 Some number-base conversions: (a) to express 0.625 in binary ($r = 2$); (b) to express 0.0325 in hexadecimal ($r = 16$)

DF	$DF \times r$	IP	New DF
0.6275	10.04	A	0.04
0.04	0.64	0	0.64
0.64	10.24	A	0.24
0.24	3.84	3	0.84
0.84	13.44	B	0.44
0.44	7.24	7	0.24
0.24	3.84	3	0.84
0.84		B	
		7	
		3	
		:	
$0.6275 \equiv (0.A0A3B73B73\ldots)_{16}$			

Figure 2.7 Conversion of 13.02 (standardized 1.6275×2^3) to hexadecimal

bit by one. Both truncation and rounding lead inevitably to a loss of accuracy in conversion for most numbers.

2.7.2 FLOATING-POINT EXPONENT

In the floating-point format using four bytes, eight bits have been allocated to represent both positive and negative exponents. Thus the number

$$A \equiv m \times 2^e$$

where e can be a positive or negative integer, the exponent is represented by the bit pattern

$$e + 127 \quad \text{and} \quad 127 \equiv (01111111)_2$$

If e is 3 then the exponent field of the real number in binary will be:

$$\begin{array}{r} 01111111 \\ +00000011 \\ \hline 10000010 \end{array}$$

If e is -6 then the exponent field will be:

$$\begin{array}{r} 01111111 \\ -00000110 \\ \hline 01111001 \end{array}$$

This now completes the description of each of the fields of the floating-point number; it remains to show some complete numbers represented.

2.7.3 FLOATING-POINT NUMBERS COMPLETE

The decimal number 13.02 has already shown to be equivalent to 1.6275×2^3.

$$\begin{aligned} \text{fraction} &= (0.\text{A0A3B5})_{16} \\ \text{exponent} + 127 &= (10000010)_2 \\ \text{sign bit} &= 0 \end{aligned}$$

S	$e + 127$	m

$\longleftarrow$ 9 bits $\longrightarrow$ $\longleftarrow$——— 23 bits ———$\longrightarrow$

$\boxed{S \mid e + 127} = (010000010)$

The final representation is obtained by putting the individual bit patterns of S, e and the *fraction* together: $(815051\text{DA})_{16}$. The last bit of the fraction given above has been used to give a 23-bit rounded result.

2.7.4 FLOATING-POINT ROUNDING ERROR

Both in the original conversion of a decimal number, and with subsequent arithmetic operations, the fraction has to be rounded to r binary digits. The error in rounding can be quantified by expressing the infinite fraction, f_I as

$$f_I = 0.b_1b_2b_3 \ldots b_r + b_{r+1}2^{-(r+1)} + \delta,$$

where

$$\delta = 2^{-(r+2)} (b_{r+2} + b_{r+3}2^{-1} + \cdots)$$

An upper bound to δ is found by setting all the binary digits to one, which gives

$$\delta \leqslant 2^{-(r+2)} \times (2) = 2^{-(r+1)}.$$

The rounded form of the infinite fraction, f_R, depends on the value of b_{r+1}:

$$\text{if } b_{r+1} = 0, f_R := 0.b_1b_2 \ldots b_r$$

$$\text{and if } b_{r+1} = 1, f_R := 0.b_1b_2 \ldots b_r + 2^{-r}.$$

The absolute size of the upper bound of the rounding error is

$$|f_I - f_R|$$

which is easily shown to be less than $2^{-(r+1)}$ in either case. Thus setting r to 23 gives a maximum rounding error of 0.000 000 06.

When compared with the representation of integers, floating point is very efficient in representing magnitude. With an eight-bit exponent the largest number that can be held is approximately 3.4×10^{38}. However, it is at the price of sacrificing accuracy. Few numbers can be held exactly and as calculations proceed there is a danger that rounding errors will make a significant difference to the result. At best with a 23-bit fraction only seven significant decimal digits can be held.

Exercises

1. Convert the following decimal numbers to binary and octal: 27, 43, 512, 997.
2. Convert the following binary numbers to decimal and hexadecimal: 00101, 1001110, 100100.
3. Perform the following additions in binary:
   (a) 1011001 + 1011000   (b) 001111 + 011100
4. Perform the following subtractions in binary (numbers given in decimal):
   (a) 128 − 53   (b) 35 − 20   (c) 236 − 193
5. Convert the following hexadecimal numbers to decimal and octal: C7B6, 239A, 2734, 9B01.
6. Convert the following binary numbers to hexadecimal and octal: 10101101, 11011011, 11001100, 00101010.
7. Convert the following decimal numbers to 10s complement: 9932, 2536, 1291.

8. Convert the following binary numbers to 2s complement: 1100, 01011, 101101, 11011100.
9. Perform the following subtractions using 10s complement:
    (a) $967 - 342$ (b) $1024 - 639$ (c) $367 - 251$ (d) $132 - 98$
10. Perform the following subtractions using 2s complement:
    (a) $10101 - 1010$ (b) $10001 - 01011$ (c) $10011001 - 10111011$
11. For the 32-bit floating-point representation as defined by IEEE, give in hexadecimal the floating-point representation for the decimal numbers $+10.04$, -10.04.

3
Parallel communications – computer bus

The previous chapter has established the primary conventions associated with the representation and coding of information used by the majority of digital computers. One of the points of the conventions is to facilitate the exchange of information not only between man and machine, but also between the various internal elements of the computer and more generally from one computer to another. In principle the conventions are very similar whether the computers are in adjoining offices or one is on Earth and the other on the Moon. However, a much shorter excursion will be examined first to establish how information is passed within a single computer; normally the journey is restricted to a few paces or in some cases to less than a metre. A model machine, the simple register machine (SRM), will be used to establish the main principles, and some of the necessary details, of how this works in practice.

3.1 Information exchange – sample computer problem

Exchanging information is a general problem that is common to both man and computer. However, in order to investigate this in more detail a very particular computer problem has been chosen that is central to how they work. The processor obeys instructions to transform the data held in its memory. If the processor can execute a million additions a second, to take advantage of this it needs to be able to store the freshly calculated number in memory once every microsecond. Frequently the components that go to make up the processor are grouped together in one area and those that constitute the memory in another as shown on Fig. 3.1.

The arrows represent the transfer of a number that is represented by 16 bits of information, either to the memory from the processor, or vice versa. In order to do this as quickly as possible all 16 bits are transferred at the same time, symbolized by the parallel lines of the diagram and frequently referred to as *parallel* communication.

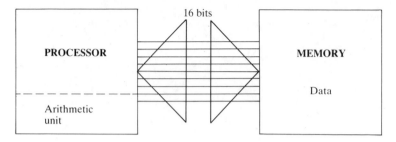

Figure 3.1   Processor and memory exchange 16 bits of information

3.1.1   OUTLINE COMPUTER SOLUTION

In order to exchange information, it is necessary to find solutions to at least the following three problems: a method of interconnection, a method of encoding the information, a method of timing and controlling the information exchange. The telephone is a common example to which this simple analysis can be applied. The instrument itself is normally connected to the system by copper wires and in a simple case a series of such wires will be sufficient to complete the connection of caller to receiver. The information for transfer is normally spoken down the telephone, which causes a microphone to send an analogue waveform down the line. This then causes the loudspeaker in the receiving instrument to produce a sufficiently close approximation to the speech of the caller that the listener is able to recognize the words of the message. The control of the telephone transaction takes place in two distinct phases. First the instrument is used to select a free line and attempt to establish contact with the recipient by dialling numbers that select the relevant exchange(s) and final destination. If all goes well the recipient answers the telephone and in the final phase the message is transferred using the normal conventions of human conversation. Notice that in this phase information proceeds not only from the caller, but also back from the recipient, in order to determine that the message has been received correctly. The timing of the various transactions is largely initiated and controlled by the speed of human conversation, though certain operations like dialling need to be critically controlled by the response time of the telephone-exchange equipment.

3.1.1.1   *Interconnection*

In the sample computer problem, the task was to exchange 16 bits of information at one time. A simple solution to this would be to provide 16 individual insulated wires that pass between the processor and the memory. Each line would convey one bit of information.

3.1.1.2   *Encoding*

Even when a simple interconnection path has been made, no information can flow successfully without some convention as to how the message is to be represented. As has been explained already most computers use the binary system to represent information and so for this transaction it would be necessary to assemble 16 binary ones or zeros for transmission. Many integrated circuits hold these binary values as different d.c. voltage levels. Often 0 volts represents zero and $+5$ volts represents one:

binary	*logic*	*electrical*
0	low	0 V
1	high	$+5$ V d.c.

Using this scheme each of the 16 lines would be set low to represent 0 or high to represent 1.

3.1.1.3   *Timing and control*

Although there are wires connecting processor to memory and a fixed convention for representing binary, information cannot flow successfully without some further coordination procedure. One simple way frequently adopted is to make

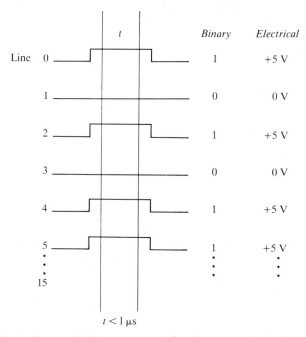

Figure 3.2   The 16 lines are held at 0 or $+5$ V for time t to indicate binary 0 or 1

one of the parties in the exchange the *master* and the other the *slave*. For the sample computer problem the processor would be the master (sender) and the memory the slave (receiver). The processor uses various control lines to tell the memory what to do next. The processor is driven by a fast oscillating crystal clock and uses this to make information available on the 16 lines for a short length of time. During this time the memory must successfully receive the information. If the processor performs a million additions per second this time should be less than 1 microsecond. This only gives an outline computer solution to show how information might be exchanged; it is necessary to examine each part of it in more detail.

3.2   Computer bus mechanics

As has already been suggested the integrated circuits that make up the logic of the processor and those that realize the memory are frequently positioned in physically distinct areas. In some computer designs these rather different functions may even be carried out on two different printed circuit boards. In order to get them to work satisfactorily together a number of parallel connections need to be made, and this set of lines and signals has come to be known as a computer bus. They usually carry both the data and address information that will determine the memory location of the data. It is a way of making 50–100 parallel connections that act as a primary highway between different parties each on their own board. These connections can most easily be made or broken by supplying each board with a plug and the 'bussed' parallel connections with a series of matching sockets, as illustrated in Fig. 3.3.

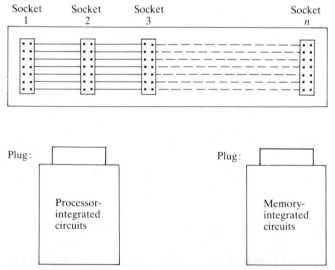

Figure 3.3   With 64/96-way indirect connectors to DIN 41612, 64 or 96 connections can be made by plugging the 100 × 160 mm board into one of the sockets

This particular standard has been illustrated to show how logical requirements can have a very simple and direct concrete expression. In current technology the central part of a computer is frequently linked together by a series of electrically conductive copper tracks.

Each of the main features of the computer bus as described in outline can take several practical forms:

1. The bus lines that connect pins 1 to 64 or 1 to 96, from one socket to the next, may be individual insulated wires attached to the pins by wire-wrap or solder techniques. This is a highly labour-intensive way of making these connections, and if only 64 are required, special ribbon cable and Euro-connectors have been developed that allow all 64 connections to be permanently made by pressing the reverse of the connector so that the relevant pins break through the insulation of the ribbon and contact is established with the appropriate copper wire. Finally, and most reliably, a special printed circuit known as a backplane is produced, which makes all the appropriate connections between the sockets that are mounted in the backplane. The backplane may also provide appropriate isolation and termination for the bus lines in order to try and ensure error-free transmission of information.

2. The bus lines are normally restricted in length. Active parallel lines in close proximity are subject to induced and other forms of noise which may produce rogue signals. Hence as well as specifying termination standards the general recommendation is to keep the bus as short as possible; for very high-speed transmission of information this might be restricted to the order of 1 metre. In general a longer bus with a higher transfer speed is more likely to produce errors than a shorter/slower one. A 1 metre bus with 64 lines and a processor running at 1 million operations/second would normally make a very robust system.

3. The plugs and sockets offer a quick and reliable way of assembling a computer that works to a standard interface. This defines mechanically which data signals are available on which pins, and logically how those signals are to behave. With the sample computer problem examined so far, it would be necessary to establish on which pins the 16 data lines were to be carried, and the time t for which the processor would make the data available to the memory. As well as logic signals the bus lines are also used to carry the voltage rails of the power supplies to the boards. Usually this will include 0 V, $+5$ V, -12 V, $+12$ V. Most boards are keyed so that they can only be inserted the right way round, as joining logic signals to power-supply levels normally destroys the logic of the board.

4. Producing boards to a standard interface makes it possible to extend the size or capability of the computer simply by plugging further boards into the bus. In addition, if the computer develops a fault, diagnosis by substituting known working boards will normally produce a fully working machine with minimum time and effort.

This description of a typical computer bus has been formed in the context of integrated circuits that use low-voltage level switching to distinguish between binary 0 and 1, and that rely on copper tracks or wires to make electrical connections between integrated circuits and boards. These simple limitations have constrained designers to build machines in a particular way; the combination of fibre optics and lasers promises in the future undreamed-of freedom in the positioning and organization of computer components.

3.3   Instruction fetch sequence and computer bus

The sample computer problem investigated so far has been based on the need for the processor to store numbers in the memory. In high-level language terms this can be represented by the statement

$$A := 43;$$

where it is assumed that the variable A is held in memory. However, in order to give a more detailed explanation of how this very simple operation is carried out, several additional quantities will have to be explained. To begin with it is assumed that the high-level language statement has been compiled correctly, and that the machine code equivalent has been placed in a location of the memory of the computer. In order to carry out the instruction the processor must first fetch it from the memory. As this is one of the commonest operations that a running computer performs there is normally a special register, known as a program counter (PC), that is used to keep track of the address of the current instruction in memory. The number in the PC gives the address in bytes of the instruction which the processor needs to fetch and execute. In this simple illustration it will be assumed that the instructions begin at location zero and the variable A is at location 100, as shown on Fig. 3.4.

Before it is able to carry out or execute the instruction the processor must first fetch the instruction by requesting the memory unit to send it the *contents* of memory location zero. When this is received by the processor it inspects the instruction to decode what operation it needs to perform: in this case $A := 43$ tells it that the number 43 needs to overwrite the contents of the memory location called A. Notice that this commonest of computer activities (executed in the order of 1 million times/s) involves both processor and memory in dealing with two distinct quantities which are accordingly both represented on the bus:

Address lines 0–15 allowing memory up to 65 K bytes.
Data lines 0–15 allowing 16 bits data transfer.

The difficulties of coordinating bus activities between the various boards require the addition of special control lines, shown diagramatically on Fig. 3.5. The arrows indicate the potential direction of information flow. One function of the control lines is to guarantee that in any single bus transaction information proceeds only from one sender to the required receiver.

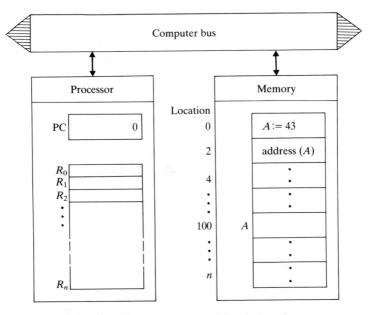

Figure 3.4 The processor executing instructions

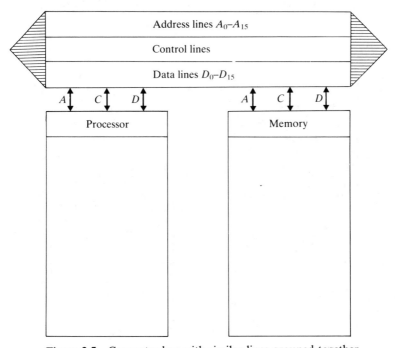

Figure 3.5 Computer bus with similar lines grouped together

3.3.1   INSTRUCTION EXECUTION STEP BY STEP

Now that an outline of instruction execution has been established this can be extended to give a more realistic idea of the logic that is required on the SRM processor and memory boards to support this, as shown on Fig. 3.6.

The processor has a program counter (PC) that contains address information, an instruction register to hold the current instruction and other registers to store intermediary quantities. These special-purpose registers are used to hold values that control the response of the processor to the current instruction. Each instruction will require a fresh value to be placed in the registers, which will in turn specify the transfer of information required for the correct execution of this particular instruction. General-purpose registers are also supported within the processor. These are more directly under program control and are frequently used to manipulate commonly met program variables. They might, for example, hold the value of a variable A if it was incremented and tested in a **for** loop. Other reasons for keeping A in a register might be that it is used frequently for assignments or comparisons. The advantage is that the value is then held in the processor, where these operations can be carried out directly by the arithmetic unit. The memory also has special-purpose registers: a select register to hold the current memory address, a data register to move information to and from the memory and the actual memory locations that store the information. The special-purpose registers on the boards are used to store intermediate values that

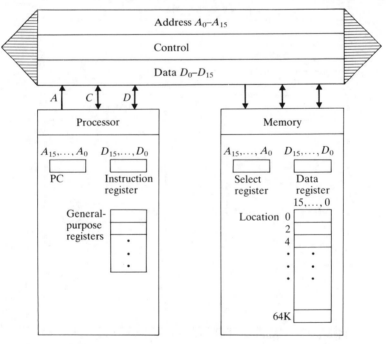

Figure 3.6   The processor executing instructions with details of the registers involved

are passed back and forth along the bus as instruction execution proceeds. As before (Fig. 3.5) it will be assumed that the following statement is for execution:

$$A := 43;$$

and that the instructions begin at memory location 0 and that the variable A is at location 100; when execution starts the PC will be set to zero (Fig. 3.7).

This may seem a very cumbersome way of setting the value of A to 43, but it does give insight into the highly repetitive and simple operations that the computer is repeatedly performing. Step 6, where the instruction is decoded and executed, varies according to the nature of the particular instruction; in this case sub-steps 6.1–6.5 are very similar to steps 1–5 of the main sequence.

More precise details of the nature of instructions and their execution are

		Processor	Memory
1.	Processor places PC address on bus with read request A_0–A_{15}:	0	
2.6	Memory receives address from bus A_0–A_{15} → select register:		0
3.	Memory uses contents select register to select memory location and place contents into data register:		$A := 43$
4.	Memory places contents data register onto bus D_0–D_{15}:		$A := 43$
5.	Processor receives data from D_0–D_{15} → instruction register:	$A := 43$	
6.	Processor decodes the instruction in the instruction register, places 43 in general purpose register and then proceeds:		
6.1	Processor increments PC and places on bus with read request A_0–A_{15}:	2	
6.2	Memory receives address from bus A_0–A_{15} → select register:		2
6.3	Memory uses contents select register to select memory location; contents of this location placed in data register:		100
6.4	Memory places contents data register onto bus D_0–D_{15}:		100
6.5	Processor receives data from D_0–D_{15} as $Addr(A)$ and sets A_0–A_{15} accordingly:	100	
6.6	Processor places contents general register (43) → D_0–D_{15}: with write request to memory	43	
6.7	Memory receives address from bus A_0–A_{15} → select register:		100
6.8	Memory uses contents select register to select memory location and write contents D_0–D_{15} to memory location (100):		43
7.	Processor increments PC appropriately: and repeat from step 1	4	

Figure 3.7 Executing an instruction

reserved for later chapters; at this stage the main points to grasp are concerned with the frequency with which bus transfers occur and the necessity to manipulate address, data and control entities in order to carry out the simplest high-level language operation.

3.4   Formal control and timing of bus activities

The model of instruction execution offered has been simplified in a number of ways to make presentation easier. One area that can now be extended is the way in which processor and memory access to the bus is coordinated. The processor is driven by a clock that ticks at a high frequency. This varies from one system to another, a typical range being 1–25 MHz; this is normally many times the frequency at which instructions are obeyed. For a computer obeying 1 million instructions/second the clock might run at 4 MHz. Because the processor is normally taken as the master device it is expected that the bus and the rest of the system will work fast enough to keep up with the demands of the processor. In order to do this the bussed exchanges of information frequently take a small number of cycles to obey a complete processor instruction. In the step-by-step execution of a statement one repeated requirement was to be able to transfer the contents of a memory location to the processor.

3.4.1   MEMORY READ AND WRITE

In practice it is convenient if read and write instructions are as symmetrical as possible and to reinforce their similarity they are described on the same diagram (Fig. 3.8). It is a timing diagram that specifies to the resolution of the clock when the various bus events should take place.

It contains the familiar address and data lines, which are shown in a box on the diagram when they contain valid information. That is when the lines have stabilized from any transition ($1 \rightarrow 0$ or $0 \rightarrow 1$), and are presenting the correct information. The control lines are used to indicate this explicitly; when $ADMEM$ is true (high) the setting of A_0–A_{15} is a valid memory address and the number presented on the bus can be used by the memory board to select the relevant memory location. The processor further controls the setting of the $READ$ and $WRITE$ lines to tell the memory in which direction the data is to pass. If $READ$ is asserted the memory must place valid data on D_0–D_{15} before the beginning of t_3, as with $ADMEM$ and $READ$ both low the memory board will cease to maintain valid data on D_0–D_{15}. If the processor asserts $WRITE$, then the memory address will be the valid destination of the data placed by the processor on D_0–D_{15}. The memory must take the data and write it into the relevant memory location before the end of t_3. Notice that it is the processor which dictates what happens next on the bus; the memory must respond correctly in the time available. If memory components rated at 200–250 ns are used setting t at 250 ns should produce a comfortable and reliable memory cycle. This is by far the simplest arrangement for the model SRM bus; many real

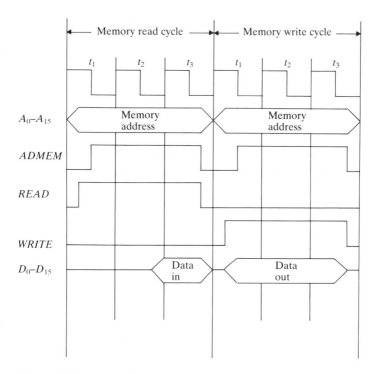

Time t = 250 ns, t_1–t_3 = 1 bus cycle

A_0–A_{15}	16 lines for carrying address range 0–64K
D_0–D_{15}	16 lines for carrying data
ADMEM	single control line to indicate valid address
READ	single control line to indicate read cycle
WRITE	single control line to indicate write cycle

Figure 3.8 Memory read and write cycle on SRM bus. Cycles are not necessarily consecutive. All control lines are shown active high (logic 1 ≡ on)

systems relax this absolute requirement at the expense of keeping the processor waiting on request from the memory, if it is using slow components.

3.4.2 PERIPHERAL INPUT–OUTPUT

The initial justification for defining a bus for the SRM was given in terms of connecting processor to memory. However for any functional system it is equally important that information can pass to or from the outside world. Hence the bussed system must be equally capable of dealing with a variety of peripherals. As with processor and memory the integrated circuits that deal with a peripheral, such as a VDU, can be conveniently grouped together. Equally important the peripheral needs to deal with both address information and data, as shown in outline on Fig. 3.9.

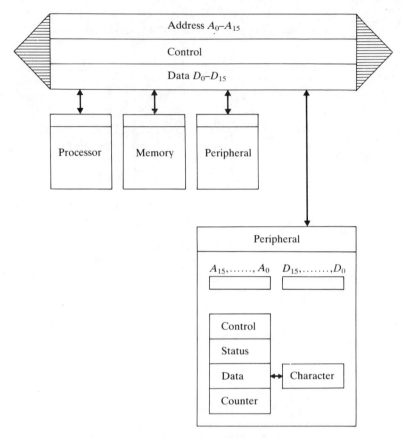

Figure 3.9   Bussed computer system with processor, memory and two peripheral boards

The address information now discriminates between one peripheral and another, with control lines again being used to coordinate activities with the processor. For SRM the peripherals are what are known as memory mapped, that is certain addresses are uniquely assigned to particular peripherals and operations performed on those addresses will work with peripheral registers as opposed to memory locations. The effect that this has will be largely dependent on the nature of the peripheral. For a VDU, it might typically display a character on the screen or accept a character typed on the keyboard. To deal with these activities four standard 16-bit registers called *control*, *status*, *data* and *counter* are provided. They are described in detail later.

3.4.3   PERIPHERAL INTERRUPT AND ACKNOWLEDGE

As far as possible the SRM deals with peripherals as though they were memory locations, the last 1K bytes of the address space being reserved for them. However, there are significant differences in the behaviour between an essentially passive memory board that the processor writes to or reads from, and a peripheral that periodically needs to call attention to itself. Normally the processor is repeatedly obeying instructions that it fetches from the memory. How can the peripheral attract the attention of the processor if it has information to transfer? One tried and tested solution to this problem is to allow devices to cause what is known as an interrupt; that is, they can force the processor to stop obeying one sequence of instructions and start another. In the new sequence of instructions the processor can then pay attention to the problems of the device causing the interrupt. SRM, in common with many other computers, allows interrupts to occur only at the end of a complete bus cycle, and has a special instruction that allows it to switch interrupts off, if necessary (interrupts inhibited). As far as possible, however, it is designed to run with interrupts enabled, thus permitting it to respond rapidly to a peripheral request. A typical interrupt cycle is shown on Fig. 3.10.

The simple register machine permits only one device to interrupt at a time. Hence logic on the peripheral boards must guarantee only a single interrupt request; this is frequently engineered via a daisy-chain line connection from the processor that passes permission to interrupt from one board to the next. A peripheral requiring attention needs to wait until it has this permission and then asserts the interrupt line (INT).

If interrupts are enabled then at the end of the current instruction the processor will obey an interrupt accept cycle. The requesting peripheral recognizes this as the processor makes interrupt acknowledge ($INTACK$) true in t_1 of the cycle. During t_3 the peripheral must have placed its address on A_0–A_{15}. The processor reads in the peripheral address and uses it to change the contents of the program counter to obey instructions (often referred to as an interrupt routine) that service the peripheral. At this time the processor may also save the value of various registers to facilitate the program change; interrupts would normally be inhibited until the peripheral has been serviced satisfactorily. On completion of the interrupt routine the SRM processor status register would need to have the external interrupt bit set to 1, thus again enabling peripherals to request the attention of the processor. This disruptive arrangement is practical only if the peripherals are relatively slow and few in number; otherwise the processor will not be able to get much other work completed.

3.4.4 PERIPHERAL CONTROL, READ AND WRITE

The peripheral board that interfaces a VDU to the bus needs to offer the programmer various options on controlling the flow of data to and from the device. These fall into four main categories and the SRM accordingly has its special registers: *control, status, data* and *counter* to deal with them (Fig. 3.9). They are made available by the peripheral at consecutive locations after the start address of the device typically set by hand on the board. The *counter* register is not normally used for single character devices. The *control* register is used to set the device into a sensible state so that it will send and receive information: for

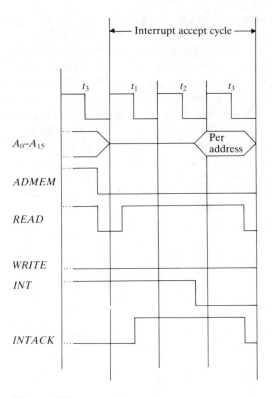

Time t = 250 ns, t_1–t_3 = bus cycle

A_0–A_{15}	16 lines for carrying peripheral address
ADMEM	not used in interrupt cycle
READ	single control line to indicate read
WRITE	not used in interrupt cycle
INT	single control line to request interrupt
INTACK	single control line to accept interrupt

Figure 3.10 Interrupt accept cycle on SRM bus. All control lines are shown active high (logic 1 ≡ on)

the VDU the speed and other characteristics of the characters, and whether the device is allowed to cause interrupts. These, and other options, can be selected by writing the relevant binary pattern to the first peripheral address. No special instructions are required as the peripheral is expected to respond to the memory read and write cycles, already defined, if its address is placed on the bus. The *status* register is inspected by reading the second word of the peripheral. This will typically show the reason for interrupt; most commonly for the VDU, it will indicate that a character has been typed and should be read, or that a character has been successfully sent to the screen and another can now be written to it. Most peripherals are subject to errors and the status register is also used to convey these. Errors vary from faulty transmission and reception of data to the fact that a device has been switched off, has run out of paper or just is not working as it should. However, putting aside these exceptional conditions, the most usual action is to read or write data. This is accomplished by addressing the *data* register. Like the other registers in SRM, it is 16 bits wide and so for byte-orientated devices only the least significant 8 bits are used for character transmission. Thus it is the *data* register that most closely corresponds with the high-level language statements

   Read (A); Write (A);

In order to carry these out, with the given board structure, the following high-level language algorithm would need to be executed, typically after interrupt:

> *device* = **record**
> *control:word*;
> *status:word*;
> *data:word*;
> *counter:word*;
> **end**

> **var** *d:device*
> *s* := *d.status*;
> **if** *s* = *ready*
>   **then if** *READ* **then** *char* := *d.data*
>   **else if** *WRITE* **then** *d.data* := *char*

In addition there would also need to be statements that dealt with the *control* and *status* registers at the beginning and the end of transactions.

3.4.5 BLOCK-TRANSFER DEVICES

It has already been suggested that causing an interrupt for every character of information transferred to or from a computer is highly disruptive of the processor. It is tolerable for devices like the VDU that work slowly transferring 10–1000 characters/second; for devices like the disk which potentially could transfer 120 000 characters/second, this would effectively prevent the processor from doing anything else. Further, devices like the disk store information most efficiently in blocks and might expect to send or receive 100 or even 1000 consecutive characters in one negotiation. In order to accommodate this, a special form of transfer needs to be implemented across the bus that permits complete blocks of information to be moved to or from the memory with minimal disturbance of the processor. This normally means that the peripheral board, as well as having control and data registers, must also have a memory buffer of its own which is big enough to contain the largest block that needs to be transferred between device and main memory. Additional logic is also required to coordinate the sending and receiving of consecutive data characters.

In outline the direct memory access (DMA) peripheral needs to proceed in this way:

1. Set up start address in memory.
2. Set up count of number of bytes to be transferred.
3. Send current byte.
4. Increment memory address, decrement counter. **if** *counter* > 0 **repeat** *step* 3
5. Block transfer complete, clear up at end of transaction.

Note that steps 3 and 4 continue automatically, without further program intervention, until the complete block of information has been transferred from the memory to the disk. In high-level language terms this is the equivalent of the element-by-element transfer of a complete array by passing the address of the array and its length to a hardware procedure.

3.4.6 DIRECT MEMORY ACCESS (DMA) PERIPHERAL

A DMA device such as a disk controller has the standard logic associated with any peripheral. It deals with the same address, data and control lines as before, and offers the special registers *control*, *status*, *address* and *counter* as shown on Fig. 3.11. It will also need the logic that causes an interrupt to signal the end of the transfer of a block of information and to indicate exceptional error conditions.

A step-by-step account will now be given of the transfer of a block of information from the main memory of the computer to a particular part of a disk using a DMA controller. The general layout of the board is shown in Fig. 3.11, while the timing of the relevant read cycle is given in Fig. 3.12.

1. Check the *status* of the DMA peripheral to see that it is ready to accept a new command.
2. Write the disk destination address to the disk through the *control* register.
3. Write the main memory start address into the *address* register.
4. Write the count of the number of word transfers required into the *counter* register.
5. Check the *status* of DMA peripheral to see set up correctly.
6. Write to the *control* register to start transfer automatically on DMA board (for timing refer to Fig. 3.12).
   6.1 DMA peripheral request bus control by setting $BUSR := 1$.
   6.2 Processor releases bus by lowering $BUSG := 0$ and DMA board then sets $BUSG := 1$ at the beginning of the next cycle (Fig. 3.12). Thus DMA peripheral now runs the bus and sets:

   $A_0-A_{15} :=$ *Address* register;
   $READ := 1$;
   $ADMEM := 1$;

   6.3 DMA peripheral releases $BUSR := 0$.

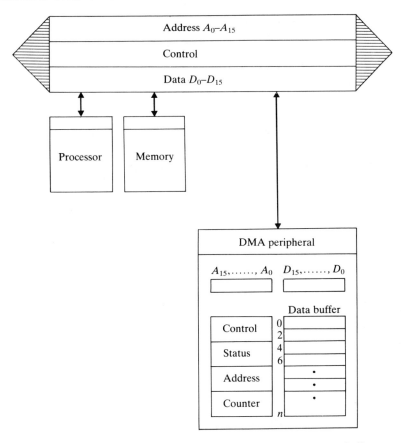

Figure 3.11 Bussed computer system with processor, memory and direct memory access (DMA) peripheral

6.4 Main memory receives address on A_0–A_{15} and places contents to D_0–D_{15} at time t_3 (Fig. 3.12).

6.5 DMA peripheral takes D_0–D_{15} and places contents in relevant on-board data buffer (Fig. 3.12); this completes the data transfer for this DMA cycle.

6.6 DMA peripheral increments *address* register, decrements *counter* and releases the bus by setting $BUSG := 0$. If *counter* $= 0$ then last character in block has been transferred, so proceed to Step 7; otherwise repeat from Step 6.1.

7. DMA transfer complete. The contents of the DMA data buffer sent to the disk; cause an interrupt to show transfer complete with success or failure indicated in *status* register.

Although there is quite a lot of preliminary information to set up for a DMA transfer in Steps 1–5, the major advantage comes in Steps 6.1–6.6, which

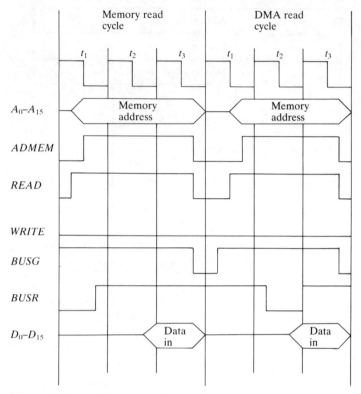

Time t = 250 ns, t_1–t_3 = 1 bus cycle

A_0–A_{15}	16 lines for carrying memory address
ADMEM	single control line to indicate valid address
READ	single control line to indicate read cycle
WRITE	single control line to indicate write cycle
BUSG	single control line to indicate bus grant
BUSR	single control line to request bus control
D_0–D_{15}	16 lines for carrying data

Figure 3.12 Memory read followed by DMA cycle on SRM bus. Cycles are not necess-arily consecutive. All control lines are shown active high (logic 1 ≡ on). Note that during memory read the processor manipulates bus lines, while with DMA read the DMA peripheral is in charge

proceed automatically without further program intervention. Hence blocks of information, consisting of hundreds of bytes, can be transferred to or from disk for the cost of only a few interrupts together with the relevant bus cycles. Only the DMA read cycle is defined in Fig. 3.12, as the write cycle is very similar. Clearly *WRITE* should be asserted instead of *READ* and D_0–D_{15} data out would be valid from t_1, as in the memory write cycle (Fig. 3.8). The data would travel from the DMA peripheral into the relevant memory location specified on A_0–A_{15} via D_0–D_{15}.

With interrupts it was essential for SRM to guarantee that only one device should request an interrupt at a time; this is equally essential for bus mastership. Hence logic on the DMA peripheral boards must guarantee only a single bus master request; this is frequently engineered via a daisy-chain line connection from the processor that passes permission to request the bus (*BUSR*) from one board to the next. A DMA peripheral (or processor), requiring the bus needs to wait until it has this permission and then asserts the bus request line (*BUSR*).

Figure 3.12 shows the processor completing a memory read cycle and then giving up the bus on request from the DMA peripheral. The requesting DMA device recognizes this when $BUSG := 0$, at the end of t_3. It then takes over the bus for a complete cycle, but after releasing *BUSR* it then recognizes its assertion by another board and duly returns the bus mastership by setting $BUSG := 0$, before the end of t_3. Hence the DMA board takes a single cycle and then relinquishes bus control. This method of working is frequently known as cycle stealing, from the fact that if the DMA peripheral takes over the bus the processor is denied it. However, the main point is that the DMA peripheral 'steals' only one cycle at a time. Cruder DMA controllers, usually without the data buffer shown on Fig. 3.11, take over the bus completely until the whole block of information has been transferred. This is usually referred to as block-transfer DMA.

This most sophisticated of parallel transfers brings to an end the account of the workings and coordination of a typical bus. It has allowed error-free transmission of data between the central components of the computer. The transfers have also proceeded as fast as the processor was able to run; this typically varies from 1–25 MHz. However, the distance over which the information can be safely transferred is normally highly restricted. This may be a few metres in a computer room, or even a single metre at the very highest speeds. But it is usually necessary to communicate with computers over much longer distances: locally a few hundred metres and remotely between one town and another, or even one country and another. These problems are the subject of the next chapter.

Exercises

1. Organize your knowledge of the telephone system (or any communications system known to you) under the following headings:
   (a) method of interconnection;
   (b) method of encoding information;
   (c) method of controlling or timing information exchange.
   For a real world system what other factors would need to be considered?
2. For a computer system to which you have access try and assemble the following information:
   (a) Does the computer have a bus?
   (b) To what standard is the bus? Is it well defined?
   (c) For the bus collect the following details: nature of backplane, length of

bus, size of boards that plug into bus and nature of connection, speed of bus data transfers.

(d) How many different printed circuit boards go to make up the computer and what are their different functions?

3. Draw a timing diagram to represent a DMA peripheral executing a typical read cycle from disk into main memory.

4
Serial communications – local and wide area

The parallel communications described in the previous chapter are vital for the high-speed working of the central part of the computer. However the distance the information travels is normally restricted to a few metres. It is essential however that information can be passed to or from computers over much longer distances, both locally within the same building and more widely between different towns and countries. The solution to these problems normally involves the serialisation of the data, which is then modulated or transformed electronically so that it can be transmitted on the media be it copper wire, fibre optics or radio waves.

4.1 Information exchange – sample computer problem

Most computers have terminals connected to them so that characters can be input from the keyboard and results displayed on the screen. Most terminals use the ASCII characters as shown in Fig. 2.4 and discussed in Chapter 2. It is usually desirable that the terminals be housed at some distance from the computer; certainly further than a metre, the distance the parallel bus defined in Chapter 3 might be restricted to. Hence, although there needs to be a peripheral board plugged into the bus, this form of communication cannot be extended directly to a VDU which might be 100 m way. Even if the parallel bus could be extended the cost and bulk of the large number of lines required would make this solution unattractive. Further, it may be necessary for the terminal to be connected to a computer in another building several hundreds of metres away, or even in another town or country. In order to keep the connecting lines as simple as possible the ASCII characters are serialized for sending down a single line; that is the 7 or 8 bits representing the character are sent bit by bit down the line. This method of solution is especially convenient for remote connections, as it is then possible to take advantage of existing telecommunications networks that typically supply two lines per instrument, one for sending and the other for receiving information.

4.1.1 OUTLINE COMPUTER SOLUTION

Connecting a terminal to a computer involves the provision of a peripheral board connected to the bus. This part of the board has already been described in the previous chapter. The other task of the board is to deal with the conventions of a remote VDU. This means that the characters sent rapidly in parallel along the bus have to be slowly serialized for the VDU.

4.1.1.1 *Interconnection*

Because of the widespread need to connect terminals to computers via the telephone system various standards have evolved to control this. The most common standard currently in use was produced by CCITT (Consultative Committee of the International Telegraphy and Telephony) and is known as RS-232-C. This covers the mechanical, electrical, functional and procedural aspects of the connection.

Figure 4.1 summarizes only the mechanical aspects with the names of the signals. The distinctive 25-way D-connector has nearly every pin named with a different signal. However, in the local connection of terminal to computer three pins are absolutely essential. These are pin 7 earth, pin 2 transmitted data and pin 3 received data using the RS-232-C/V.24 numbering system. The terminal sends the serial form of the ASCII character typed in down the transmit line, while it accepts serial information for display on the receive line. Both these lines have information proceeding in one direction only and are accordingly known as *simplex* lines.

D-type pin	Description
1	Chassis ground
2	Transmitted data
3	Received data
4	Request to send (RTS)
5	Clear to send (CTS)
6	Data set ready (DSR)
7	Common return (signal ground)
8	Data carrier detect (DCD)
12	Backward channel DCD
13	Backward channel CTS
14	Backward channel Transmitted Data
16	Backward channel Received Data
19	Backward channel RTS
20	Data terminal ready (DTR)
22	Ring indicator (RI)

Figure 4.1   RS-232-C serial interface 25-way D-type connector, selected signal names

4.1.1.2   *Encoding*

Single characters for transmission are represented by the 7/8-bit encoding using the ASCII scheme. As on the computer bus it is necessary to distinguish between zero and one; however, there are a number of possible standards that might be followed even in a local connection. Here just two of the possible mappings are shown:

Binary	Bus level	Transmission 1	Transmission 2
1	+5 V	+5 V	+12 V
0	0 V	−5 V	−12 V

The use of positive and negative voltages on the transmission lines is intended to extend the distance over which the data can be successfully received. They represent simple modulation of the original signals to suit a new medium. These local standards normally provide error-free transmission of information for at least 100 metres of cable. If actual telephone lines are to be used in the information exchange the signals will all have to pass through a *modem* that *modulates* the signals from the local levels to those required by the telephone system and *demodulates* back again from telephone to local levels. The precise electrical levels and functions that the modem needs to manage will be defined by the carrier. As well as defining electrical levels for the valid transmission of data, the modem will also be concerned to establish, control and eventually to terminate the call.

4.1.1.3   *Timing and control*

On the computer bus, data was sent in parallel at a time defined by the processor clock. This *synchronous* transmission relies on both sender and receiver essentially sharing the same clock. For serial transmission, where sender and receiver may be separated by 100 m, this is not possible directly. What happens is that both parties have a clock that ticks at an agreed frequency generated by their own crystal oscillator. Normally the terminal can be set by hand to one of several different speeds and the peripheral board also needs to be set to the same rate. Figure 4.2 shows some of the speeds which are commonly used. Compared with bus activities of 250 ns they are all very slow. At the fastest speed shown a single character takes about 1 ms to transmit. Further, instead of the single clock of the bus, there is a series of alternatives that require a variable clock time *t*, which

Transmission speed (bps)	Clock rate/bit variable t (μs/bit)	Character rate approximate (byte/s)
300	3333 μs/bit	30
600	1666 μs/bit	60
1200	833 μs/bit	120
9600	104 μs/bit	960

Figure 4.2   Selection of typical speeds used for serial terminal connection

is then taken as the time to control the serialization of a single bit. As stated before both sender and receiver need to agree in advance about the clock frequency, but to guard against them drifting out of phase with one another, each character is prefaced by a start bit that is used to start the receiver clock. This is known as *asynchronous* transmission, as the presence of the data is used to start the clock running, which should then stay aligned for long enough to recognize the bit pattern of the character, after which follow one or two stop bits to end the transaction. In Fig. 4.3 the ASCII for the character 'A' is shown as it would be transmitted.

The sequence starts with the start bit set to zero, then follow the data bits D_0–D_7, the least significant data bit leading. In addition to the seven bits of the ASCII code, D_7 is used as the parity bit. The letter P is used to signify that this bit should be set according to the *parity* required. The parity is included with the character to give an error check when it is transmitted. The parity may be *even* or *odd*. If even then a one will, if necessary, be set in the P position to make the number of bits in the character even. In the same way if odd parity is selected, the P bit will be set if needed to make the number of bits in the character odd. For example with the letter A:

$$\text{A } P100 \; 0001 \quad \frac{\text{Even parity} \quad \text{Odd parity}}{0100 \quad 0001 \quad 1100 \quad 0001}$$

The character is already even, so nothing is set for even parity; while odd parity requires the P bit to be set. The parity allows the receiver to have a simple check on whether the character accumulated is correct. Finally the sequence comes to

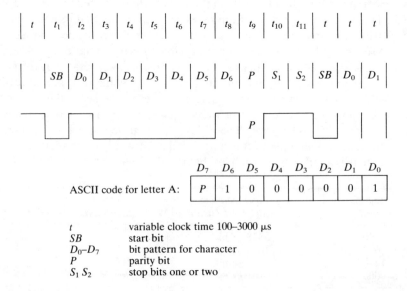

								D_7	D_6	D_5	D_4	D_3	D_2	D_1	D_0
ASCII code for letter A:								P	1	0	0	0	0	0	1

t	variable clock time 100–3000 µs
SB	start bit
D_0–D_7	bit pattern for character
P	parity bit
$S_1 \; S_2$	stop bits one or two

Figure 4.3 Serial transmission scheme for a single character: ASCII encoded letter A

an end with one or two stop bits, again something which both parties need to agree before transmission commences.

4.1.2 SERIAL PERIPHERAL BOARD

The serial encoding scheme shown is very widely used, hence there are a number of integrated circuits that implement the data encoding and decoding required. Figure 4.4 shows in outline the form a peripheral board would need to take.

The usual bus connections need to be made, and as well as interrupt control, the normal program registers – control, status, data and counter – have to be implemented. The majority of the rest of the peripheral board and the serial section of the VDU can normally be implemented by a single communications controller called a UART (universal asynchronous receiver transmitter) or ACIA (asynchronous communication interface adaptor). In the local connection shown in Fig. 4.4 only three lines are implemented: transmit, receive and signal ground. From the keyboard the 8-bit ASCII character is serially encoded by the UART, according to the speed and parity set, and sent along the transmit line. The pattern of ones and zeros will have been modulated to whatever voltage levels are deemed appropriate for the local lines. The peripheral board will decode the character sent by using the receive half of its UART; after causing an interrupt the 8-bit character can be sent by the peripheral along the bus. In a similar fashion the peripheral board can receive a character from the bus and will use the transmit section of its UART to route it to the VDU for display on the screen.

This simple model of serial communication deals with only a local direct connection. If connection is to be made to a computer via the telephone system a special device known as a *modem* (for modulator–demodulator) handles the access to the network. Normally, as stated before, the owner of the carrier network specifies the electrical characteristics as well as the logical functions that the modem needs to be concerned with. RS-232-C, defined by CCITT, is an international standard that is widely applied in this situation. In order to deal with the additional complication of accessing a telephone network several more signals lines, identified on Fig. 4.1, would have to be implemented. For example ring indicator (RI) and data terminal ready (DTR), would be needed to actually establish that a dialled-up connection had been made satisfactorily, before data could be exchanged. Request to send (RTS), clear to send (CTS) and data set ready (DSR), are concerned with *flow control* once a connection is established. That is they can be used to allow data to flow down the line, or to request the transmitter to stop sending, if the receiver cannot accept any more data. Finally once the data exchange is terminated, both parties will need to clear their calls. These additional complications require a wider examination of the topic of computer networks.

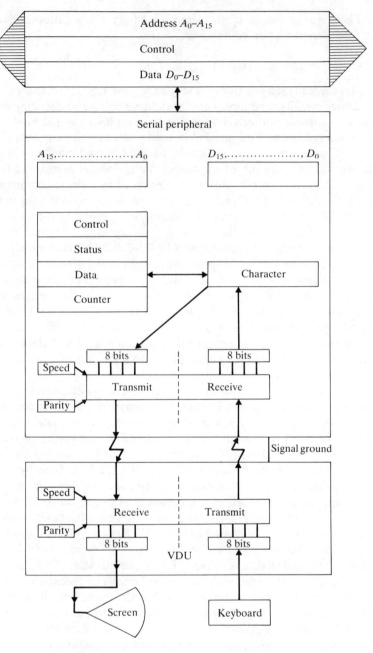

Figure 4.4 Serial peripheral board connected to a VDU

4.2 Computer networks

The existence of the world wide telephone network, potentially connecting together about 350 million subscribers, has had a profound influence on computer communications. It was the obvious network to turn to when trying to communicate with a remote computer. However, it was designed to transmit human speech in an attenuated form (normally cutting off frequencies above 3000 Hz), relying on the parties to sort out conversational misunderstandings due to noise on the line, distortion, crossed lines, inadvertent disconnection and any other practical difficulties associated with dial tones, ring tones, engage tones, and establishing contact with the desired party. This form of communication does not match the computer need to exchange discrete bodies of digital information at high speed with complete accuracy. Hence, a large amount of effort has been expended throughout the world over many years to try and satisfy the computer need by re-using the existing telephone network. In order to control this work, a large number of standards have been produced that range from detailed electrical specifications to protocols that define automatic call routeing and actual data exchange. However, none of this work can change the fact that a normal voice-grade telephone line can only support the transfer of about 500 characters/s (4800 bps) with good reception conditions. Thus the use of the telephone network frequently remains a slow and cumbersome method of computer information exchange.

The installation of new equipment, for example fibre optic cables and digital exchanges, will gradually allow a widespread distribution of much higher-speed communications better suited to computer needs. In order to consider how existing standards and new developments may be fitted together, both when using public networks (as offered by telephone companies) and private networks installed by companies and institutions on their own premises, it will be helpful to describe an overall model offered by the International Standards Organization (ISO).

4.2.1 REFERENCE MODEL FOR OPEN SYSTEMS INTERCONNECTION (OSI)

The OSI is a hierarchical model that can be used to organize and describe computer networks. A seven layer system is proposed, that should encapsulate standards and protocols from the simplest electrical connection to high-level data exchange. Figure 4.5 shows two idealized hosts that communicate via a single network node. Here direct physical communications are restricted to layer 1, but each of the higher layer protocols stays in touch via this information exchange. The duties of each of the layers will be considered in turn.

1. *Physical layer* This is concerned with the detailed definition of how control and data bits are to be represented on the transmission media and a mechanical and electrical specification of the network connection. In addition, procedures to establish, maintain and then release connections between parties on the network must be included at this level. Much of the earlier

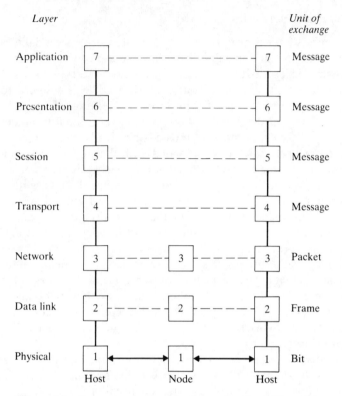

Figure 4.5 Computer communication using the OSI model

description of the pin assignments for VDUs (Fig. 4.1) and the serialization of characters with their start and stop bits, formally defined in RS-232-C, would come into this category.

2. *Data link layer* Once connection is established the physical layer transmits a sequence of bits without regard for their meaning. The data link layer has to be able to distinguish data and control groups or *frames* of bits so that it can guarantee error-free transmission between sender and receiver. Hence as well as generating acknowledgement of correctly received data, it is also vital to be able to request retransmission of data in error. As well as incorrect data, errors can also arise from data saturation. The most common cause is the transmitter sending valid data faster than the receiver is able to process it. Hence in order to guarantee error-free reception, the data link layer must also deal with *flow control* between sender and receiver. This problem also recurs in higher levels of the hierarchy.

3. *Network layer* The network layer is essentially concerned with the routing of *packets*, or small blocks of information, between hosts and network nodes. The transport layer divides its longer messages into small data segments, and the network layer adds addressing information which will determine the route of the packet to the destination. This routeing information may be fixed

or be dynamically determined according to the loading on the network. However the main point is that the network is *packet* orientated, both for addressing and for charging end users for data services.

4. *Transport layer*   This layer provides a reliable data transmission service for the session layer by dividing messages into small units that become the packets of the network layer. In the simple case a single connection will suffice. But if the transport layer requires a high data throughput, it may need to use several connections; if a high-speed connection is available it may share this with several hosts. Either way the session layer above should be unaware of these mechanisms, which will require the booking and releasing of various network connections. Host-to-host *flow control* will also be managed by this layer.

5. *Session layer*   This layer actually manages the information exchange between processes on different host machines, such as a user logged in on one computer using the services of another. Once more connection at the beginning of the session will require addresses, authentication and numerous other parameters including the nature and speed of connection required. If the connection is lost during the dialogue this layer should attempt to restore it without user interaction.

6. *Presentation layer*   Most of the work of establishing and maintaining the communications connection has been achieved by the time the session layer has been reached. However the presentation layer offers the possibility of data compression, translation or encryption.

7. *Application layer*   This is the final and highest level, where the user software dictates and generates the data that needs to be exchanged. All other layers of the protocol should be completely transparent to this layer.

It should be remembered that these seven layers for OSI remain a model for describing past systems and designing future ones. Most actual system implementations may omit layers, or divide the functions of an OSI layer between several layers.

4.2.2 MEDIA

All communications systems rely on the choice of a suitable medium for message exchange. Many networks rely on a combination of media to take maximum advantage of the characteristics of each type. One major criterion is the speed at which data can be transmitted using the medium. Figure 4.6 gives some overall guide to the possible range of speeds.

In practice this rating is partly determined by the distance a signal can travel in the medium before it is distorted or attenuated beyond recognition. Another major factor in medium choice is the cost. Twisted pair and coaxial cable have traditionally been very cheap, but the widespread use of optic fibres is constantly reducing their cost relative to performance. Equally important is the cost of installing and maintaining cables of whatever material. Radio transmission of

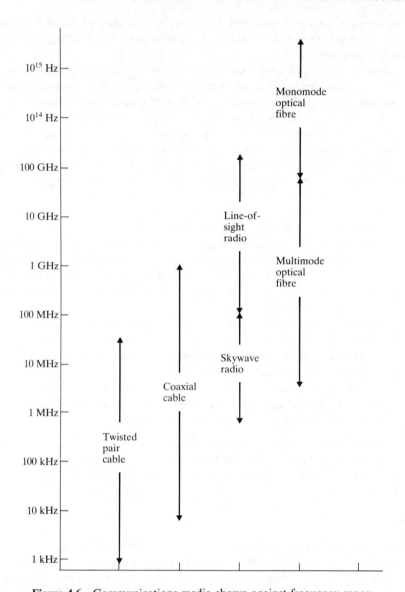

Figure 4.6 Communications media shown against frequency range

course avoids this cost, but is restricted by wave-band allocations and transmitter/receiver expense.

4.2.2.1 *Twisted-pair cable*

Two insulated wires are twisted together to reduce electromagnetic interference generated by transmitting signals along them. They are used very widely in analogue and digital communications associated with telephones and computers alike. The majority of the links run slowly with amplifiers or repeaters needed to restore the signal every 2–5 km. The medium can be used up to frequencies of 10 MHz, but would then require repeaters every 100–300 m, depending on local conditions. It is the cheapest medium: many twisted pairs are usually laid in the same cable. Typical transmission loss at 100 kHz is 3 dB/km.

4.2.2.2 *Coaxial cable*

Coaxial cable also contains two conductors, but here the arrangement is that one insulated conductor is contained within the other to provide a shielded environment. The quality and size of the cable will determine its characteristics and resistance to noise. It is of course widely used in radio and television reception, because of its high bandwidth and good noise resistance. Typical transmission loss at 100 kHz is 1 dB/km, rising to 4 dB/km at 3 MHz. Signals at 50–100 MHz are limited to a range of about 1 km. In general, signals at lower frequencies will travel further on coaxial cable than twisted pair without significant deterioration. Coaxial cables are more expensive than twisted pair, and can be very much more so depending on the construction of the cable and consequent maximum data rate.

4.2.2.3 *Radio*

Radio waves would apparently offer a very attractive path for communications offering a high bandwidth and none of the routeing problems associated with the physical laying of cables. However, skywave radio already has many of its practical bandwidths assigned and line-of-sight radio is extremely limited without the use of a satellite or other convenient relay. In either case the atmosphere is a notoriously fickle medium, which adds considerably to the cost and complexity of transmitters and receivers if they are to provide a reliable service. Nevertheless radio can provide very high-frequency communications between remote installations, some of which may even be mobile on a global scale.

4.2.2.4 *Optical fibre*

Until recently the cost of producing fibre-optic cable precluded its widespread use. Its cost/performance ratio is now comparable with coaxial cable. There are three grades of material available: step-index multimode, graded-index multimode and monomode. They each offer increasingly coherent paths to the light sources, giving increasing bandwidths from 100 MHz/km, to 3 GHz/km, to over 100 GHz/km for monomode. This amazing range of frequencies is moreover accompanied by decreases in attenuation from 10 dB/km for multimode down to 0.2 dB/km for monomode. In addition to light sources, light emitting diodes in the megahertz range and lasers above that provide signalling that is largely unaffected by electromagnetic interference. For all these reasons, fibre-optic cable is very attractive for high-speed long-haul networks, whether serving telephones, computers or combining these services together. The use of lasers and fibre optics would seem to offer great promise for the development of very high-speed networks in the future.

4.2.3 MODULATION

Modulation techniques have been developed to transform the message signal into a form suitable for transmission on the selected media. In the past this has usually been a continuous sinusoidal wave form for both analogue and digital signals. Common techniques for encoding digital data are shown in Fig. 4.7.

Amplitude modulation codes zeros as a series of small amplitude waves, while ones are represented as higher amplitude periods. On Fig. 4.7 the vertical peak-to-trough distance of the wave for a one is roughly double that used to represent a zero. *Frequency modulation* uses two different chosen frequencies to represent one and zero. Figure 4.7 shows that the horizontal peak-to-trough measure of the wave representing a one is roughly double that representing a zero. Finally in *phase modulation* both amplitude and frequency are held constant but the signal is shifted in phase to represent one and zero. In Fig. 4.7 the signals are 180° out of phase, hence producing signal reversal between one and

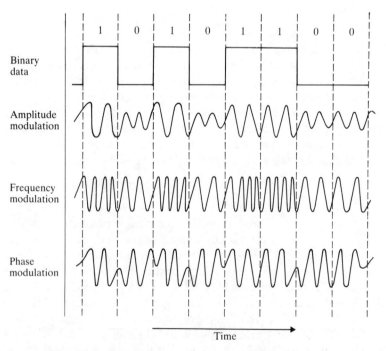

Figure 4.7 Modulation methods for encoding binary data

zero. Fibre-optics communications, frequently run from a laser source, are better adapted to pulse encoding of the information. The sending of a photon pulse from the transmitter could indicate a one rather than a zero; or the timing of the pulse might select one symbol from a set, such as the digits 0–9. Whatever form of modulation is chosen for transmission, successful reception will require the decoding of the signal, however distorted it may have become, by the process of *demodulation*.

The modulation of signals may be further complicated by the desire to share a single medium connection between several parties. The *multiplexing* is especially relevant where many slow parties can use a single high-speed connection at the same time. This can be achieved by *frequency-division multiplexing*, in which each user is assigned a separate frequency band. The number of simultaneous users will depend on the frequency range supported by the media. In telephone systems, for example, twelve 4000 Hz voice channels are multiplexed into the band 60–180 kHz. the other major form of multiplexing is *time-division multiplexing*, where each user takes over the entire bandwidth of the channel for a short time. The number of users that can be satisfactorily supported is a function of the required user transmission rate and the frequency bandwidth of the medium. Both methods of multiplexing considerably complicate the modulation/demodulation process, but give higher channel utilization, which is especially important in long-haul networks that rely on a few high-capacity connections.

4.2.4 TOPOLOGY

Most real networks have highly irregular topologies that have evolved to solve a variety of practical geographic and technical problems. Once created they can be analysed to predict their flow, capacity, reliability and saturation characteristics. However, it is also worthwhile considering some simple network models, as in most cases some simple consequences may be deduced. The point of belonging to a network is so that any part can exchange information with any other. A very simple solution is to provide a link from one node to every other. This is shown in Fig. 4.8(a) and is known as complete connection. One obvious observation about the complete solution is that it involves a large number of connections. Thus for a large number of nodes, or a large geographical area, the practical cost of realization is preclusive. However, it does mean that there is no contention between nodes for connection, and any breakdown in a connection need only affect two nodes in the system. The star network, shown in Fig. 4.8(b) drastically reduces the number of connections that need to be made between nodes. However, the node at the centre of the star must take on the critical role of relaying, or switching, messages between nodes; if it fails none of the nodes will be connected. The ring connections of Fig. 4.8(c) are also greatly reduced from the complete connection. It now follows that each node must relay messages for other nodes further round the ring, hence distributing the role of the centre node in the star system. It may also be slightly less critical if one connection is lost,

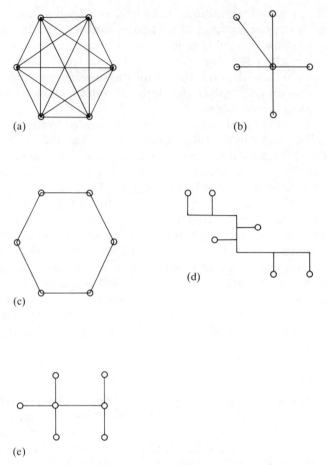

Figure 4.8 Model topologies for network connections: (a) complete; (b) star; (c) ring; (d) bus; (e) incomplete

as the nodes will still be partially connected. The bus connection (Fig. 4.8(d)) essentially joins the nodes together in a single continuous line. This should be very economical in line length and resistant to node failure. However, if the main spine connection is broken the nodes are divided into two unconnected sets, neither of which in practice may be able to function independently. Finally the incomplete connection of Fig. 4.8(e) has some of the features exhibited by each of the model networks. The consequences of the loss of a single node or connection depend on the particular topology of the network, as do the requirements of nodes to relay messages. In a practical situation this might suggest that certain nodes and connections need to be able to deal with a much higher communications bandwidth than others, and that duplicate paths should be available to increase reliability.

4.2.5 PACKET SWITCH PROTOCOL

Having reviewed how networks might be formed using a variety of physical media, it is now necessary to examine in a general way how messages are to be routed and sent across the network. In a simple model of the telephone system, call connection is managed by reserving a sequence of connections from one exchange node to another, until the required destination connection is reached. This technique is known as *circuit switching*, and although in widespread use, has a number of disadvantages as far as computer communications are concerned. To begin with, the actual process of seeking and obtaining a single connection, let alone a whole sequence, takes a long time in terms of computer data rates. Further the charge associated with the connection is for the total duration of the call connection, while data may only be exchanged periodically. In addition, the reservation of the connections in the path by definition excludes other parties from their use. This may produce bottle-necks and other undesirable side effects in the network.

One solution to these problems is to use a technique known as *message switching*. No through connection is continuously reserved, but instead the message, together with its destination address, is sent on to the network. It then travels from one switching node to the next, hence only reserving an internode connection for the duration of the message. This gives better opportunity to share connections, but now requires that each node is able to hold or buffer several complete (or near complete) messages at once. This problem of storing messages can be reduced by the use of *packet switching*. Now the message will be divided up into a number of smaller data blocks each with its own routeing information. Nodes need to be able to store only a number of complete or partially complete packages, instead of messages. Hence packet switching is the most suitable for a computer network of any size or complexity.

Packet switch networks have a number of general characteristics that can be identified independently of their physical implementation. One very obvious feature is that they all require a well-defined packet format to facilitate the information exchange. The following is typical:

Start	Source & destination address	Data	Control	Error check

The start pattern is used to alert a receiver to get in step with the beginning of a packet. The next field contains the address of the packet destination and may also indicate where it came from – useful in flow and error control. The address is highly variable in size from 8 bits in some implementations to 48 bits in others. The data field may be fixed or variable length, carrying anything from 1 to 1000 bytes. In early protocols the data was actually carried as a series of ASCII characters. More recently this has been replaced by bit-orientated data, where any bit pattern can be used. There is then a control field, which can cover a variety of functions, including the pattern of acknowledgements and flow control, as well as the status of the media and nodes being traversed. Finally an error check is provided so that the receiver can take a cyclic redundancy checksum of the packet and compare it with that computed by the transmitter. If they agree there is a good chance that the data delivered is correct. If they do not agree, retransmission may be explicitly requested, or the lack of an acknowledgement may stimulate the transmitter to send the packet again.

The protocol described so far corresponds with the physical and data link layers of the OSI model (Fig. 4.5). However, there are additional factors that enter into the protocol needed for layer 3 – the network layer. One problem already mentioned is that of *flow control*, where a fast transmitter may saturate a receiver with data. This is undesirable for the receiver and may additionally cause congestion which is undesirable for the network as well. Hence the receiver needs to be able to slow down the transmitter or request further information when it is ready. The type of service provided also needs to be determined at the network level. A *datagram* service attempts to deliver correct packets to the destination, but does not guarantee that they are all there, or that they are delivered in the order of sending. Hence the higher protocol layers would need to be active if these desirable aims were to be met. Equally a *virtual circuit* service may be offered where the network layer verifies each packet correct and in the right sequence. All error checking and retransmission would be completely transparent to the user.

Finally there is the question of addressing or identifying the destination of the packet. Many packet address fields are too small to hold the full range of destination addresses. Hence the address may only have some 'local' significance on the way to a final destination, or to an address that will forward the packet to some further intermediary node. These special nodes are known as *bridges* or *gateways* and contain special information about the connections currently established through them, including routeing. The additional addressing information required is usually conveyed using the data section of a network packet. Going from one sub-network to another of course normally introduces delays in the time taken to transmit the packet from source to destination.

4.3   Public data network – wide area

The public switched telephone network has long been used for the transmission of computer data using *circuit switched* techniques. However, despite the extremely wide distribution of telephones, it suffers from a number of disadvantages as far as computers are concerned. Amongst these are the long call set-up time, a charge based on call duration rather than data throughput, relatively high error rates and finally slow data transfer, typically less than 4800 bps. For all these reasons, attention will be restricted to the workings of public *packet switched* networks, which can offer data services at 64 Kbps or more, and match more closely the needs of computer communications.

CCITT has proposed international standard network protocols for layers 1, 2 and 3 of OSI. These standards are collectively known as *X.25*. They define the interface between the host data terminal equipment (DTE) and the carrier's data circuit-terminating equipment (DCE) via an intelligent node known as a data switch exchange (DSE). The physical layer (Layer 10, defined by standard X.21, gives the connections required for transmit, receive and control between DTE and DCE. These would most frequently be realized using conventional telephone line technology. Above this, the link layer (Layer 2) is established to exchange packets between the DTE and the local DSE. They need to guarantee error-free data transmission, and use a protocol based on high-level data link control (HDLC). This uses a series of supervisory and data frames to set up connections and exchange sequenced information by acknowledgement or re-transmission requests.

The network layer (Layer 3) is the highest level defined by X.25; above that the message transport implementation should be network independent. It offers essentially three user services called CONNECT, DATA and CLEAR. In each one of these a series of special packets is exchanged in order to realize the series. In the CONNECT phase, for example, the DTE sends a call request package to its DSE, and this is forwarded to the destination DTE, which will then return call accepted if this is possible. Various parameters controlling the data exchange may then be negotiated, such as the maximum packet length, which should be 128 bytes but could optionally be 256, 512 or even 1024 bytes. Thereafter, data can be transmitted with *flow control* available via receive ready or receive not ready packets. Finally either side can terminate the session with a clear request packet. It is important to remember that exchange of information is conducted quite independently of the nature of the medium involved or the topology of the network connections.

Most asynchronous or synchronous terminals cannot deal with the complexities of the X.25 protocol. However, it is highly desirable that they can make use of the packet switched network. Hence a standard known as *X.28* has been defined to provide a packet assembler–disassembler (PAD) interface suitable for a RS-232-C terminal. This essentially takes the characters typed by an individual user and assembles them in a suitable form for transmission across the X.25 network. Equally it will also deliver simple characters from the network back to the terminal when required. PAD implementations usually offer a number of terminal connections, hence acting as local concentrators or multiplexors to the X.25 network. This network may not offer the highest data rates technology can support, but by using advanced 'telephone' technology it offers the possibility of world wide packet switched data exchange.

4.4 Local area network – Ethernet

Local area networks (LANs) have been specifically evolved to allow very high transfer rates of information between computers or computers and peripherals. They have frequently been restricted to communications within the same building, or a group of buildings on the same site. Hence media of a high quality can be especially installed to link all the nodes of the network together. Ethernet, defined as part of the IEEE 802 local network standards, has been primarily established on coaxial cable. For a cable with a diameter of 10 mm it is designed to have a data rate of 10 Mbps, a maximum segment length of 500 m and an overall span of 2500 m. With a smaller and cheaper cable of 6 mm diameter it still runs at 10 Mbps, but has a maximum segment length of 200 m and an overall span of 1000 m. In order to cover a greater distance repeaters can be included; or fibre-optic links can be inserted at some expense, but may be crucial in linking different buildings together.

Ethernet is a broadcast bus network essentially based on a continuous coaxial cable with potential *tap* connections. Figure 4.8(d) is a model form of the topology that the network needs to follow. A tap allows a *transceiver* to make electrical contact with the bus and convey Ethernet packets to the *interface*, the *controller* and finally the host computer. Any node with a message broadcasts an Ethernet packet on the bus and hopes that the destination node will receive it correctly. The packet format is as follows:

Preamble	Destination and source address	Type field	Data	CRC

The 64-bit preamble is provided to make sure that all stations will synchronize with, and detect every packet on the network. The source and destination addresses are both 48 bits, to cover cross-network addressing. A type field of 16 bits, identifies the role of the data field. The data is of variable length, from 46 to 1500 bytes. Finally a 32-bit cyclic redundancy check is provided for error detection.

Ethernet is a broadcast network, but rather than letting a node broadcast at any time it insists that it should listen to the network first and only transmit if it is quiet, hence, it is hoped, avoiding packet collisions. The system adopted is known as multiple access with collision detection. The *transceiver* uses carrier detection to determine whether Ethernet is already being used by another node. If it is silent, transmission may begin. However, for every bit transmitted, the transceiver compares the value on the wire with that being transmitted; if it is significantly different it concludes the current packet is being interfered with. This means that two nodes are transmitting at the same time, therefore both must abandon their current packet and try again. Clearly once a collision has occurred, several nodes may wish to transmit at the same time, hence after collision detection, nodes have to back off and not try transmitting for some random time. The *interface* and the *controller* work together to transmit and receive serial Ethernet packets in order to satisfy the information needs of the host on the other side of the interface.

Although Ethernet cannot deliver data to a host at 10 Mbps, because of the packet, collision and protocol overheads, it can offer a very high-speed connection comparable with that of a disk. This level of data activity cannot be sustained for long by many hosts, hence most local area networks are idle for the great majority of the time. This network enables large numbers of terminals and computers to be linked together in such a way that most users will experience no discernible transmission delay.

4.5 Local area network – Cambridge Ring

The topology of the Cambridge Ring as its name might suggest is that of a ring, as shown in miniature at Fig. 4.8(c). It is normally run on a series of copper twisted-pair connections that run from one repeater to the next. It is frequently clocked at 10 MHz, with a repeater spacing of about 100 m depending on local conditions. Unlike Ethernet the components need to be actively powered, power supplies therefore being included as part of the ring installation. This means that repeaters can be placed wherever they are needed; though for larger spans fibre-optic links would have to be inserted. Any node on the network must have its own repeater.

Once the ring is powered up a monitor station starts the circulation of one or more slots that are big enough to contain a minipacket. The form of the 38-bit Cambridge Ring is defined by Hopper *et al.* (1986). A summary follows:

Start	Destination & source address	Data	Response

The first bit indicates the beginning of the packet and is always set to one. The second bit is the full/empty bit, which indicates whether the packet already has data in it. If full, the data should be read by the receiving station; if empty, a station wishing to transmit may place information in it. A third bit is set by the monitor station when the packet passes through its repeater. This will normally be reset when a packet is marked as empty, hence any packet passing through the monitor with the monitor passed bit set is circulating in error and can be removed. After these start bits come the source and destination addresses each of 8 bits, hence restricting the ring to 256 stations. The destination address is set by the transmitter to route the packet to the desired receiver; but it also includes its own address as source so that it can inspect the packet again as it circulates back round the ring. From the response bits, the transmitter is immediately able to tell how the receiver treated the packet. Two response bits are used in the encoding, both of which are set to one when the transmitter sends the packet. If the destination is absent or the station switched off, the bits will be returned unchanged to the source. Otherwise the destination sets the bits to show whether the minipacket was accepted, rejected because the station was busy, or rejected because the station was not listening to that particular source. The transmitter can then adjust its strategy for sending to this particular station. The final response bit is a parity bit to detect errors in the transmission system.

The data, as all other fields in the minipacket, is fixed length. It is restricted to 16 bits. This is obviously very small, and in design revisions to the ring this field was expanded. However, although only having 16 out of 38 bits valid data, the whole scale of the minipacket is small; Ethernet by contrast has a preamble of 64 bits before any of the business of the packet begins. Further, the circulation of a minipacket round the ring means that all stations get a reasonable chance to transmit if they require. In order to take advantage of the communications bandwidth offered, software protocol needs to control and route the information exchange. Data is normally transmitted across the ring using the *basic block protocol*. This provides a mechanism for delivering up to 2048 bytes of data from one host to another. It begins with a *header* minipacket, which specifies the length of the data. Thereafter follows *route* information, which contains a 12-bit port number used to direct the data to the appropriate place within the destination. Then follows the *data*, in 1–1024 minipackets, terminated by a *checksum* minipacket for error detection. In normal working the receiving station will be free, with its *source select register* set to 255 indicating its willingness to receive from any station. However, once it has accepted the header information, it will elect to receive the rest of the basic block only from that transmitter by setting its source select register to the number of the originating station.

Basic block protocol thus provides unidirectional transmission of useful sized blocks of data. Above this is provided the *byte stream protocol* that connects two hosts with bidirectional synchronized information exchange. This is achieved by implementing a number of commands. Open and close, for example, are used at the beginning and end of the byte stream session, both of which require explicit acknowledgement to keep transmitter and receiver in step. The most common command is the data command, which contains a sequence number as well as the data. In the event of a block being lost, or received incorrectly, it should be sent again by the transmitter. A timeout procedure is used to abandon byte stream connections in the event that either host fails to respond within a reasonable time, which might be in the order of 100 ms.

Thus the byte stream protocol provides a rapid means of exchanging variable sized packets of information between any two hosts connected to the ring. This may support simple terminal interaction, where the data will be dominated by multiple protocol exchanges. Equally it may be used to support a common file server, which is expected to provide files of information to a number of different computers, with little or no backing store of their own. Although fast networks like Ethernet and the Cambridge Ring cannot cover a wide geographical area, they have radically changed the way in which computers and computer systems can be linked together. They permit relatively large bodies of information to be sent where needed, in a time that is more appropriate to the potential communications speed of current computers. There will undoubtedly be much work in the future devoted to making these communications available over a wider area. Equally the speed and capacity of the medium needs to be extended, so that it can deal with the bandwidth demanded by combined speech and video exchanges.

Exercises

1. Distinguish between synchronous and asynchronous transmission. Give an example of each and explain with timing diagrams how they work.
2. Give a brief description of the following media: twisted pair cable, coaxial cable and optical fibre. In each case identify a widespread application and relate this to the physical characteristics of the media.

3. Distinguish between circuit switched and packet switched networks. Give an account of their typical use.
4. Explain what you understand by error correction. Illustrate how this may work in the context of the protocols on different communications media.
5. Using the information already given specifying Ethernet, what is the theoretical data throughput that can be achieved with maximum block sizes of 64 and 1024 bytes? Compare this with the performance achieved on the Cambridge Ring. What are your conclusions?

5
Computer peripherals

Printed documents and books are a common means by which human beings acquire and exchange information. Libraries of books act as an information store. Computer systems can create and store information with the added property of being able to manipulate it. The user of a computer system needs information represented in the form of printed marks or their equivalent on an electronic display. The computer system stores and manipulates information in a coded, machine-readable form. Computer peripherals can be divided into two classes: those which interact with users and thus convert between the human-readable and machine-readable forms and those which store machine-readable information only.

This chapter begins with a brief review of printing terms and techniques which provide a common theme to the discussion of printers, and interactive text and graphics terminals. This is followed by a survey of the common machine-readable devices, namely magnetic disks and tapes.

5.1 The printing process

The fundamental element of a page of printed text is the character. Sequences of characters are combined into words, words formed into sentences and sentences aggregated into paragraphs. In addition to letters and numbers a page of a document will contain punctuation and other special marks. The set of available characters and marks is called a font. There are many different designs of fonts, some with copyrighted names such as Times, Courier, Helvetica, etc. A named font can have different styles, e.g. Times Roman, Times Italic, and weight, e.g. normal, bold. A font can vary in size, the unit being the *point* (72 points = 1 inch). A common size of printed text is 10 point. The final characteristic of a font character is the width. This may be fixed in proportion to the point size or vary according to the character, e.g. the width of *i* is different to *m*. Fonts with variable-width characters are known as proportionally spaced fonts and have greater aesthetic appeal as well as giving a greater number of characters per line.

Figure 5.1 illustrates a number of typographical terms. The fundamental reference line for positioning text is the base line. Non-descending characters such as 'a, b, c, ...' and capitals rest on the base line. Letters with descenders, such as 'g, p, q, ...' project below the base line. The point size is the distance between the top of the ascenders and the bottom of the descenders.

In traditional printing the shape of the character is embossed on the surface of a slug of rectangular metal. A line of text is assembled or composed from these slugs by placing them one after another with spaces between words. The size of the space is varied to reduce the frequency of hyphenation. Successive lines of text have space inserted between them with the baseline spacing being set at one or two more points than the font point size. Once the complete page is composed or typeset, the embossed characters can be inked and pressed against the paper to produce the printed page.

Phototypesetting is very different to the mechanical printing system. The equivalent of a page of metal type is a photographic negative composed of small black or white dots. The resolution (number of dots per inch) is a measure of the quality of the final image. The highest-quality systems have a resolution of 1000 dots per inch. Individual character shapes must be defined as a matrix of dots or bit map. Figure 5.2 compares a selection of bit maps based on two matrix sizes: 16×20 and 5×9 dots. Clearly the larger the matrix the better the approximation to the original font shape.

(a)

(b)

Figure 5.1 Illustration of some typographical terms: (a) Times Roman – a proportional font; (b) Courier Roman – a fixed-width font

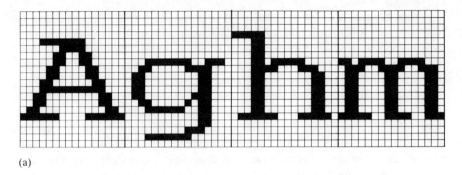

(a)

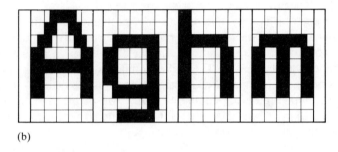

(b)

Figure 5.2   Bit maps of selected characters: (a) 16 × 20 bit map; (b) 5 × 9 bit map with intermediate horizontal positioning

5.2   Overview of the computer production of human-readable information

The function of printers and display output peripherals is to realize from a machine-readable form of text a human-readable image. This activity has strong links with printing but it is only recently that reasonably priced computer peripherals capable of producing medium quality print have become widespread. Most printers and displays can only be regarded as low quality from the typographic viewpoint. The engineering compromises required to produce a product to a price are all too evident.

The ASCII code can be divided into printing and control characters. The printing codes are mapped onto a subset of a printing font with the addition of an explicit space. The control codes of interest to printing are carriage return ($0D_{16}$), line feed ($0A_{16}$) and form feed ($0C_{16}$). Internally a piece of text is stored as a sequence of printing characters interspersed with control characters to mark the end of lines and pages.

The simplest forms of printer or display use a fixed-width font. This means a blank page can be viewed as a matrix of equal rectangular spaces butted together. Each space can contain a single character. Two integers (i, j) define a character position where i is the row index or line number and j is a column index which is the position across the page (Fig. 5.3).

A simple model of a generic printing or display device operates as follows. Suppose that the position of the last character printed is $(i, j - 1)$ and the print head is positioned over (i, j). On receipt of an ASCII code one of the following actions will occur:

printing character	select character pattern and print it at (i, j), move to position $(i, j + 1)$,
carriage return	move to the begining of the current line i.e. position $(i, 1)$,
line feed	move down one line spacing i.e. position $(i + 1, j)$,
form feed	move to new page and position $(1, 1)$.

If the device supports proportional spacing, then the same model applies except that the current print position depends on the sum of the widths of characters printed so far rather than a fixed position.

5.3 Impact printers

The adjective impact refers to the mechanical means by which a character is transferred to the paper. All printers of this class have some form of print head which is struck onto an inked ribbon to transfer the required shape to the paper. In this respect they are akin to the mechanical form of printing.

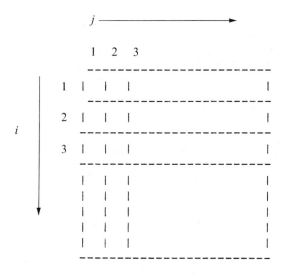

Figure 5.3 Identifying a position on the page

5.3.1 DAISY WHEEL PRINTER

The print head has embossed characters located at the end of evenly distributed arms around a wheel as shown in Fig. 5.4. Typically 96 characters are on a wheel which can be constructed of plastic or metal, the latter giving the best quality results. The character corresponding to a given code is selected by rotating clockwise or anticlockwise depending which direction gives the least movement. Once the selected character is vertical a hammer strikes it against a ribbon to make an imprint on paper.

The positioning or registration of the character is achieved with a combination of two perpendicular motions. The print head is mounted on a carriage, which can be moved horizontally and the paper movement vertically. The ribbon is generally advanced with every character printed. This implies spooling it on reels which are frequently mounted in a cartridge (see Fig. 5.5). The carriage is fixed to the print head carriage.

This type of printer gives good quality printing, sometimes termed 'letter quality', since it corresponds to that produced by an electric typewriter. Printing speeds vary from 10 to 200 characters per second. The printer is attached to the peripheral controller using either a parallel or a serial interface.

5.3.2 MATRIX PRINTER

As the name suggests this printer creates the printing mark from a matrix of

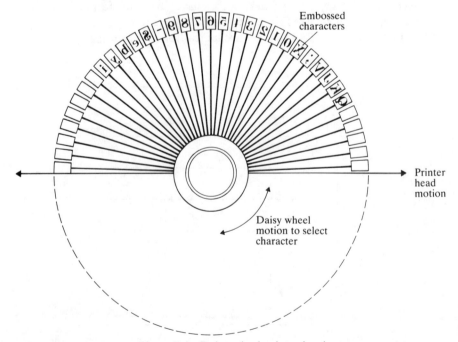

Figure 5.4 Daisy wheel printer head

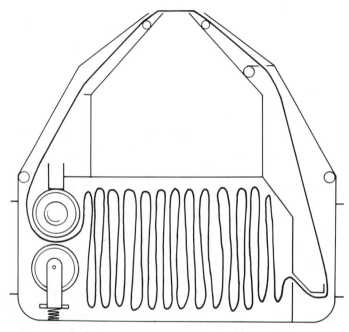

Figure 5.5 Printer ribbon cartridge

dots, as does the phototypesetter. Since it is an electromechanical device the resolution is coarse, being the order of 100 dots per inch. A 7 × 9 matrix representation is common but higher resolutions are available. The small bit map for the characters means that only two bits are used for ascenders and descenders. The print head consists of a column of 9 pins, which can be 'fired' selectively at the ribbon to create a dot on the paper. Thus the character is created one column at a time. Choosing an inter-pin spacing of $\frac{1}{72}$ inch would give a 9-point character size, which implies a pin half the diameter of a dressmaker's pin. The positioning of the print head is the same as for the daisy wheel.

The cheaper matrix printers have a fixed font. More expensive models allow a user to define and 'down load' his own font definitions. Increasingly a 'near letter quality' option is included, where the print head makes multiple passes of a line. The object is to create characters from overlapping dots. This implies fine control over head positioning. These more sophisticated printers support proportional fonts. Many of these printers allow the creation of graphical images. In this mode the picture is created using the top 8 pins of the head. The bytes supplied are interpreted as a pattern of bits and the picture is created 8 bit rows at a time.

The print speed can vary between 40 and 500 characters per second, with up to 200 being the most common range. The speed will depend on the printing mode – the higher the quality the lower the speed because of the multiple passes.

5.3.3 LINE PRINTER

As the name suggests a line of printing is created as one composite action. The matrix and daisy wheel printers are sometimes called serial printers because they have a single print head and hammer combination. Higher printing speeds are obtained if multiple heads and hammers are used. Line printers can differ in detail but they all have the following characteristics:

(a) there is a hammer for each printing position,
(b) a band or drum of embossed characters is rotated in front of the line of
     hammers.

When the correct character is in front of a particular hammer it fires to print.

Figure 5.6(a) shows the arrangement using a band. The band contains more than one set of printing characters. A complete line is printed when one set of characters has passed across the page. The inked ribbon passes between the band and the paper. An alternative to the band is a rotating drum composed of a set of bands corresponding to each printing position. Each band contains a complete printing set distributed around it (see Fig. 5.6(b)). The drum is usually inked continuously by a roll rather than using a ribbon.

Printing speeds for line printers can range up to 1500 lines per minute. This needs a block-oriented DMA peripheral interface. The speed of printing and the problem of mechanical wear means that the vertical registration of characters can vary thus reducing the quality of the result.

5.4 Laser printer – a non-impact printer

A number of techniques can be used to achieve printing without the use of hammers and print heads, e.g. thermal, inkjet, electrostatic, etc. They are potentially faster and quieter, because of the omission of the mechanical moving parts. One type of printer, the laser printer, has come to dominate this class of device. It has brought a form of phototypesetting, albeit at a reduced resolution, within the reach of a large class of computer user.

The laser printer exploits the physical phenomenon of photo-conductivity to create an initial image as a pattern of electric charge. A photo-conductive material, e.g. selenium, acts as an insulator when it is in the dark and as a conductor when it is exposed to light. A drum coated with selenium can be selectively exposed to light to leave a residual charge where black dots are required. The drum is rotated through a toner bath which contain ink particles that are attracted to the charge. The particles of ink are transferred to a sheet of paper where they are fixed by heating (see Fig. 5.7). The laser plays a key part in exposing the drum. It supplies a narrow, parallel beam of light that strikes a multiple facet mirror. The mirror rotates synchronously with the photo-conductive drum to produce a scan. The movement of one facet of the mirror causes a single horizontal scan of the drum. A dot is created by modulating the laser beam with an electro-optical shutter.

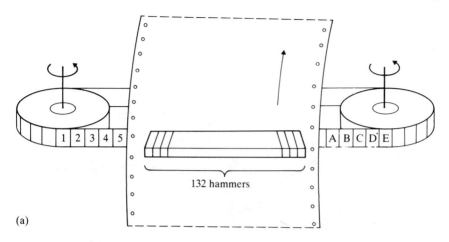

(a)

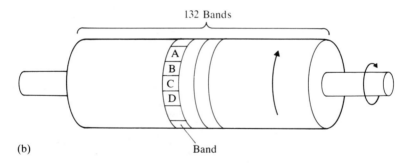

(b)

Figure 5.6   (a) Band and (b) drum line printers

Recently a number of products, based on a 300 dots per inch laser writing engine, have given exceptional print quality for the price. The printer takes A4 sized paper and can print at 8 pages a minute. The products range from a daisy wheel replacement to a sophisticated printing device driven by a graphics language. This allows documents to be created from characters drawn from a wide range of fonts and point sizes. Text may also be laid out in other than horizontal lines. A statistic worth noting is that a bit map of a page of A4 at 300 dots per inch needs about 1 Mbyte of storage.

5.5   Visual display unit (VDU)

The VDU is one of the commonest devices attached to a host computer. It supports the interactive input of characters from a keyboard and the output of

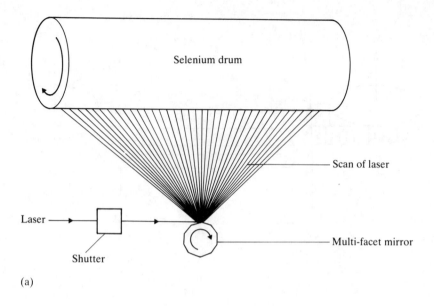

(a)

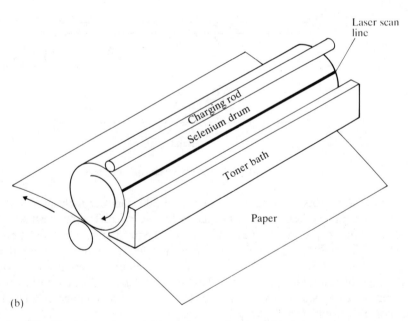

(b)

Figure 5.7 The laser printer: (a) scanning mechanism; (b) end view showing charging mechanism, toner bath and paper movement. Scan of drum takes place between charging rod and toner bath

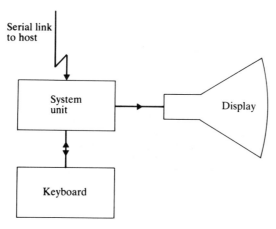

Figure 5.8   The visual display unit (VDU)

characters to display screen. Despite its name the VDU is composed of three functionally distinct units: keyboard, display and a coordinating system unit (Fig. 5.8).

The input and output of individual characters are usually part of a dialogue with the host operating system or user program. The VDU can operate in one of two modes: half-duplex or duplex. In half-duplex mode characters input from the keyboard are sent directly to the host. In duplex mode any characters input are sent both to the display and the host. In both cases characters received from the host are displayed on the screen.

5.5.1   CATHODE RAY TUBE (CRT)

The display unit is one of a number of electronic devices which are based on the CRT. A simplified diagram of a CRT is given in Fig. 5.9. The electron gun generates a focused beam of fast moving electrons which pass through a deflection unit. The deflection unit controls the spot where the beam strikes the display surface. The inner phosphor coating responds to the impact of the electrons by emitting light. The colour of the emitted light depends on the phosphor used. Common colours are white, amber, red, green and blue.

The intensity of the light spot produced is proportional to the rate of electrons striking the phosphor. The application of a negative voltage to an intensity control unit in the electron gun reduces the output of electrons. At a certain level of voltage none are emitted. The removal of the electron beam from a given position on the display surface causes the light spot to gradually fade. The beam can be deflected by the application of an electric or magnetic field. For the former this can be done by applying a voltage across two parallel plates which straddle the beam. Two independent deflections, horizontal and vertical, can be applied to the beam, allowing it to be positioned anywhere on the surface.

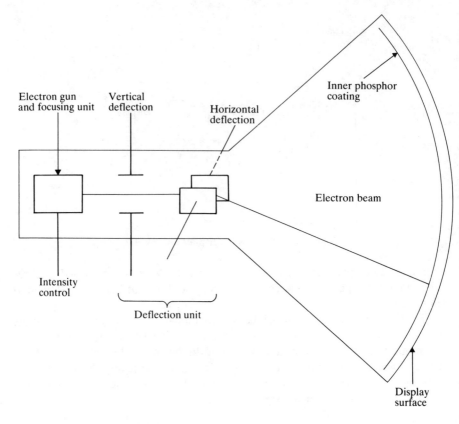

Figure 5.9 Simplified model of a cathode ray tube (CRT)

5.5.2 ADAPTING THE CRT TO DISPLAY TEXT

The problem of creating the illusion of a stable image on a transient medium is overcome by using a raster scan technique similar to television. The image is built from a series of regularly spaced lines. The electron beam repeatedly follows a pattern of the form given in Fig. 5.10(a).

A complete scan of the screen, or frame scan, starts at the top left-hand corner, the beam being swept left to right. On reaching the end of the line the beam is turned off and moved back to the beginning of the next line. This sequence is repeated until the frame scan is complete when the beam is moved back to the top left-hand corner to begin the cycle again. Frame scans take $\frac{1}{30} - \frac{1}{60}$ of a second, depending on the persistence of the phosphor. The larger the number of lines the better the quality of image created.

A monochrome television image is created by continuously varying the intensity, or modulating, the beam of electrons to give a range of grey shades. The text terminal uses only two intensities, e.g. black (beam off) or white (beam

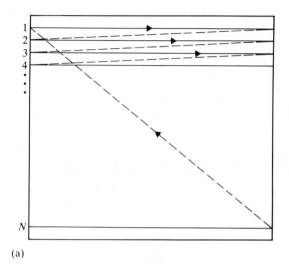

(a)

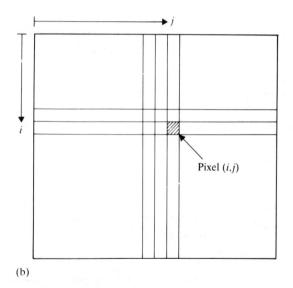

Pixel (i,j)

(b)

Figure 5.10 (a) Raster scan pattern; (b) pixel addressing

on). Each scan line is made up from a sequence of dots which can be regarded as fundamental picture elements or pixels. The total screen image can be stored as a matrix of pixel values, each value requiring a single bit of memory. The indices of an arbitrary bit position are pixel addresses (see Fig. 5.10(b)). The matrix of bits is called variously refresh memory, frame buffer or bit map.

The display controller forms a visual image from the pixel values in the refresh memory. Figure 5.11 represents a simplified view of the principal elements in the controller. The scan generator produces a sequence of pixel addresses which are used to obtain the corresponding pixel value as well as being used to generate the deflection voltage to position the beam. The pixel value is used to modulate the beam intensity to produce the light and dark dots.

As with the matrix and laser printers the resolution of the display determines the quality of the text representation. A common size of dot matrix to define a character is 7 × 9. For a terminal which displays 24 lines of 80 characters, this implies a resolution of 640 × 240 pixels. A single dot of space is allowed between each character and successive lines. The refresh memory needs to be 150 Kbits. Unlike those produced by matrix printers the dots on the display have a tendency to merge because of a halo effect which gives the illusion of a better resolution than is actually the case.

The fixed-font character set is stored in a non-volatile read-only memory (ROM). The dot matrix for each character can be stored as 10 rows of one byte, which includes the space around the character. The ROM is organized so that the ASCII character code can be used as the first address of ten rows of eight pixel values. The functional model of the display controller is now expanded as in Fig. 5.12.

It is undesirable to update the refresh memory during a frame scan. The updating is usually done between the frame scans when the beam is flying back to the top of the screen. This allows about a millisecond for the update. The updating is a memory write operation whereas the display scanning is a memory read. A text VDU usually has a flashing cursor to mark the next position a character would be printed. The unit responsible for updating the memory must contain programmable registers which control and update the cursor position.

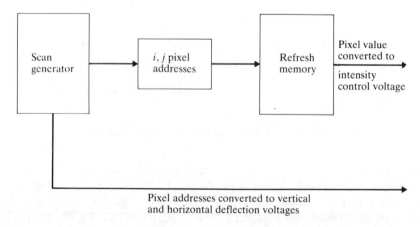

Pixel addresses converted to vertical and horizontal deflection voltages

Figure 5.11 CRT controller

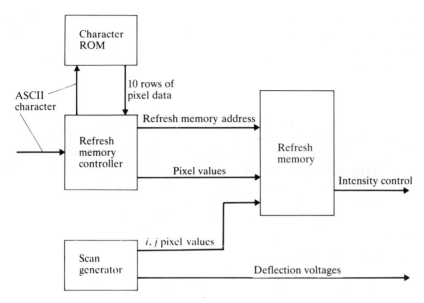

Figure 5.12   Display controller including character ROM

5.5.3 KEYBOARD

Functionally the keyboard is a matrix of about 60 keys which are used to generate the 128 characters of the ASCII code set. The QWERTY keyboard arrangement derives from typewriters, where a shift key was employed to make double use of a given key stroke, e.g. shift and 5 is %. The use of a shift key enables all of the printable subset of the ASCII code to be generated with some to spare. The control characters, except for rubout ($7F_{16}$), which has its own key, are produced by employing a second special key named control. For example,

$$\text{control and } @ = \text{null } (00_{16})$$

$$\text{control and A} = \text{SOH } (01_{16})$$

and so on. The restriction of 127 codes is circumvented by introducing a set of function keys typically between 10 and 24 in number. Depressing a function key generates a sequence of ASCII characters. The exact form of sequence is often programmable. This feature allows the writers of software packages to tailor certain operations to a single key stroke. Finally four special cursor keys are linked to the movement of the cursor on the screen.

Keyboards are designed around a matrix of isolated wires with the keys acting as switches to convert electrically a particular row and column. The wires are normally held at zero volts. If a key at position (i, j) is depressed and a voltage applied to row i it will also appear on column j. Keyboard controller integrated circuits cyclically apply a voltage to a row and scan all the columns to test for a non-zero column to determine the pair (i, j). A complete scan of the whole keyboard is performed in a millisecond. The mapping of a pair (i, j) and any shift or control depressions into a ASCII code can be handled by a single-chip microcomputer.

5.5.4   SYSTEM UNIT

The system unit coordinates the input from the keyboard, the output to the display and the communications with the host. The keyboard produces input at random but very slowly (< 10 characters per second). The characters from the host are displayed on the screen and can arrive in bursts at up to $19.2\,\mathrm{K}$ characters per second. The characters input from the keyboard are sent to the host and echoed to the display controller if the terminal is in half-duplex mode. A small microprocessor system is capable of coordinating these activities.

5.6   Graphics devices

5.6.1   USING A RASTER SCAN DISPLAY FOR GRAPHICS

The interaction between the CRT controller and the system unit of the text terminal is via ASCII codes and sequences. Crude graphical pictures can be plotted using characters but a true graphics device is created if individual pixels can be addressed rather than character blocks. Only the resolution of the device limits the monochrome drawings which can be displayed. The representation of a line requires the calculation of the sequence of pixel addresses which are closest to the true line (see Fig. 5.13). The higher the resolution of the display the less jagged the appearance of the plotted line. Any curve can be approximated by a discrete set of points. Closed areas can be filled with a regular geometric pattern or with solid colour.

5.6.2   EXTENSION OF THE CRT CONTROLLER TO DISPLAY COLOUR

Using a single bit of data per pixel in the refresh memory gives two possible intensity levels. A black-and-white television reproduces a large number of

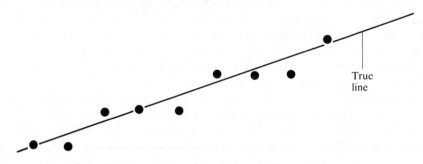

Figure 5.13   Raster scan conversion of a straight line

different intensities, or levels of grey, at any position in the picture. Increasing the number of data bits associated with each pixel increases the grey levels, e.g. 4 bits gives 16 levels, 8 bits 256 levels and so on. The use of a 1024 × 1024 resolution and 8 data bits per pixel allows a good reproduction of black-and-white photographs. The refresh memory required is 1 Mbyte. There is no substantive change to the functional diagram in Fig. 5.11 except that an 8-bit value is converted to the voltage which controls the intensity rather than a single bit value.

A colour display surface is made up of triplets of small rectangles of red, green and blue phosphor (as is a colour television). Three electron guns control the intensity of each colour individually. Thus a set of three intensities for the primary colours corresponds to a given perceived colour, e.g. equal intensities of red and green but no blue gives yellow. If each gun can be controlled to give I intensity levels, then a total of I^3 colours can be displayed.

Suppose that there are S bits per pixel in the refresh memory. The simplest modification to extend a grey scale controller to cope with colour is to divide the S bits into three equal parts, each part being an integer intensity for a colour. Most colour display controllers do not store the intensity values for each colour directly in the refresh memory. This is partly for cost reasons, but also the memory bandwidth requirement is less if a device known as a colour table, or map, is introduced. This allows a large set of possible displayable colours, the palette, with the restriction that the maximum number of simultaneously displayed colours is still 2^S (see Fig. 5.14).

The value d associated with an arbitrary pixel address (i, j) is used as index into the colour table. The contents of each entry in the table is a set of integers to control the red green and blue intensities. Suppose that the table has S entries

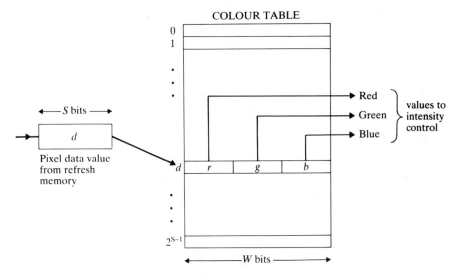

Figure 5.14 Colour table for display

each W bits wide, then 2^S simultaneous colours can be drawn from a palette of 2^W.

So far it has been assumed that a program on the host computer controls the refresh memory directly using pixel addresses. For other than trivial pictures this will involve substantial amounts of output from the graphics plotting program. This can be reduced by associating a local processor and memory which handles the communication with the refresh memory. This local, or graphics, processor is programmed to provide a range of primitive operations such as line, circle and ellipse drawing, area filling, etc. The host now issues drawing commands to the graphics processor which generates the pixel address-es and values.

5.6.3 GRAPHICS TERMINAL

Like the text terminal the graphics display is associated with one or more input devices to form an interactive graphics terminal. Graphical images are com-posed of text, line drawings, filled areas of colour, etc. As with the character-oriented displays a keyboard is required for text input, but a further requirement is a pointing device to assist in the manipulation of pictures. There are a number of pointing devices but the mouse (see Fig. 5.15) has become the most common. The mouse is a hand-held object, which can be moved about on a flat surface or specially marked tablet. The movement in two orthogonal directions is detected either mechanically or optically and the mouse outputs positional information in the form of coordinates. The graphics processor couples the mouse movement to a screen cursor, represented typically as an arrow, thus providing visual feedback to the hand movement. The mouse has a small number of buttons which act as signals.

The combination of moving a screen cursor about the display surface with signal buttons allow several styles of input. Suppose that a menu of options is displayed, positioning the cursor over one and depressing a button enables a choice to be selected. An element of a picture can be 'picked' in a similar way. Free-hand drawing can be simulated if the continuous positional information produced by the mouse is sampled by the graphics processor to produce a sequence of lines drawn on the screen.

5.6.4 GRAPH PLOTTER

The plotter was a relatively common output device for producing annotated line drawings before the introduction of graphical displays. The rapid increase in the graphical capabilities of personal computers has increased the use of plotters. There are two ways of producing a hard copy of a graphical picture: random scanning or raster scanning. The former creates the picture as a sequence of lines or vectors and the latter as the familiar image created from dots. Matrix and laser printers can act as raster-scan graph-plotting devices, although the matrix printer provides only a proof quality image.

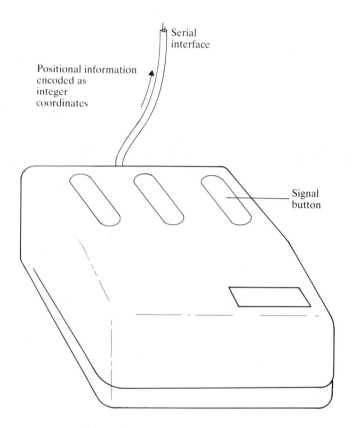

Serial
interface

Positional information
encoded as
integer
coordinates

Signal
button

Figure 5.15   Top view of a mouse

The flat bed plotter is the most common dedicated plotting device (see Fig. 5.16). This is often based on a movable gantry carrying a pen assembly, which can be moved along the gantry thus producing two perpendicular movements. Alternatively the gantry is fixed and the paper moves. These arrangements allow eight possibe drawing movements in all (Fig. 5.17).

The pen can be placed in the up position to allow free movement around the paper and in the down position when a line is to be drawn. The minimum length of pen movement is typically 0.025 mm. The size of the bed can vary from A4 to 6 × 10 ft, but the most common size is A3/A4. The plotter can have up to eight pens, allowing either a selection of colours or pen widths to be used. The A3/A4 plotter has a serial interface.

The plotter is controlled by a local processor which is programmed to respond to a fixed set of commands. The set of commands form a simple graphics language and a sequence to draw a line from position (x_1, y_1) to (x_2, y_2) could take the form of:

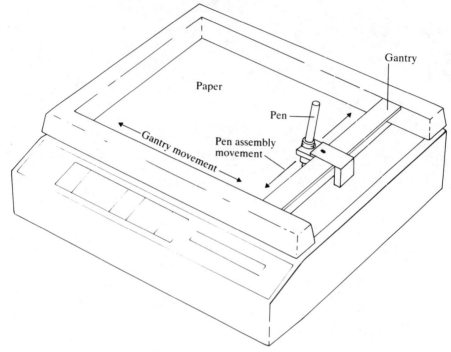

Figure 5.16   Flat bed plotter

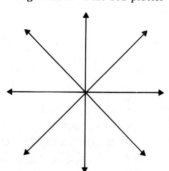

Figure 5.17   The eight possible drawing movements of the flat bed plotter

```
pen – up
move – to (x₁, y₁)
pen – down
move – to (x₂, y₂)
```

The coordinates (x_1, y_1) are an integer pair which represent an absolute position where a pen can be positioned on the plotting surface. Similar to the graphics display processor, many graph plotters have local intelligence to interpret commands to draw circles, arcs, text, area fill, etc.

The plotter ends the discussion of a selection of human-oriented devices. Most human interaction with a computer involves the use of the filing system. This interaction is either passive in the sense of loading and running existing programs or active in the creation of new files. These activities are supported by a range of machine-readable storage peripherals which are the subject of the next two sections.

5.7 Magnetic disk

Peripherals using magnetic disk and tape media provide a means of recording binary information with a high degree of stability. These devices can be regarded as an extension of the random access memory directly attached to the bus. Information is recorded by destructive writing as in the memory and can be read back many times. Disks and tapes have very different storage and timing characteristics, which determine their role in the computer system.

5.7.1 STORAGE CHARACTERISTICS

Magnetic disks are used to provide the on-line file store which is the heart of any computer system. There is a range of devices with varying capacity and performance but all are based on a similar functional model. Figure 5.18 gives a much simplified outline of the major constituents of a disk system. The disk is coated with iron oxide which can be magnetized by a write head positioned at the tip of a swinging arm. A short pulse of current in the write windings creates a small dot of magnetism on the disk.

Read windings are coincident with the write windings forming a combined reading and writing head. A dot of magnetism created previously can be detected by a pulse of induced current in the read windings.

Binary information is written in concentric circles or tracks which are located towards the circumference of the disk. The tracks are subdivided into a fixed number of sectors (N_s) where each sector contains a fixed number of bytes (N_b).

A read or write operation involves the transfer of a complete sector. To increase capacity some disk systems employ a number of disks on a spindle. Each magnetic surface has its own read/write head. Corresponding tracks on each surface are collectively termed a cylinder. The total capacity of a disk unit with N_m media surfaces, and N_t tracks per surface is simply

$$C = N_m \times N_t \times N_s \times N_b \text{ bytes}$$

Table 5.1 gives the values for three representative disk systems.

The Winchester disk system is a fixed system, in the sense that disks and actuators of the read/write heads are enclosed in a sealed unit to give a controlled environment free of dust. They are used on all sizes of computers from personal to mainframe and span the capacity range of 10 Mbytes to 1.5 Gbytes. The exchangeable disk units differ in that the spindle and disks can be removed and replaced with a different set. This allows copies of disks to be taken for security purposes.

The floppy disk system is very different in that the disk is flexible. It can be inserted and removed from the disk unit. Most personal computers have one or more of these units. They are a convenient medium for distributing software packages. There are a variety of sizes of floppy disk, for example 8, 5.25 and 3.5

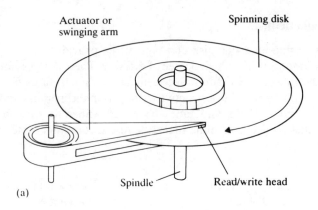

(a)

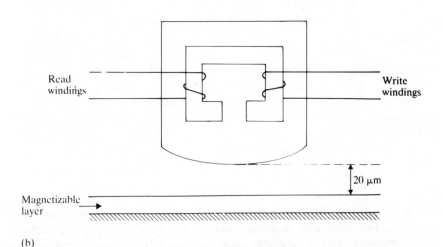

(b)

Figure 5.18 Functional model of a disk unit: (a) disk drive units; (b) read/write head details; (c) small (3.5 inch) Winchester disk showing arm and head (courtesy of Hewlett-Packard Ltd)

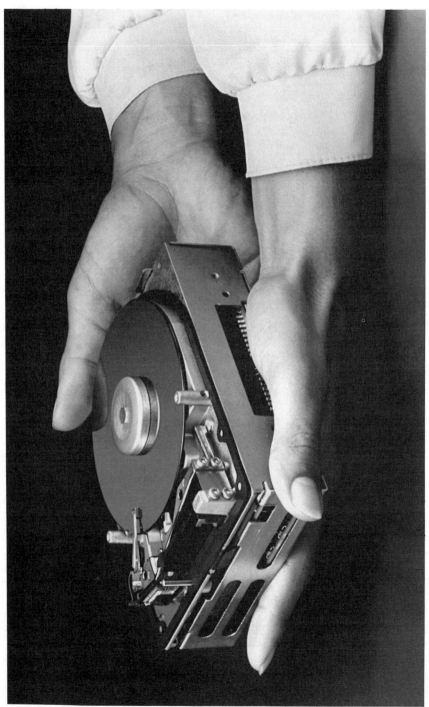

Figure 5.18 (continued)

(c)

Table 5.1 Characteristics of disk systems

	Winchester	Exchangeable	Floppy
N_b (bytes)	512	512	512
N_s	51	32	10
N_t	2496	823	80
N_m	7	19	2
C	456 Mbytes	256 Mbytes	818 Kbytes
t_s (ms)	28	30	164
t_l (ms)	8.3	8.3	100
t_t (ms)	6	6	6
P	2.2 Mb/s	1.2 Mb/s	250 Kbits/s
t_{IO} (ms)	0.22	0.43	16
$t_{\text{Read/Write}}$ (ms)	36.3	38.3	264

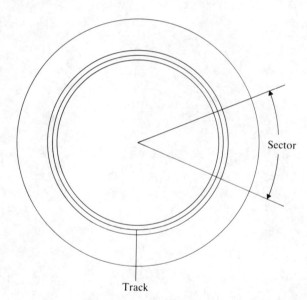

Figure 5.19   Disk organization

inch in diameter. The latter two sizes are the most common. Storage capacities range from 250 Kbytes to over 1 Mbyte.

5.7.2 TIMING CHARACTERISTICS

An important factor in the overall performance of a computer system is the time to transfer the contents of disk sectors to and from the main computer memory and the disk drive. Programs in the host have a view of the disk which is similar to that of memory. The disk is a linear set of fixed-size blocks each with a unique block address. The disk-drive unit is interfaced to the bus with a controller, which offers a block-oriented DMA interface to the processor. The controller contains local memory to act as a buffer for blocks being read or written to the disk drive. A disk read operation involves the following sequence of steps:

1. Program in host issues a read request to the disk controller specifying the block address and memory address where it is to be placed.
2. The controller maps the block address into track and sector numbers.
3. The controller initiates a head movement to seek for the required track.
4. The controller waits for the required sector to appear under the read/write head.
5. The block is transferred from disk surface to the local memory of the controller.
6. The block is transferred to the host memory using DMA.

A disk write operation will cause a similar sequence, but in a different order. The time taken to position the head over a track is called the seek time, t_s, and the time waiting for the sector to rotate under the head the latency, t_l.

The values of t_s and t_l will depend on the initial position of the read/write head with respect to the requested track and sector. Manufacturer's data quote averages for these times. The average latency is the time for the disk to perform half a revolution. The time to move from track to track, t_t, is usually quoted also. The peak transfer rate of information to and from the disk surface is determined principally by the rotation speed of the disk and the recording density (bits/inch). Denoting this peak rate by P, the time to transfer a block from the disk to the controller t_{IO} is given by

$$t_{IO} = \frac{N_b}{P}$$

The values for t_s, t_l, P, and t_{IO} are given in Table 5.1 for the three disk types considered previously. Note that t_{IO} is small compared with the sum of t_s and t_l. Thus the average time to read or write a block, $t_{Read/Write}$, can be written as

$$t_{Read/Write} = t_s + t_l$$

Note that the values of seek time, latency and read/write time for a block for a floppy disk are about an order of magnitude slower than for the other disk types.

5.8 Magnetic tape

5.8.1 STORAGE CHARACTERISTICS

Magnetic tape is a popular medium for providing 'off-line' storage. All mainframe and substantial minicomputer systems are equipped with a high-speed tape drive. The tapes are used to make security copies of the on-line disk storage and also to provide an overflow file store when the on-line capacity proves to be inadequate.

A simplified picture of a tape drive is given in Fig. 5.20. The flexible plastic tape is $\frac{1}{2}$ inch wide and is coated with a ferromagnetic material. The tape is wound onto reels which can accommodate a length of up to 2400 ft. A tape is loaded into the unit by attaching it to the supply reel drive and feeding the tape via the rollers and past the read/write heads to the take-up reel. During a read or write operation the tape is advanced past the read/write heads by pinch rollers pressing the tape against capstans, which rotate at constant speed. One of the important characteristics is that the tape can be accelerated to a constant speed and subsequently stopped very quickly. The reels are driven independently to the capstan and the loops of tape sucked into the vacuum chambers serve to decouple the two driving mechanisms and so keep the tension in the tape constant.

Binary data is written to the tape in the form of blocks or records, when it is moving at a constant speed. Since it is stationary before and after writing, an inter-block gap must occur between successive records. Usually there are nine read/write heads, which magnetize the tape in rows perpendicular to the direction of movement. Eight bits are for data, one for parity. The number of rows per inch is quoted as the density in units of bits per inch. Thus this figure is equivalent to bytes per inch for a nine-track tape.

For a disk the block size and total number of blocks storable on the disk are

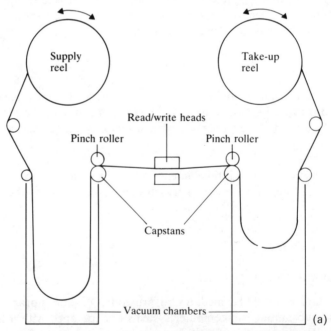

Figure 5.20 (a) Simplified model of a high-speed tape drive; (b) high-speed tape drive with 0.5 inch magnetic tape reels and smaller (0.25 inch) tape cartridge being inserted (Courtesy of Hewlett-Packard Ltd)

(b)   **Figure 5.20**   (continued)

constant. For a magnetic tape the block size, and so its capacity, can vary. The characteristics related to capacity are denoted as:

L length (inches),
ϱ recording density (bits/inch)
g inter block gap (inches),
b the block size (bytes).

Suppose there are N_b blocks when the record size is b. The capacity is thus given by

$$C = N_b b$$

The physical length of tape can be written as

$$L = N_b \left\{ \frac{b}{\varrho} + g \right\}$$

where b/ϱ is the physical length of a block. Eliminating N_b and simplifying the expression for the capacity becomes

$$C = L \frac{\varrho}{1 + g\varrho/b}$$

The smaller the ratio $g\varrho/b$ the greater the total capacity of the tape. This factor is the ratio of the gap length and the physical length of a block. Table 5.2 lists the capacity of a typical tape as a function of b.

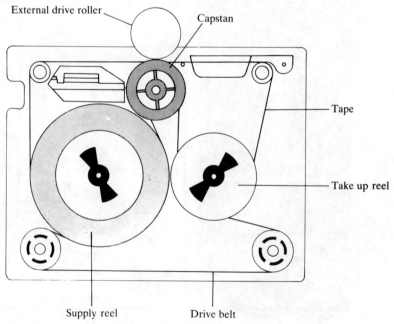

Figure 5.21   The tape cartridge

5.8.2 TIMING CHARACTERISTICS

As with the magnetic disk the host program's view of the tape is as a linear sequence of addressed blocks. In this the physical realization of blocks on the tape matches the program view. Whereas the disk is a random access device, the tape is a serial device and to access a given block requires all preceding blocks to have been read or scanned. The tape controller again offers a block-oriented DMA interface and local buffering. A tape read operation involves the following sequence of steps:

1. The host program issues a read request similar to disk read.
2. The tape controller scans the tape for the selected block.
3. The block is transferred from the tape to the local buffer.
4. The block is transferred from the local buffer to the host memory.

The time to read or write a block can be estimated from the storage characteristics plus the constant read/write speed v. Suppose that the tape has been advanced to the gap before the required block. The time to read the block is the sum of three components: the acceleration to speed v, the reading of a block size b at speed v and decelerating to rest. It is assumed that the tape accelerates and decelerates uniformly. Denoting the acceleration by α, then v is given by the equations

$$v = \alpha t \quad \text{and} \quad v^2 = 2\alpha(g/2)$$

Eliminating α, the time to accelerate to v in a distance $g/2$ is

$$t = g/v$$

The block is read in a time $b/(\alpha/v)$ and so the total time is given by

$$t_{\text{Read/Write}} = \frac{g}{v} + \frac{b}{\varrho v} + \frac{g}{v} = \left(\frac{g}{v}\right)\left\{2 + \frac{b}{\varrho g}\right\}$$

As might be expected the same dimensionless number $b/(\varrho g)$ is again an important factor. The variation of $t_{\text{Read/Write}}$ with b is also given in Table 5.2. Tape speeds can vary from 25 to 200 inches per second.

With the extensive use of Winchester disks in personal computers a less

Table 5.2 Capacity and read/write time as a function of block size

Block size (Kbytes)	Capacity (Mbytes)	Block read/write (ms)
0.5	49.4	20.0
1.0	71.3	26.6
2.0	102.1	33.1
4.0	130.3	46.2
6.0	143.5	59.3
8.0	151.2	72.4

expensive tape drive unit was required to provide the same role of back-up and overflow. Floppies have been used for this purpose but the large numbers involved are difficult to manage. Of the many designs available the cartridge tape drive is popular. A simplified picture of a tape cartridge is given in Fig. 5.21.

The tape is $\frac{1}{4}$ inch wide and is advanced from the supply to the take-up reels. The tape speed must be constant as it passes the read/write head, but the rotation speed of the reels will depend on the diameter of tape they contain. A tape-drive band that passes around both reels and a capstan solves the problems of tape tensioning and variable-speed reel drive in an ingenious way. The capstan is driven by a roller external to the cartridge. The tape does not come into contact with the capstan and external roller. Cartridges are sometimes pre-formatted to have fixed-length blocks. In fact from a software point of view pre-formatted tapes are similar to disks in that numbered blocks can be accessed albeit with a much slower access time.

There are a number of different cartridge tape systems in production. Unlike the high-speed tapes described previously the number of recording tracks can vary from 2 to 16 although the density of each track is usually about 1600 bits per inch. The capacity of tapes can vary from 256 Kbytes for a small two-track tape cartridge to 67 Mbytes for a 16-track tape 600 ft long. The read/write speeds range from 30 to 60 inches per second, although searching for a given block can be 50% faster. Peak transfer rates vary from 24 to 48 Kbits per second. The tape drives can be operated in either start–stop mode or streaming mode. The former is the technique that the open-reel tape drives are well adapted for. Streaming mode can be used when the host is able to deliver or receive a large number of blocks without any pause in between individual blocks.

5.9   Conclusions

This chapter has focused on the nature and performance of a selection of computer peripherals. Some important developments have been excluded, particularly in the technologies being used for machine-readable storage. In the area of random access devices, optical disks appear to offer significant increases in capacity where a single platter can store the order of a gigabyte of information. At present the technology is limited to write-once-only read-many-times (WORM) but it will not be long before the optical equivalent of the read/write magnetic disk is in production. Advances are happening in tape storage also. The adaptation of both video tape and digital audio tape (DAT) as computer peripherals promise to provide greater than a gigabyte of storage on a single tape.

These new capabilities will always be stretched by an increased requirement to record information. An A4 page of text encoded as ASCII coded characters needs about 2.5–5 Kbytes of storage depending on font point size and baseline spacing. The equivalent A4 bit map at 300 dots per inch needs the order of a megabyte. Increasing the resolution to 1000 dots per inch increases the storage needs by a factor of approximately 10. Page description languages represent an important development in the encoding of a page of text and graphics. Documents using a variety of fonts, point sizes and graphics can be created. The overhead incurred to get this typesetting capability varies according to the complexity of the document, but for a simple page of text a factor of three overhead over the economical ASCII encoding is incurred. This is still very small compared with an equivalent bit map. Thus an intelligent printer which interprets the page description language form to generate the bit map locally is desirable and is already available. The trend of storing and communicating information encoded with typesetting instructions, which is only recovered to human-readable form as and when required, can be expected to continue.

This completes the discussion of computer peripherals. The processor is the agent for organizing both the communication between peripherals and the manipulation of information stored on disks and tapes. The next two chapters examine both the architecture and the programming of the processor.

Exercises

1. Given that access is possible to a computer with a font editor, examine the bit maps of some fonts and determine how they are represented on disk and in memory.
2. If a matrix printer operates at an average speed of 90 characters per second, how long will it take to print an A4 page in proof graphics mode?
3. Measure how long a local serial printer takes to print a page of text. It is unlikely that the average printing speed is the same as the peak rate quoted by the manufacturer. Why should this be so?
4. Determine the factors involved in estimating a sampling rate for the graphics processor to support the capture of freehand 'drawing' by a mouse.
5. Suppose the radius of the smallest track of a disk is r inches. Derive a formula for the approximate recording density in terms of N_s, N_b, and r. Given that the rotational speed is v, estimate the peak transfer rate P.
6. Use the data given in Table 5.1 to estimate the time taken to copy a file of 500 Kbytes from the Winchester disk to the floppy disk. Assume that reading from the Winchester and writing to the floppy can proceed in parallel.
7. Calculate how long it takes to read a tape from beginning to end as a function of block size. Estimate the average access time for finding a random block on the tape.
8. Using the data in Tables 5.1 and 5.2, calculate the time to fill a magnetic tape from the exchangeable disk using 4K blocks. Is it better to use 8K blocks?

6
Assembler programming – elementary constructs

The processor can be programmed in a number of computer languages such as Basic, Pascal, Prolog and so on; it is assumed that the reader can already program in such a language. Every language has its adherents, but a major object of the high-level language designer is to provide a notation which is well suited to the expression of problem solutions. Assembler language is radically different in that it is designed to have a close relationship to the machine code of the processor and is frequently the final definition of the architecture of the machine. This closeness makes the study of assembler an important element in the development of a sound low-level model of the machine.

For most machines the assembler is an unstructured language and so any structure must be imposed by the programmer. Informal Pascal is used in this book as a design language for this purpose. A series of assembler templates for the common Pascal constructs is introduced. This technique has the advantages that:

1. programs designed in Pascal can be rapidly and accurately encoded in assembler, thus providing a structure, but in no way limiting the problems that can be solved;
2. initial insight is gained into some of the tasks carried out by a compiler and related run-time system;
3. a simple comparison between different processor architectures can be made.

The model processor architecture chosen is a simple register machine (SRM) and is summarized in Appendix 1. The instruction set is limited, but is capable of representing the data and sequencing constructs of Pascal. By comparison the instruction sets of modern 32-bit microprocessors are complex, but do not offer many more fundamental features. The equivalent templates for some popular microprocessor architectures are given in Appendices, this facilitating rapid transfer of programming skills from one processor to another.

The structure of the processor and the parallel communications mechanisms between it and the memory have been discussed in a previous chapter. Figure 6.1 reproduces the major features of interest to the assembler language programmer. The processor features form a set termed the volatile environment and represent those elements under the control of the programmer.

6.1 Memory

Memory is made up of a linear sequence of cells which can contain a single byte of information. Each cell is assigned a unique number known as an address, which is used for identification and communication purposes. The function of the memory is to hold the binary encoded data and machine code instructions that form the program to be executed by the processor. The encoding of information in binary was discussed in Chapter 2. For data other than characters a number of consecutive bytes are needed. In SRM two consecutive bytes of memory are called a word and four consecutive bytes a longword.

The memory organization of word and longword information is given in Fig. 6.2. The most significant byte of a word or longword must have an even address, i.e. be aligned on a word boundary. The address of a multi-byte data or instruction item, is the address of the most significant byte. The representation of instructions and data plus the need for exact alignment with respect to word boundaries is a fundamental characteristic of the machine. There is no intrinsic

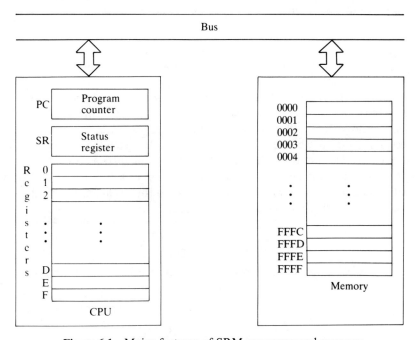

Figure 6.1 Major features of SRM processor and memory

```
            15                        8 7                        0
Word          | most significant byte | least significant byte |
```

```
            31                       16 15                       0
Long word     | most significant word | least significant word |
```

Figure 6.2   Representation of words and long words in memory

difference in form between the binary patterns representing instructions and
data. Shifting the information just a single bit with respect to word boundaries
produces an apparently similar bit pattern, but one with a different and prob-
ably nonsensical meaning.

6.2   Processor

The SRM processor has three important programmable elements: a set of
sixteen general registers $R0$–$R15$, a program counter (PC), and a status register
(SR). All registers can contain one word (16 bits) of binary information. The
functions of the processor can be summarized as follows:

1. The execution of a sequence of instructions stored in the memory.
2. Response to exceptional events such as device interrupts and serious program errors.

The PC, SR and general register set each have a role in supporting these
functions. This section will concentrate on the first function, deferring the
second until a later chapter.

   The general registers can be regarded as a local scratchpad or working
memory for the processor. A register has a 4-bit numerical address, i.e. $R10$ has
a binary address 1010_2. The contents of the PC register are interpreted by the
processor as a memory address. This address is used to fetch the next instruction
to be executed. The addition of the length of the current instruction will advance
the PC to point to the next instruction. The status register is best regarded as
a set of individually named bits, but not all 16-bit positions are used. It is divided
into two halves called the system byte and user byte.

```
            31          16 15          0
             | System byte | User byte |
```

The system byte supports the processor control of exceptional events such as
interrupts and the user byte the execution of instructions. The user byte has the
form

```
            7          3  2  1  0
             | Not used | C | V | N | Z |
```

where the letters denote:

C carry/borrow bit V signed integer overflow bit

N negative bit Z zero bit

The execution of most instructions causes the selective setting or resetting of these bits. Thus the user byte acts as a monitor of the instantaneous arithmetic state of the program being executed.

6.2.1 INSTRUCTIONS AND ADDRESSING MODES

The processor has a fixed repertoire of instructions it can execute. Consider the familiar addition of two integers. This can be written conventionally as

$$2569 + 156,$$

where the '+' character represents the operation of addition and the two integer values are the operands. Most SRM instructions perform an operation on two operands and have the general form

⟨operation⟩ ⟨specification of operand 1⟩ ⟨specification of operation 2⟩

where the operation is signified by a unique code. The specification of an operand value varies according to its position within the machine. The value can be held in a general register, a memory location or within the instruction itself. If the operand is located in a general register it is specified by that register address and an instruction which manipulates the contents of two registers has the form

⟨operation⟩ ⟨register address⟩ ⟨register address⟩.

If the second operand is a small positive constant (< 16) then it can be included as part of the instruction having the form

⟨operation⟩ ⟨register address⟩ ⟨constant value⟩.

The specification of an operand which is located in memory is more complex and will be discussed later.

The general structure of two simple instructions has been presented. The SRM machine has four classes of instruction and their detailed formats are given in Fig. 6.3. Instructions can be either short (word) or long (longword) and are divided into fixed-length fields which correspond to the operation and specification of the operands. All instructions begin with a one-byte operation code op. This is succeeded by two four-bit fields which either specify register addresses $r1$, $r2$, $x2$ or an immediate or constant value n. The long instructions have a final word field, which can be a memory address a or an immediate value d. Thus SRM is limited to a maximum memory address of 65 535 (16-bit address).

RR
register to register

15	8 7	4 3 0
op	*r1*	*r2*

RX
register to indexed memory

31	24 23	20 19	16 15	0
op	*r1*	*x2*	a	

SF
short format

15	8 7	4 3 0
op	*r1*	*n*

RI
register and immediate

31	24 23	20 19	16 15	0
op	*r1*	*x2*	d	

Figure 6.3   SRM instruction formats

The mechanisms for obtaining the operands are collectively known as the addressing modes. These mechanisms will be introduced by considering the four variants of the generic integer add instruction, each of which in Pascal notation performs the accumulation.

$$SUM := SUM + B.$$

SUM is the first operand and *B* the second operand. Pascal is too high level a notation to describe the detailed differences between the instruction formats and so an augmented notation including details of the addressing mechanisms is required.

The *RR* (register to register) class of instructions manipulate two operands, which are both in general registers. The general structure of this class is described by

RR: ⟨operation⟩ → ⟨register address⟩ ⟨register address⟩

The *RR* variant of add has the assembler mnemonic *ADDR* (add word register) and operation code $0A_{16}$. A typical assembler statement and its hexadecimal machine code equivalent is

ADDR R1, R3 | 0A | 1 | 3 |

The first operand is in register *R1* and the second in register *R3*. Executing the instruction adds the contents of the two registers assigning the result to register *R1*. Figure 6.4 summarizes the state of the general registers before and after the instruction is executed. In general terms the first operand is the contents of register *r1* and the second operand is the contents of register *r2*. Denoting 'contents of r' by (r), the first operand is written as $(r1)$ and the second as $(r2)$. The effect of executing the instruction can be described by adapting the Pascal notation to read

$$(r1) := (r1) + (r2).$$

The *RX* (register to indexed memory) instructions manipulate the first operand in a general register and the second operand in a memory location. The general structure of this class is described by

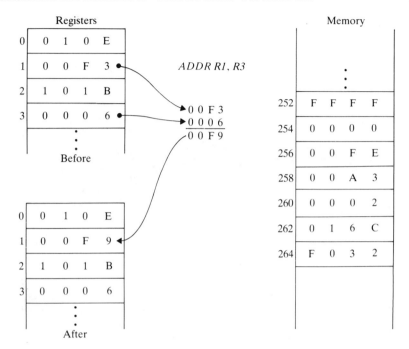

Figure 6.4   The ADDR operation

RX: ⟨operation⟩ ⟨register address⟩ ⟨index register address⟩

⟨memory address⟩

The first two elements have the same meaning as with the RR class. The last two elements

⟨index register address⟩ ⟨memory address⟩

form the complete specification of the second operand. The ⟨index register address⟩ element corresponds to the $x2$ field and the ⟨memory address⟩ corresponds to the a field of the detailed format (Fig. 6.3). Every general register except $R0$ can be used as an index register. This is when the memory address of the second operand is obtained by adding the contents of the index register to the memory address. This calculation can be written more formally as $a + (x2)$. If the $x2$ field of the instruction is zero, then this addition does not take place and the memory address of the second operand is simply a.

The RX variant of add has the mnemonic ADD (add word) with an operation code of $4A_{16}$. This form is used to add the contents of a memory location to the contents of a register. A specimen assembler instruction and its machine code (where the $x2$ field is zero) is

ADD $R2, 256$ | 4A | 2 | 0 | 0100 |

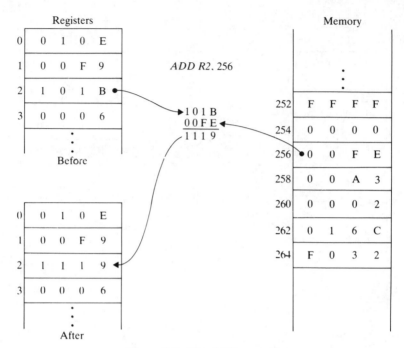

Figure 6.5 The ADD operation

This will add the contents of memory location 256 to register *r2*. Figure 6.5 summarizes this.

The formal notation for this form of *RX* instruction is simply

$$(r1) := (r1) + (a).$$

The following instruction illustrates the addressing mechanism when the *x2* field is not zero and an index register is involved

$$ADD \quad R2, 256 \ (R3) \quad \boxed{4A \mid 2 \mid 3 \mid 0100}$$

Suppose that register *R3* has the value 6 when the instruction is executed. The memory address of the second operand is given by

$$256 + 6 = 262,$$

and the result of the instruction is described in Fig. 6.6.

The effect of the instruction can be written formally as

$$(r1) := (r1) + (a + (x2)).$$

This is its most general form.

The *SF* (short format) and *RI* (register and immediate) variants, shown in Fig. 6.3, are used to add a constant to a general register. The short and long formats correspond to the *RR* and *RX* variants dealt with previously. The general structure is as follows:

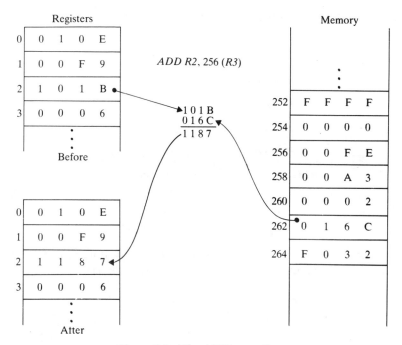

Figure 6.6   The ADD operation

$$SF: \langle \text{operation} \rangle \; \langle \text{register address} \rangle \; \langle \text{4-bit constant} \rangle$$

$$RI: \langle \text{operation} \rangle \; \langle \text{register address} \rangle \; \langle \text{index register address} \rangle \; \langle \text{16-bit constant} \rangle$$

The *SF* form of add has mnemonic *ADDS* (add immediate short) and operation code 26_{16}, the *RI* form has mnemonic *ADDI* (add word immediate) and operation code CA_{16}. In both cases the second operand is derived from the value in the last field of the instruction. For SF the second operand is the value n and so the instruction calculation is

$$(r1) := (r1) + n.$$

Since n is obtained from a 4-bit field its value is restricted to the range 0–15. The constant involved in the *RI* variant is the word field d. Similar to the *RX* variant there are two cases corresponding to the value of the $x2$ field:

either $(r1) := (r1) + d$ where $x2 = 0,$

or $(r1) := (r1) + d + (x2)$ where $x2 \neq 0.$

The addressing mechanisms or modes for obtaining operands have been introduced for the SRM machine. An examination of the Appendices will show that there are four principal addressing modes: *immediate*, *direct*, *indirect* and *indexed*. Suppose that the field of the instruction which specifies the operand has the value p. The value of the operand obtained in each case is summarized in the following:

Mode	Operand value
immediate	p
direct	(p)
indirect	$((p))$
indexed	$(p + \text{(index register)})$

Thus the *SF* and *RI* (with $x2 = 0$) variants of the add instruction

$$ADDS \quad (r1) \; := \; (r1) + n,$$

$$ADDI \quad (r1) \; := \; (r1) + d,$$

are both examples where the first operand is obtained using direct addressing and the second operand using immediate addressing. The *RX* (with $x2 = 0$) variant of add

$$ADD \; (r1) \; := \; (r1) + (a),$$

is an example where both operands are derived using direct addressing.

Suppose that n integers have been placed in successive words of memory. A program to add these all together could consist of n consecutive *ADD* instructions, which differ only in the specification of the second operand. Each instruction directly addresses a different integer. If indexed addressing is employed a single *ADD* instruction could be used, provided the contents of the index register are adjusted so that the indexed addressing mechanism selects each successive integer. This mechanism is used on SRM to change the scope of instructions dynamically. Indirect addressing offers a similar capability, but is not implemented on SRM.

A full list of all the instructions of SRM is contained in Appendix 1. Each entry gives the instruction mnemonic, operation code, full description, format and operation described in the notation just developed. Note that floating-point instructions are not present.

6.2.2 MACHINE-CODE PROGRAM AND ITS EXECUTION

At the machine-code level the programmer has considerable freedom to organize the placement of the instructions and data items in memory. The simplest form of program is one where an area of memory is divided into two parts: a contiguous sequence of instructions followed by a similar sequence of data items. Except for trivial programs the positional sequence of the instructions in memory does not correspond to the order in which they are executed.

The processor executes an individual instruction by first using the current value in the *PC* to fetch it from memory. The instruction is split into its constituent parts of operation code and the references to operands, e.g. *r1*, *x2*, *a*, etc. The operands are fetched and the operation executed. To execute a program the *PC* is initialized to the address of the first instruction and the following cycle performed:

> **repeat**
>> fetch instruction from memory using *PC* value as address
>> increment *PC* by 2 if short instruction by 4 otherwise
>> execute instruction (which may change *PC* value)
>> update the user byte of *SR*
> **until**   end of program

The simple sequencing implied by the instruction cycle can be changed using special instructions named branches, which assign an immediate value to the *PC*. Combining this mechanism with a test on the condition bits in *SR* enables a conditional branch to be performed. This gives the necessary flexibility to support all the selection and repetition constructs in Pascal. This topic will be explored at some length in later sections of the chapter.

6.3   Assembler programming

The assembler is a program translation system like a high-level language compiler. It takes a source program file as input and produces a listing file and binary program file as output. Figure 6.7 presents a very small assembler source program and an accompanying listing.

The program is composed of statements, one per line, each having a number of fixed fields. Instruction statements such as

$$ADD \qquad TEMP, J$$

having a one-to-one correspondance with a machine-code instruction. The statements such as

$$TEMP \qquad REG \quad R11$$

play a similar role to variable declarations in Pascal. Names in the language are restricted to a maximum of six alphanumeric characters beginning with a letter and only decimal and hexadecimal constants are allowed. Hexadecimal constants are preceded by the identifying character, e.g. $8BF6. For simplicity, character constants have been omitted from the model assembler.

6.3.1   SOURCE LANGUAGE FORMAT

A program statement is divided into four fields and it is the position of the field within the line which gives it significance. The general form is

$$\{\langle label\rangle\} \,\langle mnemonic\rangle\{\langle address\rangle\} \,\{\langle comment\rangle\}$$

the presence of the braces, {}, indicates that an entry in the field is optional.

(a) *Source program file*

	LD	TEMP, I	temp := i + j − 6
	ADD	TEMP, J	
	SUBS	TEMP, 6	
	HALT		
TEMP	REG	R11	
I	DC	− 10	
J	DC	26	
	END		

(b) *Listing file*

Line number	Memory location	Memory contents	Label	Mnemonic	Address	Comment
1	0000	48B0 000C		LD	TEMP, I	.temp := i + j −
2	0004	4AB0 000E		ADD	TEMP, J	
3	0008	27B6		SUBS	TEMP, 6	
4	000A	C200		HALT		
5			TEMP	REG	R11	
6	000C	FFF6	I	DC	− 10	
7	000E	001A	J	DC	26	
8	000E			END		

Symbol table
TEMP 000B *I* 000C *J* 000E

Figure 6.7 Example assembler source file and listing file

Fields are terminated by a space or end of line character.

The entry in the mnemonic field divides the statements into two broad classes reflecting the division of the program into instructions and associated data area. Thus in instruction statements the mnemonic is a symbolic representation of the machine-code operation field, e.g. *LD* and *SUBS*. Data areas are created by using assembler directives which declare variable names, e.g. *DC* and *REG*. A special assembler directive END indicates the end of the source program, as shown in Fig. 6.7(a).

The address field for instruction statements must specify symbolically the remaining fields of the machine-code instruction. Thus its detailed form will depend on the instruction format of the operation. The allowed address field formats are summarized below:

RR	$\langle r1 \rangle, \langle r2 \rangle$
SF	$\langle r1 \rangle, \langle n \rangle$
RX	$\langle r1 \rangle, \langle a \rangle$ or $\langle r1 \rangle, \langle a \rangle(\langle x2 \rangle)$
RI	$\langle r1 \rangle, \langle d \rangle$ or $\langle r1 \rangle, \langle d \rangle(\langle x2 \rangle)$

RI (branch) $\langle d \rangle$ or $\langle d \rangle (\langle x2 \rangle)$

$\langle r1 \rangle$, $\langle r2 \rangle$, $\langle x2 \rangle$, $\langle n \rangle$, $\langle a \rangle$ and $\langle d \rangle$ can be either names or constants (decimal or hexadecimal). Modified addressing is invoked by the inclusion of the factor ($\langle x2 \rangle$). A valid address field of an assembler directive is most frequently a decimal constant but can be a name or hexadecimal constant. A discussion of the various meanings will be deferred to Section 6.4.1.

The only valid entry in the label field is a name. In the context of instruction statements the entry is a true label in that it enables the instruction to be the destination of a branch or jump instruction. Names intended for use in the address field of instructions must be defined by an entry in the label field of a suitable assembler directive, i.e. the equivalent of a Pascal declaration.

The comment field must begin with a . (stop). A complete statement can become a comment if the first character of the line is a stop. The assembler will ignore comments apart from including them as part of the listing.

6.3.2   RELATIONSHIP BETWEEN ASSEMBLER AND MACHINE CODE

This relationship is easily observed by examining the assembler listing in Fig. 6.7(b). It is tabular in form with the first column containing a source line number in decimal and the last four columns containing the four fields of the source statement. The second column contains a hexadecimal number, called the memory location, which is the position in memory of the machine-code instruction or data area. The third and fourth columns contain the machine code generated from the source statement again in hexadecimal. Thus the listing contains both the assembler source program, a representation in hexadecimal of the equivalent machine code and its position in memory.

At the bottom of the listing is a symbol table. This is made up of entries of the form

$$\langle name \rangle \ \langle address \rangle.$$

No distinction is made between register and memory addresses. One of the principal tasks of the language translation process is to build this table. Given the existence of a predefined table to map mnemonics into operation codes, it is a simple matter to construct the machine-code instruction equivalent to the source as follows:

1. convert mnemonic to binary operation code using the mnemonic table;
2. replace names with binary addresses;
3. convert decimal character constant strings to binary;
4. combine the operation code, addresses and the constants according to the instruction format.

The binary program thus formed can be placed within the memory of the machine and the instructions fetched out one by one and executed by the processor.

6.4   Generation of assembler from a Pascal design

As a representative high-level language, Pascal can be used to encode solutions to a very wide variety of problems. If the main Pascal statements can be implemented in the simple register machine assembler, it follows that this will be an equally general problem solver. With practice the encoding can be performed rapidly and accurately, although the construction of large assembler programs is not to be recommended. However, the primary purpose of studying assembler in this context is to give insight into the processor architecture and how it supports common programming mechanisms. Given a systematic set of solutions for one machine, a framework is provided for enquiring and understanding others.

6.4.1   DECLARATION OF CONSTANTS AND SIMPLE VARIABLES

Consider the declaration of constants and integer variables in Pascal, e.g.

const
  $nmax = 10$;

var
  i, j, k:**integer**;

The name *nmax* will have the value 10 substituted wherever it is used; the variables i, j and k will have space reserved but do not have any defined value. The same effect can be achieved in assembler by the group of statements

        NMAX   EQU   10

        I   DS   2

        J   DS   2

        K   DS   2

Here the *EQU* (equate) directive causes the value specified in the address field to be associated with the name. The *DS* (define storage) directive takes the value of the address field as the size in bytes of the space required. An integer requires a single word. The memory address is assigned to the variable name implicitly. The assembler maintains a memory location count (see listing in Fig. 6.7) which it uses to reserve memory space for the variables, i.e. this counter is increased by the amount specified in the address field. When a name such as *J* is met in the label field of a *DS* statement the name and the current value of the memory location counter are included as a pair in the symbol table.

One feature of the SRM assembly language which is not mirrored in Pascal is the ability to name registers using the *REG* (register) mnemonic and thus use symbolic names to manipulate them. When the assembler meets the statement

        SUM   REG   R7

it adds the name *SUM* with the address value of 7 to the symbol table. Wherever the name *SUM* is used in an appropriate field of an instruction (*r1*, *r2* or *x2*) the value 7 is substituted. Since a memory location is not involved the location counter is not increased.

A second feature not available in Pascal, is the creation of named variables with an initialized value. The *DC* (define constant) mnemonic is used for this. The assembler's response to the statement

$$J \quad DC \quad 26$$

is to add the name and the current memory location counter value to the symbol table and generate the value specified in the source address field as part of the program data space (see Fig. 6.7). The memory location counter is incremented by 2, which is the length of an integer.

The presence of a name in the label field of *DS* and *DC* directives is optional. For *DS* statements this will simply cause the assembler to increment the memory location counter by the specified amount. A list of initialized values associated with a single name can be declared by

$$LIST \quad DC \quad 10$$
$$DC \quad -21$$
$$DC \quad 0$$

or more compactly as

$$LIST \quad DC \quad 10, -21, 0$$

6.4.2   ASSIGNMENT AND INTEGER ARITHMETIC TEMPLATES

The simplest construction in Pascal is the assignment of the value of a variable, or constant, to another variable e.g.

$$P \; := \; Q;$$

The SRM instructions which support assignment of integer or word values are given in Table 6.1. Two further instructions *LB* (load byte) and *STB* (store byte) manipulate byte values.

Table 6.1   Assignment instruction

Mnemonic	Full description	Format	Operation
LDR	load word register	RR	$(r1) := (r2)$
LD	load word	RX	$(r1) := (a + (x2))$
LDS	load immediate short	SF	$(r1) := n$
LDI	load word immediate	RI	$(r1) := d + (x2)$
ST	store word	RX	$(a + (x2)) := (r1)$

The selection of the suitable mnemonic(s) for any particular assignment will depend on the position of the operands i.e. in registers or memory. Suppose that both *P* and *Q* are held in registers; then the *RR* format of instruction will be needed and the encoding in assembler is simply

$$LDR \quad P,Q \quad .P := Q$$

$$P \quad REG \quad R1$$

$$Q \quad REG \quad R2$$

If *P* is a register variable and *Q* is a memory variable then *LD* is chosen. The case where both *P* and *Q* are memory variables introduces the complication of using a temporary register variable, *TEMP*, say.

$$LD \quad TEMP,Q \quad .P := Q$$

$$ST \quad TEMP,P$$

$$TEMP \quad REG \quad R2$$

$$P \quad DS \quad 2$$

$$Q \quad DS \quad 2$$

The last case of *P* in memory and *Q* in a register requires the *ST* mnemonic.

The assignment of a constant to a variable is supported by the literal addressing variants of the load instruction group, namely *LDS* and *LDI*. If the constant value is in the range 0 to 15 (i.e. can be expressed in four bits) then *LDS* can be chosen. *LDI* supports integers in the range $-32\,768$ to $32\,767$ (hex 1000 to 7FFF). Two examples are given where *P* is a register variable and *Q* is in memory.

$$LDS \quad P,7 \qquad .P := 7;$$

$$LDI \quad TEMP,387 \quad .Q := 387$$

$$ST \quad TEMP,Q$$

$$P \quad REG \quad R3$$

$$TEMP \quad REG \quad R4$$

$$Q \quad DS \quad 2$$

Integer arithmetic is supported by addition, subtraction, multiplication and division instructions which are summarized in Table 6.2. The add and subtract instructions increment and decrement the contents of a register respectively. Thus if *SUM* is a register variable the encoding of the Pascal statements

$$SUM := SUM + B; \quad \text{or} \quad SUM := SUM - B;$$

is a single assembler instruction. The choice of mnemonic depends on the operand *B* (Table 6.3).

Table 6.2 Integer arithmetic instructions

Mnemonic	Full description	Format	Operation
ADDR	add word register	RR	$(r1) := (r1) + (r2)$
ADD	add word	RX	$(r1) := (r1) + (a + (x2))$
ADDS	add immediate short	SF	$(r1) := (r1) + n$
ADDI	add word immediate	RI	$(r1) := (r1) + d + (x2)$
SUBR	subtract word register	RR	$(r1) := (r1) - (r2)$
SUB	subtract word	RX	$(r1) := (r1) - (a + (x2))$
SUBS	subtract immediate short	SF	$(r1) := (r1) - n$
SUBI	subtract word immediate	RI	$(r1) := (r1) - d - (x2)$
MULR	multiply word register	RR	$(r1, r1 + 1) := (r1 + 1)*(r2)$
MUL	multiply word	RX	$(r1, r1 + 1) := (r1 + 1)*(a + (x2))$
DIVR	divide word register	RR	$(r1 + 1) := (r1, r1 + 1) \textbf{ div } (r2)$ $(r1) := (r1, r1 + 1) \textbf{ mod } (r2)$
DIV	divide word	RX	$(r1 + 1) := (r1, r1 + 1) \textbf{ div } (a + (x2))$ $(r1) := (r1, r1 + 1) \textbf{ mod } (a + (x2))$

Table 6.3 Choice of mnemonic

Nature of B	Mnemonic choice
register variable	ADDR or SUBR
memory variable	ADD or SUB
constant < 16	ADDS or SUBS
other constants	ADDI or SUBI

If *SUM* and *B* are both in memory then the incrementing must use a temporary register, *TEMP*.

```
LD      TEMP,SUM      . sum := sum − B

SUB     TEMP,B

ST      TEMP,SUM
```

The program in Fig. 6.7 evaluates the simple integer expression $i + j - 6$, demonstrating that such evaluation is most conveniently performed using a register.

The multiplication of two word integers can generate a long word result. The *MUL* and *MULR* instructions cope with this problem by storing the result in a pair of adjacent registers. The most significant word is stored in an even addressed register $r1$ and the least significant word in an odd addressed register $r1 + 1$. *MUL* is an *RX* instruction, but exceptionally the first operand is placed in the odd addressed register $r1 + 1$. The second operand is as usual the contents of the memory address $a + (x2)$. As an example the expression

$$C := A * B;$$

will be encoded with the variables *A*, *B* and *C* being in memory. It is assumed that the multiplication produces a word result, i.e. the most significant word of the long word result is zero.

```
       LD      ODD,A      . C := A * B

       MUL     EVEN,B

       ST      ODD,C

EVEN   REG     R2

ODD    REG     R3
```

The even and odd addressed pair of registers have been explicitly named to emphasize their use.

The first operand of the division instructions *DIV* and *DIVR* is a long word dividend. As with the result of multiplication, a pair of adjacent registers with even and odd addresses are used for it. The second operand is a word integer with memory address $a + (x2)$. The operator *DIV* divides the long word integer by the word integer to yield a quotient and remainder both a word in length. The quotient result is stored in the odd register $r1 + 1$ and the remainder in the even register $r1$. Thus a single machine instruction performs both the operations of **div** and **mod** of Pascal. Suppose that A, B, Q and R are memory variables, then *DIV* can be used for either or both **div** and **mod**.

```
LDS   EVEN,0   .Q := A divB;

LD    ODD,A

DIV   EVEN,B

ST    ODD,Q

ST    EVEN,R   .R := A mod B;
```

6.4.3 HAND EXECUTION OF A SIMPLE PROGRAM

The hand or paper execution of a high-level language program serves to check the execution behaviour of the program. This technique will be used at the machine-code level to reinforce the ideas introduced describing how the machine works. The execution of a program is a dynamic process as implied by the instruction cycle. The state of the machine at the beginning of the instruction cycle can be defined as the instantaneous values contained in the processor registers (the volatile environment) and the contents of memory. Formally a state S can be written as

$$S = S(PC, SR, R, M),$$

where PC and SR have their usual significance and R is a vector containing the general register values and M is a vector of the memory contents. The execution of a program can be viewed as a sequence of changes in machine state brought about by the execution of successive instructions. The current state determines which instruction is executed next through the value of the PC register. The significant events during the execution of an instruction which determine the new state can be summarised as follows:

fetch the instruction from memory using the PC value as an address;
increment the PC by 2 or 4 depending on the instruction length;
fetch the operands and perform the operation;
update the SR register.

The PC register value is incremented automatically to point to the next instruction in memory, providing a default sequencing order. The operation can change the machine state by altering the value of a register or a memory location or the PC register. The default sequencing of instructions can only be counter-manded by operations which change the PC register explicitly. Obeying most instructions results in the status register *SR* being updated.

A simple program to evaluate an arithmetic expression was given in Fig. 6.7. A hand execution record of it is presented in Fig. 6.8. The proforma is divided into two, the upper half recording the successive states of the machine and the lower half giving details of instruction execution. Changes in memory are not shown because of space limitations, but can easily be recorded on a separate sheet. Hexadecimal notation is used throughout except for the *SR* register where only the individual bit values of *C*, *V*, *N* and *Z* are recorded. To distinguish this from hexadecimal a bit value of one is marked by a vertical bar (|) and a zero by a horizontal dash (-).

The machine is initialized to the following state S_1:

$$PC \qquad = 0000 \qquad \{\text{entry point of program}\}$$

$$SR \qquad = U \qquad \{\ \text{undefined value}\}$$

$$R0 .. R15 \ = U \qquad \{\ \text{undefined value}\}$$

and the memory containing the program and data set to:

Address	Contents
0000	48B0
0002	000C
0004	4AB0
0006	000E
0008	27B6
000A	C200
000C	FFF6
000E	001A

The *PC* value in state S_1 is 0000_{16} and points to the first instruction $48B \, 0000C_{16}$. This is an *LD* instruction which has an *RX* format and is four bytes long. This can all be determined from the operation code. Splitting the instruction into its constituent fields gives

$$op \quad 48 \qquad \{LD\}$$

$$r1 \quad B \qquad \{R11\}$$

$$x2 \quad 0 \qquad \{\text{implies no indexing}\}$$

$$a \quad 000C \quad \{\text{memory address}\}$$

Thus the first operand has register address B_{16} and the second operand has memory address $000C_{16}$. The value of operand 1 is *undefined* and operand 2 is $FFF6_{16}$. As there is no indexing the simple operation is:

$$(r1) := (a),$$

and the value $FFF6_{16}$ is copied into register *R11*. As this value is a negative number the C, V and Z bits of the SR register are reset and the N bit is set.

Now moving to the column S_2 of Fig. 6.8, the new state S_2 differs from S_1 by

$$PC = 0004$$

$$SR = \text{--}|\text{-}$$

$$R11 = FFF6$$

The second instruction at memory address 0004_{16} is the familiar ADD operation. It is an RX variant with no indexing and so the operands are obtained in the same way as in S_1. A positive result generated from operands of differing sign means a carry is generated.

Now moving to column S_3 in Fig. 6.8, the state S_3 differs from S_2 by

$$PC = 0008$$

$$SR = |\text{---}$$

$$R11 = 0010$$

The third instruction $SUBS$ is in SF format, which when broken down into its constituent fields is

$$op \quad 27 \quad \{SUBS\}$$

$$r1 \quad B \quad \{R11\}$$

$$n \quad 6$$

The first operand is the contents of register $R11$ and the second operand value is 6, because an immediate addressing mode is specified by SF instructions. The result of the subtraction is still positive and so the state S_4 differs from S_3 by

$$PC = 000A$$

$$SR = \text{----}$$

$$R11 = 000A$$

The final instruction halts the program, which is shown in column S_4.

It is suggested that this tracing technique should be applied by the reader in order to understand subsequent examples.

6.4.4 HARDWARE SUPPORT FOR DECISIONS

The decision-making capability of the machine is based on the interaction between the current contents of the user byte in the SR register and branch or jump instructions. The unconditional branch instruction (B), equivalent to **goto** in Pascal, works by changing the value of the program counter (PC). It is an RI instruction and the operation can be described by

$$(PC) := d \quad \text{or} \quad (PC) := d + (x2).$$

		S_1	S_2	S_3	S_4
	PC REGISTER	0000	0004	0008	000A
	SR REGISTER	U	- - 1 -	1 - - -	- - - -
VOLATILE ENVIRONMENT (GENERAL REGISTERS)	0	U			
	1	U			
	2	U			
	3	U			
	4	U			
	5	U			
	6	U			
	7	U			
	8	U			
	9	U			
	A	U			
	B	U	FFF6	0010	000A
	C	U			
	D	U			
	E	U			
	F	U			
INSTRUCTION STRUCTURE	INSTRUCTION REGISTER	48 B 0 / 000 C	4 A B 0 / 000 E	27 B 6	C 2 0 0
	MNEM. TYPE	LD.RX	ADD.RX	SUBS.SF	HALT
	OPER. ADDR. 1 / VALUE	B / U	B / FFF6	B / 0010	
	OPER. ADDR. 2 / VALUE	000C / FFF6	000E / 001A	- / 6	
EXECUTION	OPERATION	$(rl):=(a)$	$(rl):=(rl)+(rl)-$ (a)	$(rl):=(rl)-$ n	
	RESULT	FFF6	0010	000A	
	NEW PC	0004	0008	000A	000A
	NEW SR	- - 1 -	1 - - -	- - - -	- - - -

Figure 6.8 Record of hand execution of the program $temp := i + j - 6$

The value of d is the memory address associated with an instruction statement label. A conditional branching mechanism is achieved by selectively changing the PC register according to the success or failure of a test on the named bit values, C, N, V, Z of the SR register. Consider the operation of the BM (branch on minus) instruction. The test applied is whether the N bit in SR is set. In formal Pascal terms the operation can be described by

if N *bit in SR set*
then
$$PC := d + (x2)$$

Thus the branch occurs when N is set, and if it is reset the instruction following the branch is executed. Usually a branch does not involve using an index register.

The conditional branch instructions test the value of all the individual bits e.g. BM (branch on minus), BNM (branch on not minus) and so on. Two branches BP (branch on plus) and BNP (branch on not plus) test the values of both N and Z. This is because there is no individual condition code bit for recording greater than zero. The combination of unconditional and conditional branches is sufficient to construct assembler language templates for the sequencing and loop constructs of Pascal.

The C, V, N, Z bits are potentially altered by most instructions. This topic was covered for add and subtract instructions in Chapter 2. The load instructions set the N and Z bits according to the sign of the operand value assigned. Although most instructions set the named bits of SR, there are some instructions which leave it unaltered, namely ST, MUL, $MULR$, DIV, $DIVR$, STM (store multiple), LDM (load multiple) and the branches. Also the preceding instruction setting of SR may not be related to the test in the conditional branch. The set of compare instructions given in Table 6.4 solves this problem. These instructions compare the two operands by setting the C, N, V, Z bits in the SR register according to an effective subtraction of the two operands, leaving them unchanged. In the templates that follow an appropriate compare will always accompany a conditional branch instruction even when it is not strictly required.

6.4.5   IF . . . THEN . . . ELSE . . . TEMPLATE

Consider the informal Pascal model **if** statement

$$\textbf{if } A \ = \ B \textbf{ then } S1 \textbf{ else } S2,$$

Table 6.4   Compare instructions

Mnemonic	Full description	Format
CMPR	Compare word register	RR
CMP	Compare word	RX
CMPI	Compare word immediate	RI

where *S1* and *S2* are arbitrary statement sequences (compound statements). Assuming that *A* and *B* are register variables the assembler template equivalent to this statement is as follows:

```
              CMPR      A,B        .if A  =  B
              BNE       ELSE       .then

                .
                S1                   S1
                .

              B          NEXT
   ELSE        .                    .else

                .
                S2                   S2
                .

   NEXT
```

The *BNE* instruction is used rather than the *BE* instruction because a true result of the test on the *Z* bit of the *SR* register must select the **else** clause. Once the *S1* sequence has been executed the unconditional branch omits the **else** clause. *NEXT* labels the first statement after the **if** statement.

As with arithmetic expression evaluation the choice of compare instruction will depend on the location of the operands in the relational expression. A temporary register would have to be employed if both *A* and *B* are in memory.

Table 6.5   Branch mnemonics

Relational	Mnemonic
$A = B$	BNE
$A \# B$	BE
$A > B$	BNP
$A > = B$	BM
$A < B$	BNM
$A < = B$	BP

Table 6.5 gives the branch mnemonics to choose to implement the various relational expressions. As a simple example, the following program fragment records the maximum of two variables *a* and *b* in the variable *max*:

```
         if a  > =  b
         then
             max :=  a
         else
             max :=  b;
```

Supposing that all the variables are named registers the template encoding is

```
         CMPR   A,B      .if a > = b
         BM     ELSE     . then
```

```
              LDR     MAX,A   .  max := a
              B       NEXT    . else
     ELSE     LDR     MAX,B   .  max := b;
     NEXT
     A        REG     R0
     B        REG     R1
     MAX      REG     R2
```

IF A, B and MAX are memory variables, then a superficially more complex encoding of the same form is required:

```
              LD      TEMP,A    .if a > = b
              CMP     TEMP,B
              BM      ELSE      . then
              LD      TEMP,A    .  max := a
              ST      TEMP,MAX
              B       NEXT      . else
     ELSE     LD      TEMP,B    .  max := b;
              ST      TEMP,MAX
     NEXT
     TEMP     REG     R0
     A        DS      2
     B        DS      2
     MAX      DS      2
```

Relational expressions are frequently combined with the logical operators **and**, **or** and **not** to form logical expressions. Assembler templates for two typical cases are given in Fig. 6.9.

```
(a)           CMPR    A,B       .if (A = B) and (C > 0)
              BNE     NEXT
              CMPI    C,0
              BNP     NEXT      .then
                .
                S               .  S
                .
     NEXT

(b)           CMPR    A,B       .if (A = B) or (C > 0)
              BE      THEN
              CMPI    C,0
              BNP     NEXT      .then
     THEN       .
                S               S
     NEXT
```

Figure 6.9 Examples of **if ... then** templates with logical expressions

Note that when the logical **and** operator is used with two relationals, the first occurrence of a false condition can be exploited to omit the **then** clause (Fig. 6.9(a)). Similarly with the **or** operator the first occurrence of a true result selects the **then** clause (Fig. 6.9(b)).

6.4.6 WHILE AND REPEAT LOOP TEMPLATES

When generating a template **while** and **repeat** loops differ only in the position where the test for the termination of the loop is made. For a **while** loop the test is applied before every execution of the loop body and for the **repeat** the test is carried out at the end. An example of each type will be given

(a) **while** $A \neq 0$ **do** S;

```
WHILE      CMPI    A,0       .while A ≠ 0
           BE      NEXT      .do
            .
            S                 S
            .
           B       WHILE
NEXT
```

NEXT labels the first statement after the **while** loop. It was assumed that A was a register variable.

(b) **repeat** S **until** $A >= B$;

```
REPEAT         .                      .repeat

               .
               S                        S
               .

               .
UNTIL      CMPR    A,B        .until A >= B;
           BM      REPEAT
```

REPEAT labels the first statement of the compound statement S. The need for an explicit *UNTIL* label will depend on the details of S, but it does aid readability to include it even if it is not strictly necessary.

As an illustration of a simple **while** loop the statement $a := a \textbf{ div } b$ will be implemented in assembler from the algorithm

```
temp := a;
a := 0;
while temp > b
do begin
    temp := temp - b;
    a := a + 1;
end
```

If all the variables are in named registers the encoding is as follows:

```
          LDR      TEMP,A      . temp := a;
          LDS      A,0         . a := 0;
WHILE     CMPR     TEMP,B      . while temp  > b
          BNP      NEXT        . do begin
          SUBR     TEMP,B      .   temp := temp − b;
          ADDS     A,1         .   a := a + 1;
          B        WHILE       .   end
NEXT
A         REG      R0
B         REG      R1
TEMP      REG      R2
```

An algorithm to find the highest common factor (hcf) of two positive integers provides an example which uses all the sequencing and loop constructs discussed so far. Given two integers m and n where $m > n$, replace m by the value $m\,mod\,n$. Continue replacing the larger of the numbers by the *mod* of the smaller until the result is zero. The non-zero integer will be the hcf of m and n. To demonstrate the encoding of a **while** loop within a **repeat** loop, the *mod* function will be implemented by successive subtraction. A Pascal design algorithm follows:

```
repeat
  if m < n
  then begin
        t := m;
        m := n;
        n := t
  end;
  while m > = n
  do
        m := m − n;
until m = 0;
res := n;
```

The assembler encoding is given in Fig. 6.10.

6.4.7 **FOR** LOOP TEMPLATE

A typical form of this loop is

$$\textbf{for } i := j \textbf{ to } n \textbf{ do } S;$$

where i is known as the control variable and is most frequently an integer. i has an initial value of j and is incremented by one every time the compound

```
                LD        M,A        .Get m & n from initialized
                LD        N,B        .memory variables
    REPEAT      CMPR      M,N        .repeat
                BNM       WHILE      .  if m < n
                                     .  then begin
                LDR       T,M        .        t := m;
                LDR       M,N        .        m := n;
                LDR       N,T        .        n := t
                                     .     end;
    WHILE       CMPR      M,N        .  while m > = n
                BM        UNTIL      .  do
                SUBR      M,N        .     m := m − n;
                B         WHILE
    UNTIL       CMPI      M,0        .until m = 0;
                BNE       REPEAT
                LDR       RES,N      .res := n;
                HALT

    M           REG       R0
    N           REG       R1
    T           REG       R2

    RES         REG       R3
    A           DC        64
    B           DC        296

                END
```

Figure 6.10   Assembler encoding of Pascal *hcf* algorithm

statement is executed. The loop is terminated when S has been executed with i equal to n. If $i > n$ initially the statement S is not executed. Thus in developing a suitable template, the test for completion is performed before S and i is incremented after S. Suppose that i is a register variable and j and n are in memory. The template is thus

```
                LD        I,J
    FOR         CMP       I,N        .for i := j to n
                BP        NEXT       .do
                 .
                 .
                 .
                 S                    S
                 .
                 .
                 .
                ADDS      I,1
                B         FOR
    NEXT
```

By changing the *BP* and *ADDS* mnemonics to *BM* and *SUBS*, the template is transformed to implement the **for** loop:

$$\textbf{for } i := j \textbf{ downto } n \textbf{ do } S$$

As a last example in this chapter an algorithm is presented to calculate Fibonacci numbers. Such numbers are defined by

$$F_0 = 0,$$
$$F_1 = 1,$$
$$F_n = F_{n-1} + F_{n-2} \quad (n \geqslant 2)$$

and can be easily evaluated using a **for** loop. The Pascal algorithm to calculate the fifth Fibonacci number and record it in the variable *fnew* is given below:

```
fold := 0;
fnew := 1;
for i := 2 to 5
do begin
        t:= fold + fnew;
        fold := fnew;
        fnew := t
end;
```

Figure 6.11 gives the assembler encoding.

	LDS	FOLD,0	.*fold* := 0;
	LDS	FNEW,1	.*fnew* := 1;
	LDS	I,2	
FOR	CMPI	I,5	.**for** *i* := 2 **to** 5
	BP	NEXT	.**do begin**
	LDR	T,FOLD	. *t* := *fold* + *fnew*
	ADDR	T,FNEW	
	LDR	FOLD,FNEW	. *fold* := *fnew*;
	LDR	FNEW,T	. *fnew* := *t*
	ADDS	I,1	. **end**;
	B	FOR	
NEXT	HALT		
FOLD	REG	R0	
FNEW	REG	R1	
T	REG	R2	
I	REG	R3	
	END		

Figure 6.11   Assembler encoding of Pascal algorithm to calculate the fifth Fibonacci number

So far the emphasis has been on the fundamental declarations and sequencing constructs of a typical high-level language as they have to be expressed in an assembler language program. In the next chapter it will be shown that the SRM machine is capable of supporting advanced data structures such as records and arrays together with the procedure mechanism.

Exercises

1. Table 6.6 lists a set of variables names with associated addresses and values. *I*, *J* and *K* are register variables and *P*, *Q* and *R* are memory variables. The addresses and values are in hex.
    (a) Generate machine code instructions (in hex) from the following assembler source instructions:

(a)	*SUBS*	*I*,3
(b)	*ADD*	*I*,*P*
(c)	*SUBI*	*J*,256
(d)	*ADDR*	*I*,*K*
(e)	*LD*	*K*,*P*(*I*)
(f)	*LDI*	*J*,*R*
(g)	*ST*	*K*,*Q*

    (b) Taking the same initial values of the variables given in the table, execute each instruction independently, recording both the result and the settings of the *C*, *V*, *N*, *Z* in the *SR* register.

Table 6.6

Name	Address	Value
I	8	0004
J	9	0100
K	A	7FFF
P	0020	FFF0
Q	0122	1000
R	3524	0010

2. Write an assembler program to evaluate the integer expression where the variables are either all located in registers or all in memory.
3. Code the following fragment of Pascal in assembler:

$$\textbf{if } a = b$$
$$\textbf{then}$$
$$e := 1$$
$$\textbf{else}$$
$$e := 0;$$

Consider the cases

(a) a, b and e are register variables,

(b) a and e are register variables and b is a memory variable,

(c) a, b and e are memory variables.

Use a proforma as given in Fig. 6.8 to execute the assembler encoding for the cases when $a = b$ and $a \neq b$.

4. Given the internal dimensions of a box (height, width and length) and the external dimensions of a cylinder (diameter and height), design a Pascal algorithm to determine whether the cylinder will fit into the box. Assume the dimensions are integral. Encode the solution in assembler.

5. Design an assembler template for the following informal Pascal statements:

(a) **while** $(a \neq 0)$ **or** $(b > c)$
 do
  S;

(b) **repeat**
  S_1;
  if $a < = b$
  then
   S_2
  else
   S_3;
  until $(a = b)$ **and** $(c = 0)$;

6. One Pascal construction not discussed in the chapter was the **case** statement. Explore ways of implementing this in assembler.

7. Design a Pascal program to find the number of decimal digits in a positive or negative word integer. Translate the solution into assembler.

8. Design a Pascal program to calculate the smallest power of two greater than a given integer n. Use addition rather than multiplication to generate successive powers of 2. Translate the algorithm into assembler.

7
Assembler programming – advanced constructs

The last chapter introduced the details of the SRM processor and developed assembler templates for the Pascal constructs for assignment, integer arithmetic, selection and repetition. Although the mechanism of indexing was described it was not exploited. This chapter explores the use of this mechanism in providing a systematic means of encoding typical high-level language constructs: single-dimensional arrays, records, procedures and functions.

Both arrays and records are examples of structured types, and variables of such types have more than one element. An element can be a simple type such as an integer, or a structured type. Thus an element of a record could be an array or another record. Arrays and records differ in the mode of access of the elements, but indexed addressing is needed in both cases.

The procedure is included in all worthwhile high-level imperative languages. It is an essential part of the programming technique known as structured decomposition, which breaks down a given task into sub-tasks. Each sub-task is then represented explicitly as a procedure. It is important therefore to study how a procedure-call mechanism can be constructed from simple machine-code elements.

7.1 Arrays

An array is an ordered sequence of elements all of the same type. This type is known as the base type, which can be simple or structured. The group of elements is denoted by a single name and the order is defined by an index type. Each element is associated with a value of the range of the index type. The most common index type is a subrange of the positive integers which in Pascal is defined by

$$\langle LB \rangle .. \langle UB \rangle,$$

where *LB* and *UB* denote the lower and upper bounds of the range respectively. The declaration of a small array of integers in Pascal is

> **type**
>   *vector* = **array** [1 .. 20] **of integer**;
> **var**
>   *v*: *vector*;
>   *i*: **integer**;

The name of the array is *v* and the base type is integer. The lower bound is 1, the upper bound is 20 and there are 20 elements in all. The index type is integer and if *i* is an integer variable the *i*th element is accessed by using the subscripted form of the variable *v*[*i*].

The type declaration defines three key pieces of information

1. the lower bound (*LB*),
2. the upper bound (*UB*),
3. the element type and thus implicitly the memory storage requirement of each element (*ES*).

The array elements of an array of integers such as *v* are arranged in sequence in memory (Fig. 7.1).

The total storage requirement for the array of integers is given by

$$(UB - LB + 1) * ES \text{ bytes,}$$

and the memory address of the element with index *i* is

$$a + (i - LB) * ES.$$

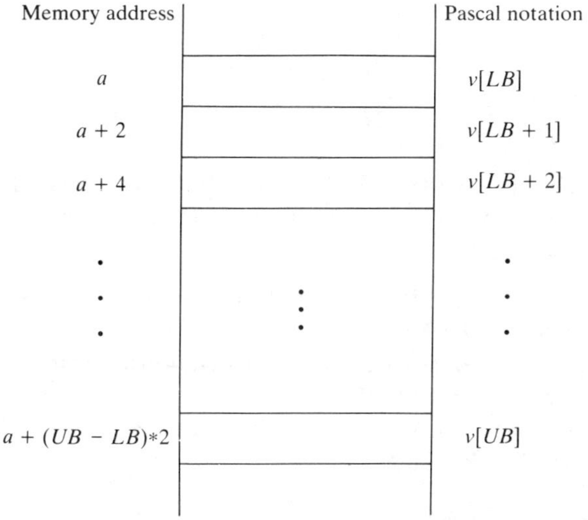

Figure 7.1 Storage of an array of integers

The address a is commonly termed the base address of the array and the expression $(i - LB) * ES$ the relative address (or offset) of the element $v[i]$ with respect to a. Although the upper bound UB does not enter the calculation of the element address, it could be used in conjunction with LB to check that the value of i is within bounds.

The declaration of an array in assembly code must take account of the type information (LB, UB and ES) and the storage requirement. One way to declare two variables $v1$ and $v2$ of type vector is as follows:

```
VECLB    EQU   1    . type
VECUB    EQU   20   . vector  =  array [1 .. 20] of integer
VECES    EQU   2
                    . var
V1       DS    40   . v1, v2:vector;
V2       DS    40
```

Note that the typing information is declared only once and, as for simple variables, the name of the vector variable is associated with the most significant byte of the required area of memory.

The construction of a template for Pascal statements involving arrays uses indexed addressing, i.e. the RX format of instruction with the $x2$ field being any register from $R1$ to $R15$. The problem in translating a statement of the form

$$v[i] := 42;$$

is the calculation of the address of $v[i]$. Suppose the following registers are declared

```
I        REG   R0
S        REG   R1
EVEN     REG   R2
ODD      REG   R3
PTR      REG   R4
ES       REG   R5
```

The adjacent pair of registers $EVEN$ and ODD are declared for use in a multiplication operation. If the register variable I contains the index value, then the assignment can be encoded as:

```
LDI      PTR,V          . v[i] := 42
LDR      ODD,I          . {
SUBI     ODD,VECLB      . Calculate offset from
LDI      ES,VECES
MULR     EVEN,ES        . (I − VECLB) * VECES
ADDR     PTR,ODD        . }
LDI      S,42
ST       S,0 (PTR)
```

The first five instructions are a straightforward translation of the address calculation given earlier. The absolute memory address of $v[i]$ is held in the register *PTR*. Since the complete address has been calculated the a field of the *RX* instruction must be zero. An absolute address used in this way is frequently called a *pointer* to a variable.

As a second example a simple list-processing problem will be used. A typical class of such algorithms is represented by the informal description:

initialization
while not end of list
do begin
   process item
   get next item
end

Suppose that the array v contains a list of integers terminated by zero. A Pascal version which finds the maximum value in the list is

max := 0;
i := 1;
item := $v[1]$;
while *item* $\#$ 0
do begin
  if *item* > *max*
  then
    max := *item*;
  i := $i + 1$;
  item := $v[i]$
end

The assembler coding is given in Fig. 7.2.

If elements in a list are processed sequentially, the calculation of the address of an element can be much simplified. Successive values of the pointer can be calculated iteratively as follows:

$$PTR_{i+1} = PTR_i + ES,$$

where PTR_i is the address of the ith element. The value of PTR_{LB} is the base address of the array since this is equivalent to the address of the first element. The sequence of instructions involving the multiplication can be replaced by

    ADDI   *PTR,VTYPES*
    LD   *ITEM,* 0(*PTR*)

The original complete form of pointer calculation must be used if random accesses to the list are made.

```
          LDS      MAX, 0          .max :=0;
          LDS      I,1             .i := 1;
          LDI      PTR, V          .item := v[1];
          LD       ITEM, V
WHILE     CMPI     ITEM, 0         .while item ≠ 0
          BE       OUT             .do begin
          CMPR     ITEM, MAX       .  if item  >  max
          BNP      NEXT            .  then
          LDR      MAX, ITEM       .       max := item;
NEXT      ADDS     I,1             .  i := i + 1;
          LDR      ODD, I          .  item := v [i];
          SUBI     ODD, VECLB
          LDI      ES, VECES
          MULR     EVEN, ES
          ADDR     PTR, ODD
          LH       ITEM, 0(PTR)
          B        WHILE           .  end
OUT       HALT
MAX       REG      R0
I         REG      R1
EVEN      REG      R2
ODD       REG      R3
ITEM      REG      R4
PTR       REG      R5
ES        REG      R6
                                  .type
VECLB     EQU      1              .  vector  =  array [1 . . 20]
VECUB     EQU      20                             of integer
VECES     EQU      2              .var
V         DS       40             .  v: vector
```

Figure 7.2 Assembler encoding of list-processing algorithm

7.2 Records

A record is like an array in that it is a variable with several elements or components. The components of a record can be of different types. The component is said to occupy a field of the record and each field has a distinct name associated with it. The access to the field is via the name. As a simple example of a record, the time of day is expressed as the pair of integers *hours* and *minutes*. The Pascal declarations for a record of type *time* and two variables *t1* and *t2* of that type follow:

type

    time = **record**

         hours:**integer**;

         mins:**integer**;

    end;

var

    t1,t2:*time*;

To select a field of a record variable, the variable name is followed by the field name, the names being separated by a dot. Thus

$$t1 \, . \, hours \; := \; 20; \; t1 \, . \, mins \; := \; 6;$$

are legal assignments to the *hours* and *minutes* field of *t1*.

In a similar way to arrays the components of a record are arranged consecutively in memory. For a variable of type *time* this is as shown in Fig. 7.3.

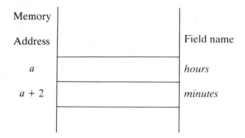

Figure 7.3 Storage of a record

Again *a* is called the base address and the fields *hours* and *minutes* have relative addresses 0 and 2 with respect to *a*. The total memory requirement of the record is simply the sum of the individual requirements of each field. The relative address of a given field is the sub-total of the memory requirement of the fields which precede it. The declaration in assembler for records of type *time* is as follows:

```
                         . type
                         .   time = record
HOURS       EQU     0    .       hours:integer;
MINS        EQU     2    .       mins:integer:
                                 end
                         . var
T1          DS      4    .   t1, t2:time;
T2          DS      4
```

Thus the assembler names *HOURS* and *MINS* have the relative addresses of the respective field names associated with them. The encoding of the assignment

$$t1 \; := \; t2;$$

is as follows:

```
          LDI      T1PTR, T1                    . t1 := t2
          LDI      T2PTR, T2
          LD       S, HOURS(T2PTR)
          ST       S, HOURS(T1PTR)
          LD       S, MINS(T2PTR)
          ST       S, MINS(T1PTR)

T1PTR     REG      R1
T2PTR     REG      R2
S         REG      R3
```

The relative address of a field name is constant and so can be used in the *a* field of an *RX* format instruction.

The solutions to programming problems frequently employ data structures, which are combinations of arrays and records. Consider the simple problem of accumulating the weekly total of the time worked by an employee from his daily returns. An informal algorithm using an array of records is given below:

```
var
    daytot:array [1 .. 7] of time;
    wtot:time;
    sumhr,sumin:time;
    i:integer
begin
    sumhr := 0;
    sumin := 0;
    for i := 1 to 7
    do begin
        sumhr := sumhr + daytot [i]. hours;
        sumin := sumin + daytot [i]. mins;
        if sumin > = 60
        then begin
                sumin := sumin - 60;
                sumhr := sumhr + 1
        end
        wtot . hours := sumhr;
        wtot . mins := sumin
    end;
```

The algorithm and its assembler equivalent are given in Fig. 7.4.

7.3   Procedures

As for the simpler Pascal instructions an assembler template can be constructed for procedures. To identify the problems that need solving, consider the follow-ing procedure definition of the highest common factor (*hcf*) algorithm discussed

```
          LDS    SUMHR,0              .sumhr := 0;
          LDS    SUMIN,0              .sumin := 0;
          LDI    PTR,DAYTOT           .{initialize PTR to base address of daytot}
          LDS    I,1                  .for i := 1 to 7
FOR       CMPI   I,7                  .do begin
          BP     OUT
          ADD    SUMHR,HOURS(PTR)     .    sumhr := sumhr + daytot[i].hours;
          ADD    SUMIN,MINS(PTR)      .    sumin := sumin + daytot[i].mins;
          CMPI   SUMIN,60             .    if sumin >= 60
          BM     NEXT                 .    then begin
          SUBI   SUMIN,60             .          sumin := sumin − 60;
          ADDS   SUMHR,1              .          sumhr + 1
NEXT      ADDS   I,1                  .          end;
          ADDI   PTR,DAYES
          B      FOR                  .    end;
OUT       LDI    PTR,WTOT             .{initialize PTR to base address of wtot}
          ST     SUMHR,HOURS(PTR)     .wtot.hours := sumhr;
          ST     SUMIN,MINS(PTR)      .wtot.mins := sumin;
          HALT

I         REG    R0
SUMHR     REG    R1
SUMIN     REG    R2
PTR       REG    R3
                                      .type
                                      .  time = record
HOURS     EQU    0                    .                hours:integer
MINS      EQU    2                    .                mins:integer
                                      .           end;
DAYLB     EQU    1                    .var
DAYUB     EQU    7                    .daytot:array[1..7]of time;
DAYES     EQU    4                    .  wtot:time;
DAYTOT    DS     28

WTOT      DS     4
```

Figure 7.4   Assembler encoding of weekly times calculation

in the last chapter:

```
procedure hcf (m,n: integer; var r:integer);
var
    t:integer;
begin
  repeat
    t := m mod n;
    m := n;
    n := t;
  until n = 0;
  r := m
end;
```

$$hcf\ (25,\ 10,\ res);$$

Where the constants 25 and 10 and the variable *res* are termed actual parameters. The call transfers control to the code body of the procedure, which is executed with the actual parameters substituted for the corresponding formal ones. When the last statement has been executed, control is returned to the program statement immediately following the call.

The actual parameters and the local variables of the procedure exist only for the duration of the call. The activated procedure can change the contents of a value actual parameter, e.g. the statement $m := n$ in *hcf*. This affects only the actual parameter and does not alter the variables in the calling routine. This limitation enables expressions, variables and constants of the correct type to be substituted for value parameters. Excluding global variables, the only means of changing the contents of variables in the calling routine is via a reference parameter. The effect of the call of *hcf* above is to change the value of the actual parameter *res*.

The problems posed in devising an assembler template for procedures can be summarized as:

1. a call-and-return mechanism;
2. the creation of actual parameters and local variables upon activation and the deletion of them upon return;
3. the translation to machine code of the procedure body that references the actual parameters and local variables, complicated by the fact that the absolute memory location of these entities is unknown until the activation.

7.3.1 CALL-AND-RETURN MECHANISM

The transfer of control from a calling routine to a procedure and the subsequent return is supported by two instructions (Table 7.1).

The execution of the instruction corresponding to the assembler statement

$$CALL \qquad R15,HCF,$$

will first save the memory address of the instruction following the call in register *R15*, and second branch to the assembler instruction labelled by *HCF*. The *RET* instruction is an unconditional branch to the instruction whose address is in *r1*.

Table 7.1 CALL and RET

Mnemonic	Full description	FORMAT	Operation
CALL	Call procedure	RI	$(r1):=(PC)+4$
			$(PC):=d+(x2)$
RET	Return from procedure	RR	$(PC):=(r1)$

The first version of a template for procedures is

> .
> .
> .

| CALL | R15,HCF | call to activate procedure |

> .
> .
> .

HCF ⟨first instruction of the procedure code⟩

> .
> .

⟨code body of procedure⟩

> .
> .

| RET | R15 | return to calling routine |

A convention is introduced that *R15* is reserved for the return address or link from procedure. The link register will be given the global name *LK*:

$$LK \quad REG \quad R15$$

Note that if one procedure activates a call to another the link is overwritten. The original value must be preserved. This is the first example of such a problem and rather than solve it in an *ad hoc* manner a general solution will be given in a later section.

7.3.2 DYNAMIC ALLOCATION AND DEALLOCATION OF MEMORY USING A STACK

The memory space for actual parameters and local variables is only needed when the procedure is called. The use of the *DS* directive to allocate space creates a fixed or static area of memory which exists for the life of the program. Compilers for Pascal and other similar languages allocate memory dynamically. This solution will be used as it also gives insight into the important programming concept of the stack.

The implementation of a stack is based on a contiguous area of memory and a variable called a stack pointer (Fig. 7.5.). At any instant the stack contains both allocated and free space. The stack pointer variable contains the memory address of the most significant byte of the last area allocated, which is conventionally called the top of the stack. The direction of allocation is from the high address to the low address of the stack.

Reserving a second register *R12* named *SP* for the stack pointer, ⟨n⟩ bytes can be allocated on the stack by subtracting ⟨n⟩ from the stackpointer:

$$SUBI \quad SP, \langle n \rangle.$$

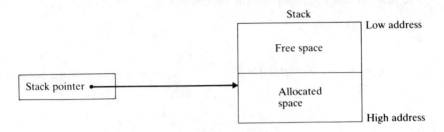

Figure 7.5   A stack and its associated pointer

The deallocation of $\langle n \rangle$ is achieved by adding $\langle n \rangle$ to *SP*:

$$ADDI \qquad SP, \langle n \rangle.$$

If $\langle n \rangle$ is less than 16, the short format instructions can be used (*SUBS* and *ADDS*).

In the ensuing discussion, it will be assumed that a stack exists with *SP* initialized for parameters and local variables.

7.3.3 PARAMETERS

The procedure heading defines both the number, order and the nature of the parameters. For example the procedure heading for the *hcf* example is

procedure *hcf* (*m*, *n*:**integer**; **var** *r*:**integer**);

where *m* and *n* are known as value parameters and *r* is a reference parameter. A mechanism is required that enables the translation of the procedure body together with the substitution of actual parameters at the activation stage. The actual parameters can be organized as a consecutive sequence in memory, the total group being known as a parameter block. The internal structure of the block, like a Pascal record, is determined by the individual components. For the *hcf* algorithm the structure is shown in Fig. 7.6. In general, a value parameter requires sufficient storage to accommodate a copy of the actual parameter value. For a structured type this is the total size of the record or array. A reference parameter always requires one word to contain the memory address of the actual parameter variable.

The parameter block and its contents, the actual parameters, are created by the calling routine and placed on the stack. Thus the base address is not fixed until just prior to the call. The calling routine has to pass the address of the block to the called routine. This can be done by reserving a second register, *R14*, which will be given a name *PB* to signify its role as a pointer to the parameter block. Thus immediately after the call of *hcf*, the stack has the form shown in Fig. 7.7.

The translation of a statement involving a parameter requires a specification of the appropriate memory address. The above diagram shows the difference

Formal name	Address	
m	*a*	integer value
n	*a* + 2	integer value
r	*a* + 4	address of *r*

Figure 7.6   Storage of parameters

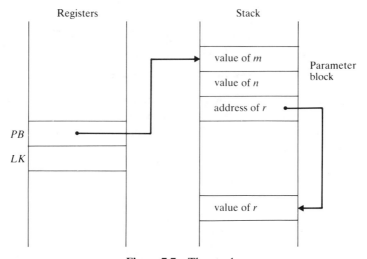

Figure 7.7   The stack

between accessing value and reference parameters. A systematic means of translation is achieved by associating the formal parameter names with relative addresses signifying their position in the parameter block:

$$
\begin{array}{lll}
M & EQU & 0 \\
N & EQU & 2 \\
R & EQU & 4
\end{array}
$$

The formal parameter names are used in the same way as field names in a record. The calculation of the relative addresses and the total size is the same. Thus using *PB* as the index register, the assignment *n* := *m* can be encoded as

$$
\begin{array}{lll}
LD & TEMP,M\ (PB) & .n := m; \\
ST & TEMP,N\ (PB) &
\end{array}
$$

This is similar to the accessing of fields within records. The assignment $r := m$ encodes as

```
LD      TEMP,M (PB)          .r := m;
LDI     RPTR,R (PB)
ST      TEMP,0 (RPTR)
```

In this case the address of r must be loaded into an index register named $RPTR$ before the value can be assigned. Thus the procedure can be coded without explicit knowledge of the position of the parameter block, which is determined only at the time of activation. It is only the relative addresses of the parameters that are fixed.

7.3.4 LOCAL VARIABLES

As with the actual parameters, the local variables of a procedure exist only when it has been called; they are destroyed on exit to the calling routine. Thus a similar mechanism to that used for parameters, involving a reserved register pointing to a local variable block on the stack, can be employed. Consider the declaration

var *Lv1, Lv2, Lv3*:**integer**;

in a procedure. The local variable block requires six bytes of space on the stack. Supposed that the address of the block on the stack is assigned to the reserved register *R13*, which will be called *LT*. The organization of the three variables on the stack is shown in Fig. 7.8.

As with formal parameter names, the local variable names are associated with their relative address with respect to the value in *LT*:

```
LV1     EQU     0
LV2     EQU     2
LV3     EQU     4
```

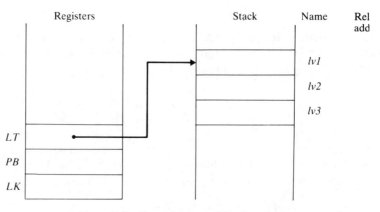

Figure 7.8   Organization of local variables

The assignment $lv3 := lv1$ translates to

$$LD \quad TEMP,LV1 \ (LT)$$
$$ST \quad TEMP,LV3 \ (LT)$$

7.3.5 SECURITY OF THE REGISTERS

When developing a template for the procedures, the problem of the security of registers has been temporarily overlooked. It has been assumed that the reserved registers SP, LT and PB point to correct positions on the stack and LK contains the correct link address. The remainder of the register set is available as temporary workspace for the procedure to use. Provided no action is taken to preserve the register values, when one procedure calls another the reserved registers and possibly others will be overwritten. The simplest solution to the problem of register corruption (both actual and potential), is to save all the values of the general registers on the stack before the call of a procedure and then to restore them after the return from the procedure.

Two SRM instructions directly support the saving and restoring of registers (Table 7.2). The action of the store multiple instruction is to save the registers from $r1$ to $R15$ in sequence, starting from the memory address $a + (x2)$:

$$(a + (x2)) := (r1)$$
$$(a + (x2) + 2) := (r1 + 1)$$
$$(a + (x2) + 4) := (r1 + 2)$$

$$\cdot$$
$$\cdot$$
$$\cdot$$

$$(a + (x2) + (15 - r1)*2) := (R15).$$

The load multiple instruction performs the converse:

$$(r1) := (a + (x2))$$
$$(r1 + 1) := (a + (x2) + 2)$$
$$(r1 + 2) := (a + (x2) + 4)$$

$$\cdot$$
$$\cdot$$
$$\cdot$$

$$(R15) := (a + (x2) + (15 - r1) * 2)$$

The allocation of space and subsequent saving of all the registers on the stack is achieved by

Table 7.2 STM and LDM

Mnemonic	Full description	Format
STM	Store multiple	RX
LDM	Load multiple	RX

$$\begin{array}{ll} SUBI & SP,32 \\ STM & 0,0(SP) \end{array}$$

and the restoration of a register set by

$$\begin{array}{ll} LDM & R0,0(SP) \\ ADDI & SP,32 \end{array}$$

7.3.6   COMPLETE TEMPLATES FOR PROCEDURES AND THEIR ACTIVATION

The complete templates for the encoding of procedures and the sequence for an
activation in SRM machine code are given in Fig. 7.9(a) and (b) respectively.

The translation of the parameter list involves calculating the relative address
of every parameter and associating it with the formal parameter name using the
EQU directive. Value parameters need sufficient space to hold the actual parameter value and reference parameters a single word to hold an address. Local
variables are declared in a similar way. The size of the local variable block is
determined by accumulating the total of the individual space for each variable.
With each addition the running total is the relative address of the next variable
name.

(a) *Procedure encoding template*

⟨declaration of parameter list⟩

⟨declaration of local variables⟩

| ⟨procedure name⟩ | SUBI | SP,⟨1⟩ | .allocate space for local variables |
| | LDR | LT,SP | .initialize *LT* |

⟨code body⟩

| | ADDI | SP,⟨1⟩ | .deallocate local variables |
| | RET | LK | |

(b) *Procedure activation template*

	SUBI	SP,32	.save registers
	STM	R0,0(SP)	
	SUBI	SP,⟨p⟩	.allocate ⟨p⟩ bytes for parameters
	LDR	PB,SP	.initialize *PB* for called procedure

⟨add parameters to block in order of procedure definition⟩

| | CALL | LK,⟨procedure name⟩ | .call procedure |

	ADDI	SP,⟨p⟩	.deallocate parameter block
	LDM	R0,0(SP)	.restore registers
	ADDI	SP,32	

Figure 7.9   Templates for a procedure and its activation

The procedure code begins with the allocation of space for the local variables on the stack and the initialization of the reserved register LT, which points to the top of the local variable block. This is followed by the code body of the procedure that could contain activations of other procedures. The translation of expressions involving parameters must use indexed addressing with PB as the index register. Thus the use of a parameter in an expression will translate into RX or RI instructions, with the second operand of the form

$$\langle \text{parameter name} \rangle \; (PB).$$

Similarly for local variable references the assembly code instructions have a second operand of the form

$$\langle \text{local variable name} \rangle \; (LT).$$

The procedure code terminates with the deallocation of the local parameter block and the RET instruction to return to the calling procedure or main program.

The template for the calling sequence of a procedure (Fig. 7.9(b)) begins by saving the current register set on the stack. This is followed by the creation of the parameter block on the stack. It is the calling routine's responsibility to allocate the space for the block, initialize the reserved register PB and copy the actual parameters into it. The procedure is activated by the CALL instruction transferring control to its first instruction. After the procedure returns control to the instruction following the call, the parameter block is deallocated. Finally the original register set is restored. Note that in the absence of global variables, the only way a procedure can have an effect is via reference parameters. The effect of assignments on value parameters does not affect the environment outside the procedure itself.

The encoding of the *hcf* procedure is given in Fig. 7.10. This illustrates many of the different features of a Pascal procedure. It has two value and one reference parameter and a single local variable. The contents of the value parameters change as the calculation proceeds, thus this example demonstrates that such parameters can be regarded as initialized variables as far as the procedure is concerned. The assignment to the reference parameter is preceded by an instruction to load the reference into the register PTR, which is then used as a pointer for the assignment instruction. In some cases it would be beneficial to reserve registers for such pointers.

Figure 7.11 gives an example of a main program which calls the *hcf* procedure. In addition to illustrating the calling sequence, it presents the necessary code for declaring and initializing the stack and declaring the reserved register names. It is the responsibility of the main program to initalize the stack once, for the life of the program.

7.4 Functions

A Pascal function definition is similar to a procedure definition. A function to

```
                                              .procedure hcf(m,n:integer;
                                                  var r:integer);
M           EQU       0
N           EQU       2
R           EQU       4
                                              .var
T           EQU       0                        .   t:integer
                                              .begin
HCF         SUBS      SP,2
            LDR       LT,SP
REPEAT      LDS       EVEN,0                    .   repeat
            LD        ODD,M(PB)                 .       t := m mod n;
            DIV       EVEN,N(PB)
            ST        EVEN,T(LT)
            LD        SCR,N(PB)                 .       m := n;
            ST        SCR,M(PB)                 .
            LD        SCR,T(LT)                 .       n := t;
            ST        SCR,N(PB)
            BNE       REPEAT                    .   until n = 0;
            LD        SCR,M(PB)                 .   r := m;
            LD        PTR,R(PB)
            ST        SCR,0(PTR)
            ADDS      SP,2
            RET       LK                        .end

SCR         REG       R0
PTR         REG       R1
EVEN        REG       R2
ODD         REG       R3
```

Figure 7.10   Assembler encoding of *hcf* procedure

calculate the sum of the first *n* numbers follows:

```
function sumn (n:integer):integer;
var
    i, s:integer;
begin
    s := 0;
    for i := 1 to n
    do
        s := s + i;
    sumn := s
end;
```

Whereas a procedure has an effect, a function yields a value of the type indicated after the parameter list. Typically it is called as part of an expression, for example:

$$a := sumn(4) + b;$$

The value is returned by the execution of at least one assignment of the form

			.program *ex73*;
RES	EQU	0	**.var** *res*:**integer**
	LDI	SP, STACK	.{initialize stackpointer}
	ADDI	SP, STSIZ	
	SUBS	SP, 2	. {allocate space for local variables}
	LDR	LT, SP	. {initialize LT for main program}
	SUBI	SP, 32	. {save register set}
	STM	0, 0(SP)	
	SUBS	SP, 6	. {allocate six bytes on stack and initialize PB}
	LDI	TEMP, 25	. {add actual parameters to block}
	ST	TEMP, 0(PB)	
	LDS	TEMP, 10	
	ST	TEMP, 2(PB)	
	LDI	TEMP, RES(LT)	
	ST	TEMP, 4(PB)	
	CALL	LK, HCF	. *hcf* (25, 10, *res*);
	ADDS	SP, 6	. {deallocate parameter block}
	LDM	0, 0(SP)	. {restore register set}
	ADDI	SP, 32	
	HALT		**.end**
TEMP	REG	R0	
SP	REG	R12	.pointer to top of stack
LT	REG	R13	.pointer to local variable block
PB	REG	R14	.pointer to parameter block
LK	REG	R15	.link
STSIZ	EQU	100	.stack size
STACK	DS	STSIZ	.stack

Figure 7.11 Assembler encoding of main program which calls *hcf* procedure

⟨function name⟩ := ⟨return value⟩;

The template for procedures already returns values. For functions the problem is simplified, in that there is only a single value to return, instead of a variable number for a procedure. The easiest modification to the existing procedure template is to reserve register *R0* for this return value. The template for the function calling sequence must exclude *R0* from the general register save. The modified calling sequence is given in Fig. 7.12.

Within the function code body there are one or more instances of an assignment such as

LD   R0, ⟨return value⟩,   ⟨function name⟩ := ⟨return value⟩

In this case the return value required is situated in memory. Figure 7.13 gives the encoding of *sumn*.

7.5   Conclusions

Assembler templates for **SRM** have been developed for single-dimensional

A PROGRAMMER'S INTRODUCTION TO COMPUTER SYSTEMS

```
SUBI   SP, 30            .save registers R1–R15
STM    R1, 0(SP)
SUBI   SP, ⟨p⟩           .allocate ⟨p⟩ bytes for parameter block
LDR    PB, SP            .initialize PB for function
```

⟨add parameters to block in order of function definition⟩

```
CALL   LK ⟨function name⟩   .call function

ADDI   SP, ⟨p⟩           .deallocate parameter block
LDM    R1, 0(SP)         .restore registers R1–R15
ADDI   SP, 30
```

⟨use value in *RO* in an expression evaluation⟩

Figure 7.12   Calling sequence for a function

arrays, records, procedures and functions. The presence of a mechanism such as modified addressing has been shown to be essential for the implementation of these constructs. A number of special instructions directly support the procedure mechanism, namely *CALL, RET, LDM* and *STM*.

The objective has been to develop the templates in as general a way as possible. The one problem not tackled explicitly was global variables. The global variables belonging to the main program can be declared using the assembler directive *DS*, thus not using the stack. These variables may be accessed in the usual way. The problem of a procedure declared within another procedure, with local variables of one being global to the other, has not been solved. The added complexity of a general solution to local variables was felt to be beyond the scope of this book.

A second problem that has not received explicit treatment is that of recursion. Recursion is a programming mechanism, where a procedure can call itself and is supported by languages such as Pascal. As a simple example the sum of the first n positive integers can be defined as follows:

$$S_n = S_{n-1} + n, \qquad S_1 = 1$$

which naturally codes into the following Pascal:

```
function sumn (n:integer):integer;
begin
  if n > 1
  then
    sumn := sumn (n − 1) + n
  else
    sumn := 1
end
```

The templates formulated for procedures and functions can deal with this mechanism, because of the explicit use of a stack to support the dynamic allocation of parameters and local variables.

```
                                        .program ex77;
RES      EQU     0                      .var res:integer;
         LDI     SP, STACK              .
         ADDI    SP, STSIZ              .
         SUBS    SP, 2                  . {initialize LT}
         LDR     LT, SP
         SUBI    SP, 30                 . {save registers R1–R15}
         STM     R1, 0(SP)
         SUBS    SP, 2                  . {add actual parameter}
         LDR     PB, SP
         LDS     TEMP, 5
         STH     TEMP, 0(PB)
         CALL    LK, SUMN               . res := sumn (5);
         ADDS    SP, 2
         LDM     R1, 0(SP)              . {restore registers R1–R15}
         ADDI    SP, 30
         ST      R0, RES(LT)
         HALT

TEMP     REG     R0
                                        .function sumn(n:integer):integer;
N        EQU     0
                                        .var
RI       REG     R2                     . i, s: integer;
S        EQU     0
                                        .begin

SUMN     SUBS    SP, 2
         LDR     LT, SP
         LDS     SCR, 0                 . s := 0;
         ST      SCR, S(LT)
         LDS     RI, 1                  . for i := 1 to n
FOR      CMP     RI, N(PB)              . do begin
         BP      OUT
         LD      SCR, S(LT)             .   s := s + i;
         ADDR    SCR, RI
         ST      SCR, S(LT)
         ADDS    RI, 1
         B       FOR                    .    end;
OUT      LH      RO, S(LT)              . sumn := s;
         ADDS    SP, 2
         RET     LK                     .end

SCR      REG     R1
```

⟨plus declarations of reserved registers and stack as in Fig. 7.11⟩

Figure 7.13 Assembler encoding of *sumn* function together with a calling program

The overhead associated with procedure calls is large. Some optimization is possible in a systematic way:
1. map the local variables onto registers rather than the stack;
2. for small numbers of parameters map the parameter block onto the registers;

3. save only those registers which are used by the called routine.

Such optimizations are relatively easy for a disciplined programmer to incorporate, but may be more difficult for compilers to employ automatically.

The last two chapters have given a detailed treatment of the characteristics of the SRM machine using Pascal and its systematic translation into machine code as a theme. Having established a sound model of the processor at a low level, the next chapter returns to a higher-level view of the computer system as a whole and how it is organized to offer a computing service.

Exercises

1. Extend the example program of Fig. 7.2 to record the position(s) of the maximum values in a second array, and recode in assembler.
2. The following Pascal type declaration supports short fixed-length strings of characters:

> **type**
> *string* = **array** [0 .. 20] **of char**

A string is always terminated by a null character. Although the assembler for SRM does not support character constants, byte operations and hexadecimal constants allow character manipulation to be explored. Write an assembler program to compute the length of a string.
3. In a two-dimensional world each point is represented by a pair of coordinates (x, y). Assuming x and y are integers, design a data structure of type *coordinate*. Given that the vertices of a four-sided figure are stored in an array of type *coordinate*, design an algorithm to test whether the figure is a square or not and implement it in assembler.
4. Rewrite the program given in Fig. 7.4 as a procedure with the daily times and weekly sum as parameters. Explore the difference in solution between having the array of times as a value or reference parameter.
5. Design a data structure to represent long-word integers. Write two procedures in assembler to add and subtract such integers.
6. Rewrite the program to calculate Fibonacci numbers as a function to calculate F_n.
7. Using the definition of strings in Exercise 2, design algorithms and implement assembler versions of functions to:

    (a) copy a string from one variable to another returning the length of the string copied;
    (b) compare two strings returning a value 1 if they are equal and 0 if not.

8. Implement the recursive form of calculating the sum of the first n numbers which was discussed in the conclusions of this chapter. Develop diagrams of the state of the stack at the entry and exit to the function.

8
Introduction to operating systems

The earlier chapters of this book have built up a hardware model of the computer to explain how it works. Particular attention has been paid to the way in which the architecture of the machine affects its programming, by examining assembler notation. These major influences on the form computer systems take are concluded by examining the operating system itself. For it is this that finally determines the user's image of the system. The overall purpose of an operating system is to help computer users to solve problems. It should free them from detailed concerns about how the machine works or how their information is stored. It needs to share out machine resources equitably and safely between competing demands and at all times to present a helpful image to the user.

8.1   Typical user interaction

It is supposed that a user will usually access a computer from a terminal. After logging in, the user might select an editor to allow the input of text into a file; the result of this will frequently be to write a modified version back to the file store. If the text formed part of a program the file might in turn form the input to a compiler that checked the program and produced as output both a listing and a sequence of machine instructions ready to run. Finally the programmer might actually run the new program; this in turn would typically input some information, do some calculations and produce some results.

8.2   Operating system view

From many such user interactions it is not difficult to propose a simple model; input, followed by computation, followed by output. This is typically the sequence of events that the operating system will be asked to supervise.

8.2.1 SERIAL SYSTEM

In a simple serial system it will be supposed that each user interaction begins immediately after the preceding one with no gap in time. If the input, compute and output times of a typical user interaction are represented by i, c, o respectively, then a sequence of users could be represented as in Fig. 8.1.

8.2.2 INPUT–OUTPUT OVERLAP

In a more realistic system it is assumed that the input and output of characters for different users may proceed at the same time as shown in Fig. 8.2. Even with this simple assumption the operating system has taken far less time to process the four user jobs and this time gained is in itself a justification for having an operating system. With a multi-access system several people may use the computer at the same time; the pauses in activity represented by the slow speed of typing, as well as complete gaps while people 'think', will make it possible to make the central processing unit available to other users. In practice, the operating system performs many duties on behalf of the user, including input–output. As well as allowing overlap of activities this also has the advantage of freeing people from having to know precise details of how the peripherals work and must be coordinated. Hence the user can direct information with the same command to terminal, line printer or disk and the system will guarantee that it is transferred correctly. Many other functions have also been taken on by operating systems: some of these will be briefly reviewed before beginning a more detailed study.

8.2.3 SCHEDULING, ACCOUNTING, LOGGING

It may be necessary to make a charge for the use of a computer system. With serial access, as represented by Fig. 8.1, the amount of time that a user is charged for could be simply represented by the total elapsed time spent at the terminal. However, with a multiaccess system two people may have sat at the terminal for the same length of time, but have asked the computer to do very different things. It is normally expected that any charge made should relate to the work done, regardless of terminal 'think' time or the activities of other users on the system which will both affect the elapsed time. Hence the operating system itself will

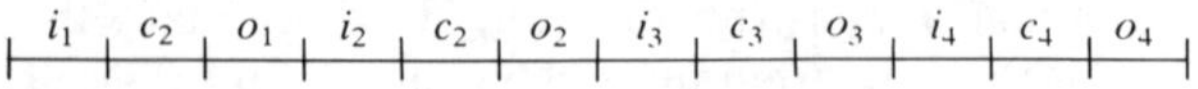

Figure 8.1 Serial system showing a sequence of four users

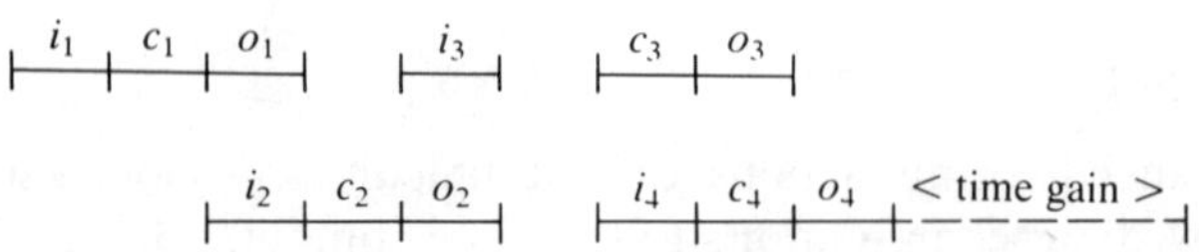

Figure 8.2 Input–output overlapped with four users

need to accumulate information on exactly what the user did in the terminal session. As far as processor time is concerned the system is peculiarly well placed to record this as it manages input–output as well as switching the computer's attention from one user to another. The scheduler is a key system routine that effectively determines which tasks should be executed next on the computer; this routine will need to keep logging information about the start and stop times of each user task if a realistic charge is to be made.

8.2.4 FILE SYSTEM AND PROTECTION

Most modern operating systems offer users facilities to store both programs and data directly on the computer. These are normally placed in named files on the backing-store of the computer and a list of them is kept in the owner's directory. The users are allowed to create, modify and delete their own files. In addition the file system may allow the safe sharing of information by allowing read access to selected files. This would normally require the use of a double-barrelled name of the form

$$directoryname–filename$$

where the owner of *directoryname* had given another user permission to access his particular *filename*. This will work as a useful facility if the operating system guarantees to protect user files by allowing only the appropriate access.

8.3   User task representation

Enough has been said in outline about an operating system to establish that it has a variety of functions to fulfil. It will now be possible to examine in more detail some of the mechanisms that are frequently used in the solution of the complex timing and coordination problems that result.

8.3.1 SINGLE-USER VIEW OF TASK

As far as the operating system is concerned, each user that is logged in has to be regarded as a potentially active master task that may create further sub-tasks. The structure of Fig. 8.3 shows how the system must preserve the context in which the user is working; this is directly analogous with the block structure of high-level languages. It is also instructive to represent the same simple session using a timing diagram as in Fig. 8.4.

8.3.2 SYSTEM VIEW OF TASK → PROCESS

The operating system needs to keep track of all tasks that may become active. Hence in a busy multi-access system there will be a large number of requests for work to be carried out. In order to cope with this problem the operating system needs to have a simple uniform way of dealing with all requests. The normal reaction of most systems is to create a *process* to deal with each of the tasks.

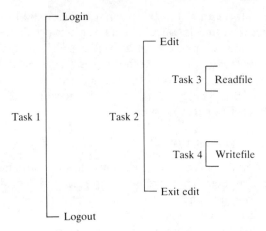

Figure 8.3   Single user creates system tasks

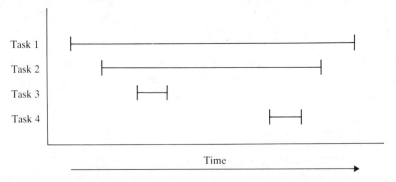

Figure 8.4   User session potentially active tasks

These processes are of course programs with or without data, many of which are direct calls on the software of the system. They range from login–logout, through input–output to the use of large sub-systems such as editors or compilers. However, as far as the operating system is concerned, they can all be treated in a uniform way by regarding each as a process.

The overall system view of processes has now become quite complex and it is helpful to construct some further rather more realistic timing diagrams. In order to do this the time scales used need to be placed in some realistic context. It is vital to be able to relate these to typical operations performed on the computer. It has already been suggested that the machine can obey instructions quickly, about 1 million operations per second. Putting this another way it takes about $1\,\mu\text{s}$ per average instruction. This contrasts sharply with the speed of input–output operations:

$$\text{VDU input 10 bytes/s} \;\equiv\; 100\,\text{ms/byte} \;\equiv\; 100\text{K instructions}$$

$$\text{VDU output 100 bytes/s} \;\equiv\; 10\,\text{ms/byte} \;\equiv\; 10\text{K instructions}$$

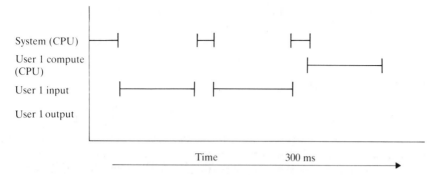

Figure 8.5 Single serial system transition from input to compute phase

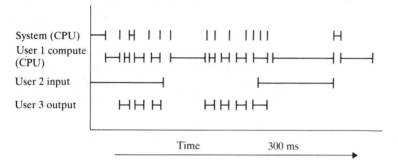

Figure 8.6 Multiple users with input–output overlaps

Using these approximations it is now possible to show timing diagrams to give a more realistic model of the process transitions that occur on a real system. The simple serial use of a system postulated at the beginning of this chapter would in reality look much more like the situation shown in Fig. 8.5. Here each character input taking about 100 ms causes the operating system to take action to receive it. The last two characters are shown arriving for user 1, and at that point the system is able to set the processor to work on the user's computing task. Until that time the processor is mostly idle, only being active to accept input characters. Equally, in this simple serial system, user 1 output cannot begin until the compute phase has finished.

As before it is observed that most operating systems attempt to overlap input–output with computing in order to offer more efficient use of the computer. This inevitably leads to a much more complicated timing picture. Several activities are now proceeding in parallel, leading to many potentially active processes. The processor activity in Fig. 8.6 is shown divided between user 1 intensively computing and the occasional activities of the system (shown by a blip). The transitions are caused by the input–output activity of users 2 and 3, leading to small numbers of instructions being obeyed on their behalf. This model is now sufficiently realistic to show the typical pattern of a system where the processor is carefully managed by the system, but input–output is allowed to proceed in parallel and produces an apparently random series of events concerned with the arrival and departure of characters which force the operating system to respond.

8.4   Interrupts and processes

Because input–output is such a frequent activity most machines make special provision for this by allowing the processor to receive what is known as an *interrupt*. As the word suggests it normally causes the processor to abandon the current task or process and begin another process. Each interrupt signals the occurrence of an event in the computer system. The process change allows the system to identify the precise nature of the event, and to take appropriate action. As suggested, the most frequent sources of interrupts are the peripherals requesting input or output of information. Most of the time the system is prepared to be interrupted, but there are certain critical operations which must be completed without interference and for this reason the system is able to switch interrupts off. This is also referred to as running with interrupts inhibited rather than enabled. If information is not to be lost the system should normally run with interrupts enabled and only switch them off (inhibit them) for very short periods of time.

8.4.1   INTERRUPT ROUTINE FUNCTIONS

The combination of the frequency of interrupts and their specialist nature has led most systems to develop a series of special programs known as interrupt routines. Regardless of the reason for the interrupt they need to perform a number of standard duties:

1. *Switch interrupts off.* Once interrupt processing has begun it is normally good practice to completely clear the work needed by the current interrupt. As interrupts occur at random, there is nothing to prevent a second interrupt happening immediately after the first. A simple way to guarantee integrity is to switch interrupts off until the current one has been dealt with.
2. *Make safe.* The interrupt process must guarantee that when it has finished the system can return to the precise state it was in before the interrupt occurred. To facilitate this the interrupt routine stores the values of previous program variables, the location counter, registers and other essentials of the volatile environment. These must all be carefully restored at the end of the routine as the interrupt process itself must inevitably change program counter and register values to carry out its job.
3. *Find source of the interrupt.* Although interrupt mechanisms vary widely in their sophistication, it is normally necessary to check a series of status indicators in the processor and the peripherals in order to determine the precise cause of the interrupt.
4. *Service interrupt.* The action taken by the routine depends on the cause of the interrupt. Essentially the action should be kept as brief as possible so that

interrupts can be switched on again. The most frequent task will be to take
a character from a device and place it in the memory of the machine or send
a character from memory to peripheral. Clearly rather different action will
be taken when dealing with a disk or other backing store device. Equally an
internal clock may have caused an interrupt and as well as incrementing a
counter to keep track of time, the precise value of the counter may indicate
that the system should take some special action. Normally this will not be
taken directly by the interrupt routine, but passed on to some other system
process for obeying later when interrupts are enabled.
5. *Return.* Once the routine has finished it will restore the previous environment
   and return control to the operating system, with interrupts again enabled.

8.5   Process representation

The frequent occurrence of interrupts on a busy multiaccess system leads to a
large number of program changes. Hence it has to be expected that any user task
will be started and stopped many times before it is completed. In order to
facilitate this the system adopts a central data structure that allows it to keep
track of all processes in a uniform way.

The system data includes a statement of what version of the operating system
is being run as well as the date. In addition a link or pointer is kept to the many
process descriptors which will contain information vital to running a particular
process. Each process descriptor is in turn linked to the next descriptor, forming
a queue maintained in what is known as a linked list. In a similar way the system
also maintains a queue of all runnable processes; the linked form (shown by
arrows on Fig. 8.7) makes it easy to change the order of the run queue as well
as its membership. This is simply achieved by changing the pointers rather than
moving all the information held within the process descriptor.

8.5.1   PROCESS STATUS AND SERVICE

Each process descriptor contains vital information that allows tasks to be
stopped and then re-started later from exactly the previous state. Thus the
volatile environment has to be saved and restored, including the program
counter, the value of the processor registers and other status information. Each
descriptor also has a name given to it by the system so that it can distinguish
between original user tasks and sub-processes created to deal with the additional
problems of running the user program. Finally the process is marked by the
system as being in one of three well-defined states: running, runnable or unrunnable. With a single-processor machine there can only be one *running* process
that is actually using the processor at that time. After that there is normally a
queue of processes that could use the processor when it becomes available
shown as *runnable*. The remaining processes kept in the system are still potentially runnable, but for the moment cannot make use of processor time and are
consequently marked as *unrunnable*. These changes of status and the consequent

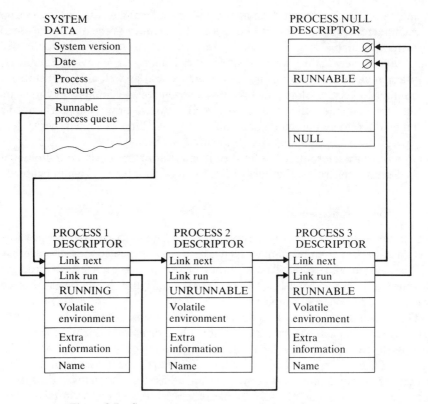

Figure 8.7   System structure to represent process queue

re-ordering of the process descriptor queues are crucial to the central management of the system and indeed require specific routines to achieve this.

8.5.2   PROCESS SYNCHRONIZATION

Operating systems have adopted a number of different methods to solve the problems of starting, stopping and coordinating processes. The primitives that will be described show the underlying operations that need to be performed without commitment to any particular management policy. They would normally form part of the central system nucleus and once started would have to run to completion, that is they would run with interrupts switched off, thus isolated from the effects of input–output and process change.

1. *start-process* (*name, time-out*);
   This primitive tries to find a compiled program file *name*, load it into memory, prime a process descriptor with the relevant information and add it to the process queue. If this is successful it will mark the process as RUNNABLE. The details may include how much processor time the process should be allowed in *time-out*. If this is exceeded the process will be stopped

and the system may decide to remove the process altogether and even other related processes as well.

2. *suspend-process* (*name*, *time*, *action*);
   The process itself may recognize that it can no longer continue to use the processor, but it has not finished its task. Hence it requests voluntary suspension, but may request that it should be restarted after a certain *time* or after a certain *action* has taken place. Hence the system should change the process descriptor from RUNNING/RUNNABLE to UNRUNNABLE.

3. *resume-process* (*name*);
   The situation of a suspended process may have changed either because the specified *time* has elapsed or because the specified *action* has taken place. Hence the process descriptor should now be changed from UNRUNNABLE to RUNNABLE.

4. *stop-process* (*name*);
   This primitive may be invoked because a process recognizes that it has finished its task. However, in other cases the termination may be forced because it has exceeded its ration of processor time given in *timeout* or because there is some hardware or software error condition that cannot be cleared. In all cases, however, the current process should be stopped and the process descriptor cleared and made available to a fresh process.

8.6 Dispatcher (low-level scheduler)

The dispatcher is the name given to a system routine that actually supervises the change from one process to the next according to the information given in the process descriptors. It is normally run when the current process cannot continue. The most frequent reasons for this are an interrupt from input–output activity or the clock, an error condition from hardware of software, or voluntary process suspension. Whatever the reason for its being started the dispatcher takes various standard actions:

1. Interrupts are switched off to prevent process disturbance. If the current process is still the best for running, then it will restore the volatile environment from the process descriptor, load the program counter, switch on interrupts and pass control back to the process.
2. If the current process is not to be run, then its volatile environment should be stored in its process descriptor.
3. The dispatcher should select the next RUNNABLE process.
4. Restore the volatile environment of the new process descriptor, load the program counter, switch on interrupts and pass control back to the new process.

Thus the overall action of the dispatcher is simply to work down the queue of runnable processes. Normally system processes have a special priority and for this simple model it is suggested that this will be adequately reflected if system

CPU utilization

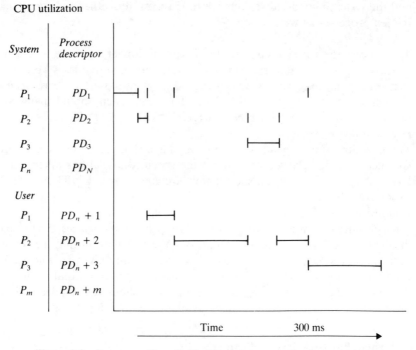

Figure 8.8 Processor time divided between system and user processes

processes are always placed at the head of the run queue; the dispatcher must always clear system tasks at the head of the queue before beginning user processes lower down. In this way the dispatcher acts as a low-level scheduler of processes, leaving to the main scheduler the job of further altering process priorities by reordering them on the run queue. The situation of system and user processes can be shown on the timing diagram of Fig. 8.8. The diagram of processor utilization shows system processes being allocated the first n process descriptors, while users take up the succeeding m descriptors. The dispatcher always clears all system processes that are runnable, before passing control in turn to the user processes further down the queue.

8.7   Scheduler

The scheduler has the power to order processes in the process queue according to predetermined priorities. It automatically places all system processes at the head of the queue and will normally make sure that the scheduler and dispatcher have highly privileged positions within that. After these follow the users: the simplest policy to adopt with them would be to obey each process to completion in the order they occur on the run list. However, with a multi-access system it can immediately be seen that the first few users in the queue will get their tasks finished quickly, but that the rest will have to wait idly until their turn comes. If the times for job completion are significant, it might mean that user 99 was waiting for hours before any of his work was done. Clearly this would not be a very popular multi-access system; most systems guarantee to serve each user in turn by adopting a round-robin scheduling algorithm.

8.7.1 ROUND-ROBIN

Evolved specifically for multi-access systems to give users a reasonably rapid response. The scheduler allocates a fixed quantum of processor time to each user in turn. When a user has exhausted his processor cycles the process is suspended and the next person receives a turn. In order for this to be effective the time quantum must be kept small, normally between 1 s and 100 ms, depending on the system and the numbers of users. If too small a time quantum is selected little work will get done on a busy system, as the time spent changing from one process to the next will significantly reduce the number of processor cycles available to users. Equally if the quantum is too large, the system will appear to 'sleep' from time to time while it attends to other users.

More complex scheduling algorithms attempt to get the best of both worlds by placing people on different queues according to their needs. Those who seem to require rapid response are placed on a queue with a small time quantum of say 20 ms. Others requiring more processor activity are given a much larger quantum of say 1 s, but the queue is served less frequently. These and other strategies are all the responsibility of the scheduler with an obedient dispatcher working down the ordered queue of processes.

8.7.2 CHARGING AND RATIONING

This complex situation is clearly very different from the single-user model of a computer introduced at the beginning of this chapter, where if a charge were to be made for computer use a simple record of elapsed time would suffice. For a fully developed multi-access system it is only the system that knows what work a user has done, while connected to the computer, and this record has to form the basis for a charge.

With a sophisticated system certain facilities may not be available to all users. Plotting large complex graphs on a plotter or accessing expensive facilities on other machines may only be available to certain named users and the system will have to restrict access. Equally it may be that a user is given a budget of a particular resource and it is up to the system to enforce the rationing. This normally requires an account file for each user which is credited or debited up to a certain budget; once this is exceeded the system must terminate the user task and refuse to allow further expenditure on that account. More often the user is allowed to proceed and a charge is made for the facilities used. Some systems may only charge for processor use, which makes the accounting easy but may not encourage good habits in the user community. Hence a formula that includes several factors can be employed. This would typically combine separate measures of the activity of the user logged into the system:

$$units\text{-}used := 133 * P + 6 * C + 3 * K + 5 * W$$

where P = processor time (s);
       C = terminal connect time (s);
       K = number of memory blocks used;
       W = number of disk transfers.

The formula is still heavily weighted to processor time, but does take some account of memory and storage activity which would also affect the response that other users on the system would experience. Additions can easily be made to reflect direct inconvenience to the system such as mounting a magnetic tape, use of a graph plotter, use of special paper on a line printer or just excessive amounts of output. Again with a view to influencing the behaviour of users, the charging formula can be made responsive to the time of day by making higher charges at popular times to try and even out demand throughout the 24 hour period. Hence charging formulae can be used to fulfil a number of functions, in addition to making the system show a profit from its users.

8.8   File handler

All modern computer systems encourage users to store their programs and data online. Under normal circumstances this should mean that information input or created on the system at any time is immediately available. Hence the file system has become one of the central facilities essential for the smooth working of both system and user alike.

8.8.1   USER FACILITIES

File systems vary in their complexity and the sophistication of the facilities offered; however, to be worthy of the name they need to provide most of the following functions:

1. *Creation and deletion of files.* The most basic requirement is that the user needs to be able to direct information to a file for subsequent recall and to remove it when it is no longer useful. The file should have a symbolic name of the user's choice; file and other commands should all allow the user to reference the information by this name. Systems vary in the freedom they allow in name creation, but they usually start with a letter which can be followed by a limited series of printable characters. Whatever form the name takes it should have no effect on where the file is placed. It is entirely the duty of the system to allocate space for the file and manage secondary storage throughout the life of the file without further intervention by the user.
2. *Directory provision.* File systems usually keep a special directory of all the files belonging to one user. If the files are listed alphabetically this forms a

most convenient way for the individual to keep track of the files created both when it comes to the creation of new file names and the deletion of old ones no longer in use. Some systems allow the user to create new directories so that all the information relevant to a particular task can be grouped together. This facility is vital if the user is going to be able to work on a large number of tasks at the same time.

3. *File-access controls.* The user is usually able to restrict the form of access to a particular file. Read only access can be used to protect program or data from inadvertent change; attempting to write into the file will cause the system to trap and disallow the operation. The files may also be of different types, so that for example data and program files can be separately identified. This again enables the system to disallow inappropriate operations – for example, trying to compile a data file or loading and running a symbolic program file rather than the binary version.

4. *Sharing of files between users.* In the context of a multiaccess system it is natural to expect to be able to share information with other users. However, if this is to be practical the access has to be carefully controlled. Normally the access categories granted to the owner of the file can be selectively offered to other users of the system. This can either be offered globally to everyone or to some sub-set of friends. Read access may be offered to all users, but the ability to change or write to the file needs to be reserved for a few people.

8.8.2   FILE DIRECTORY STRUCTURE

The structure of the file system varies to some extent according to the facilities offered. However, there are basically three different types of information that must be accommodated: a list of authorized users, a file directory for each user and the actual files themselves. Figure 8.9 shows a single directory for each user; more sophisticated systems would allow additional directories for groups of files under the same user.

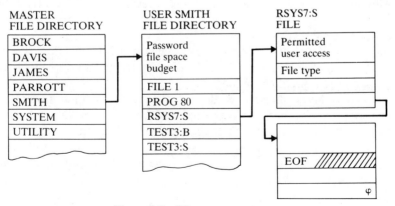

Figure 8.9 File system structure

The master file directory has access reserved for the manager of the system, as this contains a list of all the authorized users of the system. There is then a file directory for each user. The head of this file contains the user password, the amount of file space occupied, as well as other budgetary and accounting information. This allows monitoring of the time the user spends logged on the system and of the amount of resource used such as processor time. The main body of the file directory will contain an alphabetical list of the user files. Each file entry contains a pointer to the start of the file itself. The head of the first block of the file gives the access rights of the file and may in addition grant special access to a list of authorized users or friends. Attempts to access another user's files normally needs a double-barrelled name such as SMITH-FILE 1. Additional monitoring information may also be stored here such as file size, date when last read from or written to. The file type indicates what sort of information follows in the main body of the file, the main distinction usually being between text and binary files. Any file may consist of several blocks of information which need to be linked together by pointers. The last block of the file requires an end-of-file marker as well as a null pointer.

8.8.3   FILE ACCESS

It has already been suggested that it is useful to be able to share files on a multi-access system. However, the permitted access has to be monitored by the system and for this purpose a range of access may be defined for different classes of user. Normally at least three groups are recognized: the owner of the file, named users or friends and the rest of the users of the system. The range of access offered can be graded in the following list of increasing permissiveness:

1. *Execute.* This is where the user is able to run the program contained in the file, but nothing else. Clearly this can be offered as a widespread facility without compromising the information in any way.
2. *Read.* This access is only sensible to offer on text files and can be widespread without risk of the file being changed. However, if people can read the file there is nothing to stop them copying it and then making their own version of the original text or program.
3. *Append.* Although the existing file is safeguarded from deletion, this access allows the addition of material to the file. Clearly this is normally offered to a small group of collaborating users.
4. *Write.* This gives complete freedom to change the file in any way. Clearly under normal circumstances this is reserved for the owner. Depending on the file system this may also include the creation and deletion of files.
5. *Directory.* The final category of access is also normally reserved for the owner because it not only allows creation and deletion of files, but also the ability to change any of the directory entries defining access rights.

8.8.4   RELIABILITY

Clearly if a file system is to be widely used it must be reliable. The access checks must work correctly so that users are protected against inadvertent or intentional contravening of access rights. If the operating system itself goes wrong in any area it is normally expected that this will not affect the file system. This is to some extent helped by the fact that the information is held on a backing store, but may be further aided by careful planning in the system. It is normally considered good practice to minimize the number of different places in the system where the file store may be updated. Changes to the file store should also be applied to the files on backing store with reasonable regularity.

However, there are always unforeseen circumstances and hardware failures that directly affect the backing media such as magnetic disks. Individuals can take action by choosing to make copies of their files onto tapes or disks that are then held securely off line. If a file is lost the user may then go back to the last version that was dumped off line. However, these *ad hoc* arrangements take time and effort for each user to organize and a simple strategy frequently adopted is to make a copy of the whole of the file system. One easy way of organizing this is to take over the whole of the computer system periodically and to make a complete copy of the file system onto disk or tape. While this is happening none of the users can be logged in and if the file store is large this activity may take a long time. However, it does give a secure and reliable way of restoring the file store.

An improved method of guaranteeing the reliability of the file store is by using an incremental dump strategy. Here a continuous record of the changes made to the filestore is kept, usually on magnetic tape. The advantage of this scheme is that the system is not closed down and that the file changes are very much more up to date. However, restoration of the filestore can be very long and tedious as it will be necessary to replay all the modifications that have been so painstakingly recorded on tape.

Both periodic and incremental dumping needs to be accompanied by additional system software if an error-free file system is to be maintained. These programs need to be able to make consistency checks in both directories and data files. If errors are found they need to automatically restore directory and data blocks as required.

This concludes a summary of the main features of an operating system. It gives the final flavour to the model of computing offered to the user. Underneath it exist many layers of software and hardware. This book has given models of the processes that must exist in these layers in order to realize a complete system. They have been described as programs with special properties, or as subsystems combining hardware and software closely together, or just hardware with particular performance characteristics. In all these cases, emphasis has been laid on what the programmer needs to know in order to understand a complete computer system in outline. It is hoped that these beginnings can be further added to through the books in the bibliography and programming experience of systems problems with a microprocessor or other computer system.

Exercises

1. Make use of the conventions established to time processes and represent them on a timing diagram. Show a typical set of transitions and provide notes to explain them for the following processes:
   (a) system processes such as scheduler and dispatcher;
   (b) three user processes operated on a round-robin basis.
2. Use high-level algorithm techniques to fulfil the duties of an interrupt routine. Use the SRM computer with the details given in Appendix 1.
3. Give an orderly account of a computer file system as seen by a user. Give examples of the commands available and illustrate their effect on a system known to you.

Bibliography

T. C. Bartee (1985), *Digital Computer Fundamentals*, (6th edn), McGraw-Hill
K. G. Beauchamp (1987), *Computer Communications*, Van Nostrand Reinhold
F. Halsall (1988), *Data Communications, Computer Networks and OSI* (2nd edn), Addison-Wesley
A. Hopper, S. Temple and R. Williamson (1986), *Local Area Network Design*, Addison-Wesley
A. M. Lister (1984), *Fundamentals of Operating Systems* (3rd edn), Macmillan
J. Peterson and A. Silberschatz (1985), *Operating System Concepts* (2nd edn), Addison-Wesley
A. S. Tanenbaum (1981), *Computer Networks*, Prentice-Hall

Appendix 1
Summary of the simple register machine (SRM)

This appendix summarizes the complete simple register machine for comparison with others. It includes some items which have not been used explicitly in the main text. Apart from exception handling and input–output, SRM has been realized as an assembler/emulator system which has been used for a number of years for teaching purposes.

A1.1   The processor

The processor contains three principal constituents: the status register (*SR*), the program counter (*PC*) and a set of sixteen general registers. All registers are sixteen bits or one word in length. The combined values of the *PC* and *SR* registers is called the context of a program or process.

A1.1.1   STATUS REGISTER

This register combines support for both the operating system and user programs. It consists of a set of individually named bits organized into the following format:

```
15  14  13  12  11        8 7       3  2  1  0
  S  | E | II | DI | FI |  Not used  | C | V | N | Z
  ←——————System byte ————→ ←———— User byte ——→
```

Bit name	Function
S	set for supervisor mode, reset for user mode,
E	set for external interrupt enable, reset for disable,
II	set for illegal instruction interrupt enable, reset for disable,
DI	set for fixed-point divide fault interrupt enable, reset for disable,

FI	set for floating-point fault interrupt enable, reset for disable,
C	set if carry generated, reset otherwise,
V	set if signed integer overflow generated, reset otherwise,
N	set if result of operation is negative, reset otherwise,
Z	set if result of operation is zero, reset otherwise.

In user mode certain sensitive instructions such as changing the value of the *SR* register are illegal. The remaining bits of the system byte enable or disable the automatic response of the processor to interrupts. The change between user and supervisor mode can take place in two ways:

1. the execution of a supervisor call instruction (*SVC*) by a user program,
2. the occurrence of an interrupt.

The *C*, *V*, *N* and *Z* bits in the user byte act as a monitor of the arithmetic result of the current instruction. The rules governing the setting of these bits for integer arithmetic instructions were discussed in Chapter 2. The load instructions (*LD, LDR, LDS, LDI*) set *N* and *Z* according to the sign of the operand as do the logical operations (AND, OR, exclusive OR). All other instructions such as branch instructions leave them unaffected.

A1.1.2 PROGRAM COUNTER

This register contains the memory address of the location of the most significant byte of the next instruction to be obeyed. After the execution of most instructions the *PC* is incremented by two or four according to whether it is a short or long instruction.

A1.1.3 GENERAL REGISTERS

There are sixteen general registers denoted by *R0, R1*, and so on up to *R15*. The first operand of an instruction is frequently obtained from a register. Registers *R1–R15* inclusive can be used for indexing.

A1.2 Instruction formats

There are four classes of instruction with the following formats:

RR
register to register

```
15        8 7   4 3   0
+---------+-----+-----+
|   op    | r1  | r2  |
+---------+-----+-----+
```

RX
register to indexed memory

```
31         24 23  20 19  16 15            0
+----------+------+------+--------------+
|   op     |  r1  |  x2  |      a       |
+----------+------+------+--------------+
```

SF
short format

```
15        8 7   4 3   0
+---------+-----+-----+
|   op    | r1  |  n  |
+---------+-----+-----+
```

RI
register and immediate

```
31         24 23  20 19  16 15            0
+----------+------+------+--------------+
|   op     |  r1  |  x2  |      d       |
+----------+------+------+--------------+
```

r1 and *r2* denote generic 4-bit register addresses, i.e *R4* has numerical address 4, *R10* address 10 and so on. *x2* denotes a register used as an index register. *a* is a 16-bit memory address, whereas *n* and *d* are interpreted as immediate or literal values. *n* is a 4-bit and *d* a 16-bit value.

A1.3   Instruction set

Mnem.	op	Full description	Format	Operation
ADD	4A	add word	RX	$(r1):=(r1)+(a+(x2))$
ADDI	CA	add word immediate	RI	$(r1):=(r1)+d+(x2)$
ADDR	0A	add word register	RR	$(r1):=(r1)+(r2)$
ADDS	26	add immediate short	SF	$(r1):=(r1)+n$
B	60	branch unconditional	RI	$(PC):=d+(x2)$
BC	69	branch on carry	RI	if C set then $(PC):=d+(x2)$
BE	61	branch on equal	RI	if Z set then $(PC):=d+(x2)$
BM	63	branch on minus	RI	if N set then $(PC):=d+(x2)$
BNC	6A	branch on not carry	RI	if C reset then $(PC):=d+(x2)$
BNE	62	branch on not equal	RI	if Z reset then $(PC):=d+(x2)$
BNM	64	branch on not minus	RI	if N reset then $(PC):=d+(x2)$
BNO	68	branch on not overflow	RI	if V reset then $(PC):=d+(x2)$
BNP	66	branch on not plus	RI	if N set or Z set then $(PC):=d+(x2)$
BO	67	branch on overflow	RI	if V set then $(PC):=d+(x2)$
BP	65	branch on plus	RI	if N reset and Z reset set then $(PC):=d+(x2)$
CALL	41	call subroutine	RI	$(r1):=(PC)+4$ $(PC):=d+(x2)$
CMP	49	compare word	RX	$(r1):(a+(x2))$
CMPI	C9	compare word immed	RI	$(r1):d+(x2)$
CMPR	09	compare word reg	RR	$(r1):(r2)$
DIV	4D	divide word {*r1* even, 32-bit dividend required}	RX	$(r1+1):=(r1,r1+1)\,\mathbf{div}\,(a+(x2))$ $(r1):=(r1,r1+1)\,\mathbf{mod}\,(a+(x2))$
DIVR	0D	divide word {*r1* even, 32-bit dividend required}	RR	$(r1+1):=(r1,r1+1)\,\mathbf{div}\,(r2)$ $(r1):=(r1,r1+1)\,\mathbf{mod}\,(r2)$
HALT	C2	halt program execution		
LDB	D3	load byte	RX	$(r1):=(a+(x2))$
LDBR	93	load byte register	RR	$(r1):=(r2)$
LD	48	load word	RX	$(r1):=(a+(x2))$
LDI	C8	load word immediate	RI	$(r1):=d+(x2)$
LDR	08	load word register	RR	$(r1):=(r2)$
LDS	24	load immediate short	SF	$(r1):=n$
LDM	D1	load multiple *r1–r15*. Contents *r1–r15* loaded from successive words	RX	$(r1):=(a+(x2))$
LCXT	C1	Load context	RX	$(SR):=(a+(x2))$ $(PC):=(a+(x2)+2)$
MUL	4C	multiply word {*r1* even, 32-bit result}	RX	$(r1,r1+1):=(r1+1)*(a+(x2))$
MULR	0C	multiply word register {*r1* even, 32-bit result}	RR	$(r1,r1+1):=(r1+1)*(r2)$
AND	44	logical AND word	RX	$(r1):=(r1)$ AND $(a+(x2))$
ANDI	C4	logical AND word immed	RI	$(r1):=(r1)$ AND $d+(x2)$
ANDR	04	logical AND word reg	RR	$(r1):=(r1)$ AND $(r2)$
OR	46	logical OR word	RX	$(r1):=(r1)$ OR $(a+(x2))$
ORI	C6	logical OR word immed	RI	$(r1):=(r1)$ OR $d+(x2)$
ORR	06	logical OR word reg	RR	$(r1):=(r1)$ OR $(r2)$
RET	03	return from subroutine	RR	$(PC):=(r2)$
SUB	4B	subtract word	RX	$(r1):=(r1)-(a+(x2))$
SUBI	CB	subtract word immed	RI	$(r1):=(r1)-d+(x2)$
SUBR	0B	subtract word reg	RR	$(r1):=(r1)-(r2)$
SUBS	27	subtract immediate short	SF	$(r1):=(r1)-n$
STB	D2	store byte	RX	$(a+(x2)):=(r1)$
STBR	92	store byte register	RR	$(r2):=(r1)$
ST	40	store word	RX	$(a+(x2)):=(r1)$

STM	D0	store multiple *r1–r15*.	*RX*	$(a + (x2)) := (r1)$
		Contents *r1–r15* stored		
		in successive words		
SVC	E1	supervisor call	*RX*	see Section A1.4.3
XOR	47	exclusive OR word	*RX*	$(r1) := (r1)$ XOR $(a + (x2))$
XORI	C7	exclusive OR word immed	*RI*	$(r1) := (r1)$ XOR $d + (x2)$
XORR	07	exclusive OR register	*RR*	$(r1) := (r1)$ XOR $(r2)$

A1.4   Memory map

0	External interrupt table
256	Fault interrupt table
26E	Reset
276	SVC table
29E	
	. .
	. .
	. .
FE00	Memory-mapped device space

There are two contiguous blocks of memory which are reserved. The first block is divided into three tables supporting external interrupts, fault interrupts and supervisor calls, sometimes called collectively exception handling. The second block is the reserved addresses for memory-mapped input–output.

A1.4.1   EXTERNAL INTERRUPT DEVICES

An external peripheral device is assigned an address $0,1,2 \ldots 31$. Each of the 32 devices has a corresponding four word entry in the external interrupt table. The detailed form of the first few entries in the table is given below:

0	Old context: Device 0
4	New context: Device 0
8	Old context: Device 1
C	New context: Device 1
10	Old context: Device 2
14	New context: Device 2

Given that external interrupts are enabled, the processor responds to a device interrupt with the following actions:

1. acknowledges the interrupt to determine the device address n (say);
2. saves the current context in the *old context* field of entry n,

3. loads the new context into *SR* and *PC* from the *new context* field for device *n*.

The new value of *SR* must change the processor mode from user to supervisor state and disable external interrupts. The new value of *PC* must point to the first instruction of an interrupt service routine which deals with the interrupt event.

A1.4.2   FAULT INTERRUPT TABLE

The details of the table are given below.

256	Old Context: Illegal Instruction
25A	New Context: Illegal Instruction
25E	Old Context: Divide Fault
262	New Context: Divide Fault
266	Old Context: Floating Point Fault
26A	New Context: Floating Point Fault

Each fault has its own entry and the values are used in exactly the same way as for device interrupts.

A1.4.3   SUPERVISOR CALL TABLE

There are sixteen supervisor calls selected by the value of the *r1* field in the *SVC* instruction. This instruction provides a controlled software event mechanism for changing from user to supervisor state. The mechanism is based on the third fixed table with the form

276	$a + (x2)$
278	Old context
27C	SR for new context
27E	PC for *SVC 0*
280	PC for *SVC 1*
282	PC for *SVC 2*

and so on. The execution of the *SVC* causes the processor to perform the actions:

1. save the second operand address $a + (x2)$ in the *SVC* table (this provides a means for passing parameters),
2. save the *old context* of the user program in location 278 of the table;
3. load the *new context* taking the *SR* word from location 27C and the *PC* word from $27E + r1 * 2$.

A1.4.4   MEMORY-MAPPED DEVICE TABLE

This table of addresses is situated from memory address FE00 to FFFF inclusive. It is divided into four word entries, one for each device attached to the bus. The entry for device 0 is at FE00, device 1 at FE10 and so on. The entries have two forms:

1. Character-oriented device

Control
Status
Data
Counter

The individual fields are one word long and map directly onto the device controller registers. The *counter* field records the number of buffered characters in the device interface.

2. Block-oriented device

Control
Status
Memory address
Counter

Again the one-word fields are mapped into controller register. The *memory address* field is set to the start address field of a block of memory and the *counter* field to its size in words. The direction of transfer and the signal to start are set by writing to the *control* address.

Appendix 2
Summary of the Motorola 68000 processor and high-level language templates

This appendix summarizes the features of the Motorola 68000 (MC68000) processor so that equivalent templates to those developed in Chapters 6 and 7 can be presented. For reasons of space this will be a partial view and the reader is referred to the manufacturer's documentation (*M68000 Programmer's Reference Manual* (5th edn), 1986) for more information. This uses a slightly different register transfer notation to that developed in this book. Only a selection of instructions are described that allow the encoding of the HLL templates. The principal omissions include the manipulation of system registers, logical instructions and bit-manipulation instructions.

A2.1 Processor

The processor contains four principal elements: a set of eight data registers, nine address registers, the program counter (*PC*) and the status register (*SR*).

D0	
D1	
D2	
D3	
D4	
D5	
D6	
D7	

```
A0  [                          ]
A1  [                          ]
A2  [                          ]
A3  [                          ]
A4  [                          ]
A5  [                          ]
A6  [                          ]

A7  [                          ]  User stack pointer (USP)
    [                          ]  Supervisor stack pointer (SSP)

PC  [                          ]

SR         [        |         ]
```

The status register is 16 bits long and the remaining registers are 32 bits long. There are eight 32-bit data registers denoted by D0–D7. They are used for byte, word or long-word operands. Byte and word operands are positioned in the least significant part of the register. All the data registers can be used for indexing.

There are seven address registers denoted by A0–A6 and a user stack pointer (A7 or USP). When the processor is in supervisor state it normally uses a second stack pointer, supervisor stack pointer (SSP), that is not accessible to user programs. Address registers are used to hold memory addresses and can also serve as software stack pointers. All eight registers can be used as index registers. Only word and long-word operations can be carried out on address registers.

The PC register contains a 32-bit memory address of the location of the next instruction to be obeyed. The register is incremented by the length of the current instruction unless it is a branch or subroutine call.

The status register combines support for both the operating system and user programs. It consists of a set of individually named bits organized as follows:

```
 15      13          10  9  8        4   3   2   1   0
[ T |   S  |     | I₁| I₂| I₃|    | X | N | Z | V | C ]
        system byte          |          user byte
```

Bit name	Function
T	set if trace mode is on
S	set when processor is in supervisor state and reset when in user state
I_2, I_1, I_0	interrupt mask bits
X	copy of C bit after add, subtract, negate, shift and rotate instructions
N	set if result of operation is negative, reset otherwise
Z	set if result of operation is zero, reset otherwise
V	set if signed integer overflow generated, reset otherwise
C	set if carry generated, reset otherwise

The interrupt mask defines an interrupt level between 0 (low) and 7 (high). Every peripheral device may be allocated to a level. If the mask has value i the processor will ignore interrupts from levels i and below. As with the simple register machine (SRM) the transition between user and supervisor states happens when an external interrupt occurs, a TRAP instruction (supervisor call) or a serious program error occurs.

A2.2   Instruction formats and addressing modes

The MC68000 has a much greater range of operations and addressing modes than SRM. Again all the instructions involving two operands have the general form:

$$\langle operation \rangle \ \langle specification \ of \ operand \rangle \ \langle specification \ of \ operand \rangle,$$

but the addressing mechanisms (or modes) are much more extensive. In describing the modes the following notation will be used:

Dn	data register with address n
An	address register with address n
Xn	data or address register with address n
m_{16}	16-bit memory address
m_{32}	32-bit memory address
d_8	8-bit constant
d_{16}	16-bit constant
d_{32}	32-bit constant
n	operand size in bytes

The subset of the addressing modes required for this Appendix is summarized in the following table:

Mode	Operand address	Operand value	Assembler sym
Immediate		d_8 or d_{16} or d_{32}	# $\langle data \rangle$
Data register direct	Dn	(Dn)	Dn
Address register direct	An	(An)	An
Absolute short	m_{16}	(m_{16})	$\langle label \rangle$
Absolute long	m_{32}	(m_{32})	$\langle label \rangle$
Register indirect	(An)	$((An))$	(An)
Post-increment register indirect	(An) $(An) := (An) + n$	$((An))$	$(An) +$
Pre-decrement register indirect	$(An) := (An) - n$	$((An))$	$-(An)$
Register indirect with offset	$(An) + d_{16}$	$((An) + d_{16})$	$d_{16}(An)$
Indexed register indirect	$(An) + (Xn) + d_8$	$((An) + (Xn) + d_8)$	$d_8(An, Xn)$

The specification of the operand address is termed the *effective address* or *ea* for short. This term is used to cover the variety of ways in which the operand address is computed from more primitive elements that appear in the instruction itself.

The instruction formats of the MC68000 are not fixed in the way as SRM. To avoid a long list of detailed bit values and fields, the general structure of the principal non-privileged instructions will be described in the following table:

Assembler mnemonic	Instruction structure
MOVE	⟨operation⟩ ⟨size⟩ ⟨destination *ea*⟩ ⟨source *ea*⟩
MOVEA	⟨operation⟩ ⟨size⟩ ⟨*An*⟩ ⟨source *ea*⟩
MOVEM	⟨operation⟩ ⟨direction⟩ ⟨size⟩ ⟨register list⟩
MOVEQ	⟨operation⟩ ⟨*Dn*⟩ ⟨8 bit data⟩
LEA	⟨operation⟩ ⟨*An*⟩ ⟨*ea*⟩
ADD, SUB, CMP	⟨operation⟩ ⟨*Dn*⟩ ⟨direction⟩ ⟨size⟩ ⟨*ea*⟩
ADDA, SUBA, CMPA	⟨operation⟩ ⟨*An*⟩ ⟨size⟩ ⟨source *ea*⟩
ADDQ, SUBQ	⟨operation⟩ ⟨3-bit data⟩ ⟨*ea*⟩
ADDI, SUBI, CMPI	⟨operation⟩ ⟨size⟩ ⟨destination *ea*⟩ ⟨constant⟩
CLR	⟨operation⟩ ⟨size⟩ ⟨*ea*⟩
DIVS, MULS	⟨operation⟩ ⟨*Dn*⟩ ⟨source *ea*⟩
BRA	⟨operation⟩ ⟨8- or 16-bit displacement⟩
Bcc	⟨operation⟩ ⟨condition⟩ ⟨8- or 16-bit displacement⟩
JSR	⟨operation⟩ ⟨destination *ea*⟩
RTS	⟨operation⟩

The contents of the size field determine the size of the operand value (byte, word, longword) involved in the operation. The 8- and 16-bit constants and displacements are treated as signed quantities. The 3-bit constant in the ADDQ or SUBS instruction maps onto the small positive integer range 1–8. The length of an instruction depends mainly on the effective address (*ea*) and this is potentially composed of three elements:

⟨addressing mode⟩ ⟨register address⟩ { ⟨extension word (s)⟩ }.

The braces { } indicate that the extension words may or may not be present according to the value of the mode field. For example register direct and indirect addressing modes only require a mode value and register address and no extension words. In this case the instruction is one word in length. If an addressing mode involves a 16-bit memory address, displacement or constant, then one extension word is required; for 32-bit addresses or constants two extension words are needed. Thus a *MOVE* instruction can vary from one to five words in length depending on the addressing modes involved. It is the only instruction that can have both operands in memory; the remainder of two operand instructions must have at least one operand in a register.

The subset of the instruction set required for the high-level language templates is summarized below using the following conventions. In general a final letter A in the mnemonic denotes instructions which manipulate the contents of an address register as a destination operand. Similarly Q and I letters indicate that the source operand is an immediate value. The mnenonic *Bcc* is a generic name for a family of conditional branches, where the letter pair *cc* denotes a given condition such as minus. The table relates the instruction mnemonic to the assembler syntax and the operation specified in the notation discussed in Chapter 6. The last column lists any addressing modes which cannot be used as substitutions in the *ea* field of the instruction. Considering the ADD instruction there are two variants:

$$ADD \quad \langle ea \rangle, Dn$$
$$ADD \quad Dn, \langle ea \rangle$$

For the first variant there are no restrictions on $\langle ea \rangle$, whereas for the second variant *An*, *Dn* and #$\langle$data$\rangle$ are excluded. An *ADDA* instruction must be used if *An* is the destination address and *ADDI* if it is #$\langle$data$\rangle$. The exclusion of *Dn* stems from the direction field of the *ADD* instruction. At the assembler level there is no distinction.

Name	Assembler syntax	Operation	Illegal $\langle ea \rangle$
Add	$ADD \langle ea \rangle, Dn$	$(Dn) := (Dn) + (\langle ea \rangle)$	
	$ADD \; Dn, \langle ea \rangle$	$(\langle ea \rangle) := (\langle ea \rangle) + (Dn)$	$An, Dn, \#\langle data \rangle$
Add address	$ADDA \langle ea \rangle, An$	$(An) := (An) + (\langle ea \rangle)$	
Add quick	$ADDQ \; \#\langle data \rangle,$ $\langle ea \rangle$	$(\langle ea \rangle) := (\langle ea \rangle) + \langle data \rangle$	$\#\langle data \rangle$
Add immediate	$ADDI \; \#\langle data \rangle, \langle ea \rangle$	$(\langle ea \rangle) := (\langle ea \rangle) + \langle data \rangle$	$An, \#\langle data \rangle$
Branch conditionally	$Bcc \langle label \rangle$	**if** branch condition is true **then** $(PC) := (PC) + d$	
Branch always	$BRA \langle label \rangle$	$(PC) := (PC) + d$	
Clear an operand	$CLR \langle ea \rangle$	$(\langle ea \rangle) := 0$	
Compare	$CMP \langle ea \rangle, Dn$	$(Dn) - (\langle ea \rangle)$	
Compare address	$CMPA \langle ea \rangle, An$	$(An) - (\langle ea \rangle)$	
Compare immediate	$CMPI \; \#\langle data \rangle, \langle ea \rangle$	$(\langle ea \rangle) - \langle data \rangle$	$An, \#\langle data \rangle$
Divide signed	$DIVS \langle ea \rangle, Dn$	$(Dn) := (Dn)/(\langle ea \rangle)$ 32-bit dividend, 16-bit divisor. Least significant word of result contains quotient, most significant word the remainder.	An
Jump to subroutine	$JSR \langle ea \rangle$	$(SP) := (SP) - 4;$ $((SP)) := (PC);$ $(PC) := \langle ea \rangle$	$An, Dn, (An) +$ $-(An), \#\langle data \rangle$
Load effective address	$LEA \langle ea \rangle, An$	$(An) := \langle ea \rangle$	$An, Dn, (An) +$ $-(An), \#\langle data \rangle$
Move data from source to destination	$MOVE \langle sea \rangle, \langle dea \rangle$	$(\langle dea \rangle) := ((\langle sae \rangle))$	$\langle dea \rangle = An$
Move address	$MOVEA \langle ea \rangle, An$	$(An) := (\langle ea \rangle)$	
Move multiple registers	$MOVEM \langle register$ $list \rangle, \langle ea \rangle$	save registers in memory	
	$MOVEM \langle ea \rangle,$ $\langle register \; list \rangle$	restore registers from memory	
Move quick	$MOVEQ \; \#\langle data \rangle,$ Dn	$(Dn) := \langle data \rangle$	
Multiply signed	$MULS \langle ea \rangle, Dn$	$(Dn) := (Dn) * (\langle ea \rangle)$ Both operands must be 16-bit, result is 32-bit.	
Return from subroutine	RTS	$(PC) := ((SP));$ $(SP) := (SP) + 4;$	
Subtract	$SUB \langle ea \rangle, Dn$	$(Dn) := (Dn) - (\langle ea \rangle)$	
	$SUB \; Dn, \langle ea \rangle$	$(\langle ea \rangle) := (\langle ea \rangle) - (Dn)$	$An, Dn, \#\langle data \rangle$
Subtract address	$SUBA \langle ea \rangle, An$	$(An) := (An) - (\langle ea \rangle)$	$\#\langle data \rangle$
Subtract immediate	$SUBI \; \#\langle data \rangle, \langle ea \rangle$	$(\langle ea \rangle) := (\langle ea \rangle) - \langle data \rangle$	$An, \#\langle data \rangle$
Subtract quick	$SUBQ \; \#\langle data \rangle, \langle ea \rangle$	$(\langle ea \rangle) := (\langle ea \rangle) - \langle data \rangle$	

A2.3 High-level language templates

The assembler source has the usual fixed format structure of label mnemonic
and address followed by an optional comment. A comment is preceded by a star
(*) character. The assembler directives *DS, DC* and *EQU* have the same effect
as for *SRM*. The mnemonic can be qualified by a letter to indicate size as
illustrated below:

DS.B	10	*reserve 10 bytes of memory,
DS.W	10	*reserve 10 words of memory,
DS.L	10	*reserve 10 long words of memory.

The size of the operands of a given instruction can be determined in the same
way, e.g

ADD.B	*D1, D2,*
ADD.W	*D1, D2,*
ADD.L	*D1, D2,*

all perform the generic add operation $(D2) := (D1) + (D2)$ on *D1* and *D2*, but
add the least significant bytes, least significant words and long words contained
in the registers respectively. If a qualifier is omitted the default operand size is
words. One feature not present in the assembler is the ability to name register
variables. Register variables must be quoted by the fixed named *D0, A0, D1, A2,*
and so on.

A2.3.1 SIMPLE ASSIGNMENT TEMPLATES

The *MOVE* group of instructions support the assignment function. If *P* and *Q*
are two variables in memory the following sequence of instructions demonstrates various assignments:

	MOVE	*D0, P*	*$*P := D0$;
	MOVE	*Q, D4*	*$*D4 := Q$;
	MOVE	*P, Q*	*$*Q := P$;
P	*DS*	1	
Q	*DS*	1	

Two differences from *SRM* should be noted: the order of operands quoted in
the address field of the instruction is reversed and memory-to-memory transfers
can be effected in a single instruction. The assignment of constants to registers
and simple memory variables is illustrated below:

MOVE	#245, P	*$*P := 245$;
MOVEA	#P, A0	*$*A3 := \langle$memory address of *P*$\rangle$
MOVE	#9, D3	*$*D3 := 9$;

A2.3.2   INTEGER ARITHMETIC

The recoding of the simple arithmetic expression $t := i + j - 6$; in MC68000 assembler is as follows:

```
        MOVE    I, D0      *t := i + j - 6;
        ADD     J, D0
        SUBQ    #6, D0
        MOVE    D0, T
    I   DC      26
    J   DC      -10
    T   DS      1
```

As the data registers are 32-bit, the multiply instruction is somewhat easier to use than *SRM*. The encoding of $C := A*B$ where all the variables are in memory is

```
        MOVE    A, D1    *C := A*B;
        MULS    B, D1
        MOVE    D1, C
```

A2.3.3   HARDWARE SUPPORT FOR DECISIONS

The branching mechanism of the MC68000 is based on adding a *displacement* to the *PC* register. The *displacement* can be either an 8- or 16-bit signed value. The group of conditional branches operate by testing the value of the one or more of the condition code bits (N, Z, V, C). The mnemonics and the corresponding tests are given in the following table:

Mnemonic	Description		N	Z	V	C
BCC	branch carry clear		x	x	x	0
BCS	branch carry set		x	x	x	1
BEQ	branch equal		x	1	x	x
BGE	branch greater than or equal		1	x	1	x
		or	0	x	0	x
BGT	branch greater than		1	0	1	x
		or	0	0	0	x
BHI	branch high		x	0	x	0
BLE	branch less than or equal		x	1	x	x
		or	1	x	0	x
		or	0	x	1	x
BLS	branch low or same		x	1	x	1
BLT	branch less than		1	x	0	x
		or	0	x	1	x
BMI	branch minus		1	x	x	x
BNE	branch not equal		x	0	x	x
BPL	branch plus		0	x	x	x
BVC	branch overflow clear		x	x	0	x
BVS	branch overflow set		x	x	x	1

The values of the condition code bits that would result in a branch occurring are indicated. The letter x in the settings indicate a 'don't care' value; it can be either a one or zero but this does not affect the execution of the operation. The *Bcc* group of conditional branches and the *BRA* (branch always) instruction form the basis for selection and sequencing constructs of a high-level language.

A2.3.4   THE IF...THEN...ELSE TEMPLATE

The encoding of the model Pascal **if** statement

$$\textbf{if } A \ = \ B \textbf{ then } S1 \textbf{ else } S2;$$

is as follows:

```
            MOVE    A, D0    * if a = b
            CMP     B, D0    * then
            BNE     ELSE
              .
            S1                        S1
              .
            BRA     NEXT
    ELSE      .                       * else
              .
            S2                        S2
              .
    NEXT
```

A2.3.5   WHILE AND REPEAT LOOP TEMPLATES

An example of each type of loop will be given; the variables a and b are assumed to be located in memory:

(a) **while** $a \ne 0$ **do** S;

```
    WHILE   CMPI    #0, A    *while a ≠ 0
            BEQ     NEXT     *do
              .
            S                          S
              .
            BRA     WHILE
    NEXT
```

(b) **repeat** S **until** $a > b$;

```
    REPEAT    .                        *repeat
              .
            S                          S
              .
              .
    UNTIL   MOVE    A, D1    *until a > b;
            CMP     B, D1
            BLE     REPEAT
```

The *hcf* algorithm, used in Chapter 6, will be recoded in MC68000 assembler to show a complete program with **repeat**, **while** and **if** constructs.

```
REPEAT    MOVE    M, D0       *repeat
          CMP     N, D0       *  if m < n
          BGE     WHILE       *  then begin
          MOVE    M, T        *       t := m;
          MOVE    N, M        *       m := n;
          MOVE    T, N        *       n := t;
*                                 end;
WHILE     MOVE    M, D0       *  while m > = n
          CMP     N, D0       *  do
BMI       UNTIL
          MOVE    N, D1       *    m := m − n;
          SUB     D1, M
          BRA     WHILE
*
UNTIL     CMPI    #0, M       *until m = 0;
          BNE     REPEAT
          MOVE    N, RES      *res := n;
          STOP
*
M         DC      258
N         DC      9
RES       DS      1
T         DS      1
          END
```

A2.3.6 **FOR** LOOP TEMPLATE

A typical form of this loop is

> **for** $i := j$ **to** n **do** S;

and its template encoding is as follows:

```
          MOVE    J,I         *for i := j to n
FOR       MOVE    I,D0        *do
          CMP     N,D0
          BGT     NEXT
          .
          .
          .
          S                        S
          .
          .
          .
          ADDQ    #1,I
          BRA     FOR
NEXT
```

In this solution all the variables are assumed to be in memory. Clearly it makes sense to use a data register for the control variable if it is available.

A2.3.7 ARRAYS AND RECORDS

Array variables can be declared in the same manner as for *SRM*.

```
VECLB      EQU     1      *type
VECUB      EQU     20     *    vec = array [1 .. 20] of integer
VECES      EQU     2
                          *var
V          DS      20     *    v: vec;
```

The encoding of the simple assignment

$$v[i] := 42;$$

is easily achieved by exploiting the indexed register indirect addressing mode. One address register, $A0$, is used to contain the base address of the array and a second, $A1$, the result of the offset calculation $(i - LB)*ES$.

```
MOVEA.L    #V,A0          *v[i] := 42;
MOVEA.L    I,A1
SUB        #VECLB,A1
MULS       #VECES,A1
MOVE       #42,(A0,A1)
```

If a pointer to the array elements is maintained in register $A2$, the assignment of the constant would become

$$MOVE \#42,(A2)$$

The declaration of records follows the same pattern as with *SRM*.

```
                          *type
                          *    time = record
HOURS      EQU     0      *              hours:integer
MINS       EQU     2      *              mins:integer
                          *          end;
                          *var
T1         DS      2      *    t1, t2:time
T2         DS      2
```

The accessing of individual fields of records can normally use the register indirect with offset addressing mode. The address register contains the base address of the record and the relative address of the field maps onto the 16-bit offset. The encoding of the assignment

$$t1 := t2;$$

is as follows:

```
MOVEA.L    #T1,A1                          *t1 := t2;
MOVEA.L    #T2,A2
MOVE       HOURS(A2),HOURS(A1)
MOVE       MINS(A2),MINS(A1)
```

If the base type of an array is a record, then the same addressing mode can be used with the address register containing a pointer to the array element. The encoding of the weekly times example from Chapter 7 follows:

```
         CLR      SUMHR                   *sumhr := 0;
         CLR      SUMIN                   *sumin := 0;
         MOVEA.L  #DAYTOT,A0              *{initialize A0 to point to daytot [1]}
         MOVE     #1,I
FOR      CMPI     #7,I                    *for I := 1 to 7
         BGT      OUT                     *do begin
         MOVE     HOURS(A0),D0            *   sumhr := sumhr + daytot[i].hours;
         ADD      D0,SUMHR
         MOVE     MINS(A0),D0             *   sumin := sumin + daytot[i].mins;
         ADD      D0,SUMIN
         CMPI     #60,SUMIN              *   if sumin > = 60
         BMI      NEXT                    *   then begin
         SUBI     #60,SUMIN             *        sumin := sumin - 60;
         ADDQ     #1,SUMHR               *        sumhr := sumhr + 1
NEXT     ADDQ     #1,I                    *      end;
         ADDA.L   #DAYES,A0
         BRA      FOR                     *   end;
OUT      MOVEA.L  #WTOT,A1
         MOVE     SUMHR,HOURS(A1)        *wtot.hours := sumhr;
         MOVE     SUMIN,MINS(A1)         *wtot.mins := sumin;
         STOP
                                          *type
                                          *   time = record
HOURS    EQU      0                       *           hours:integer;
MINS     EQU      2                       *           mins:integer
                                          *         end;
DAYLB    EQU      1                       *var
DAYUB    EQU      7                       *   daytot:array[1..7] of time;
DAYES    EQU      4                       *
DAYTOT   DS       14
I        DS       1                       *   i, sumhr, sumin:integer;
SUMHR    DS       1
SUMIN    DS       1
WTOT     DS       2                       *   wtot:time;
         END
```

A2.3.8 PROCEDURES AND FUNCTIONS

Chapter 7 discussed a straightforward model of procedure support that was built around the use of a stack. The stack data structure was used for saving

registers, and for the dynamic allocation of parameter blocks and local variables. Four registers were dedicated to facilitating the procedure mechanism. The
equivalent template encoding for the MC68000 will be built around three dedicated address registers: the user stackpointer (SP or $A7$) points to the current
top of stack, $A6$ contains the base address of the current parameter block and
$A5$ contains the base address of the current local variable area. The stack grows
from a high address to a low address.

The instructions to implement the procedure call and return are JSR (jump
to subroutine) and RTS (return from subroutine), which make explicit use of the
stack:

$$JSR \langle ea \rangle \qquad (SP) := (SP) - 4; ((SP)) := (PC); (PC) := \langle ea \rangle;$$

$$RTS \qquad (PC) := ((SP)); (SP) := (SP) + 4;$$

The JSR instruction first adds the return address to the stack and then transfers
control to the effective address specified in the instruction. The RTS instruction
uses the entry on the top of the stack and assigns it to the PC.

Registers are saved and restored by using the $MOVEM$ instruction. The
assembler instruction

$$MOVEM.L \qquad D0\text{--}D7/A0\text{--}A6, (SP)-$$

saves all the registers, except $A7$, on the stack in sequence. The post-decrement
addressing mode updates the stackpointer automatically. The restore operation
is achieved by

$$MOVEM.L \qquad +(SP), D0\text{--}D7/A0\text{--}A6$$

Again the stack pointer is automatically adjusted by the pre-increment addressing mode and finishes pointing to the new top of stack.

Formal parameters are declared using the EQU directive to assign an offset
(relative address) with respect to the base address of the block to a parameter
name. The encoding of the formal parameters of the hcf example used in
Chapter 7

procedure hcf (m, n:**integer**; **var** r:**integer**);

is

$$
\begin{array}{lll}
M & EQU & 0 \\
N & EQU & 2 \\
R & EQU & 4 \\
\end{array}
$$

The allocation of $\langle p \rangle$ bytes of space on the stack for the parameter block and
updating of $A6$ is achieved by the instructions:

$$SUBA.L \# \langle p \rangle, \qquad SP$$

$$MOVEA.L \qquad SP, A6$$

The register indirect with offset is the most suitable addressing mode to access actual parameters, e.g. the assignment $n := m$ can be encoded as

$$MOVE \qquad M(A6), N(A6) \qquad *n := m;$$

The assignment $r := m$ encodes as

$$MOVEA.L \qquad R(A6), A4 \qquad *r := m$$
$$MOVE \qquad M(A6), (A4)$$

The declaration of local variables and allocation of space on the stack is done in a similar way, as is the access, except that the stack pointer SP is used as the register address.

The template for constructing a procedure is

$$\langle \text{declare formal parameters} \rangle$$

$$\langle \text{declare local variables} \rangle$$

$\langle procname \rangle$	$SUBA$	$\#\langle l \rangle, SP$	*allocate space for local variables
	$MOVEA.L$	$SP,A5$	

.
.

$$\langle \text{procedure code body} \rangle$$

.
.

	$ADDA.L$	$\#\langle l \rangle, SP$	*remove local variables from stack
	RTS		

The template for calling the procedure is:

$MOVEM.L$	$D0-D7/A0-A6, -(SP)$	*save registers
$SUBA.L$	$\#\langle p \rangle, SP$	*allocate space for parameters
$MOVEA.L$	$SP, A6$	*set $A6$ to base address of parameter block
	$\langle \text{add parameters} \rangle$	
JSR	$\langle procname \rangle$	*activate procedure
$ADDA.L$	$\#\langle p \rangle, SP$	*remove parameter block from stack
$MOVEM.L$	$(SP) +, D0-D7/A0-A6$	*restore registers of calling routine

The *hcf* example given in Figs. 7.10 and 7.11 recoded in MC68000 assembly language is given below:

			*program ex7-3;
RES	EQU	0	*var res:integer;
	MOVEA.L	#STACK,SP	* {initialize stack pointer}
	ADDA.L	#STSIZ,SP	
	SUBA.L	#2,SP	* {allocate space for local variable
	MOVEA.L	SP,A5	* & initialize A5 for main program}
	MOVEM	D0-D7/A0-A7, -(SP)	* {save main program registers}
	SUBA.L	#8,SP	* {allocate parameter block
	MOVEA.L	SP,A6	* & initialize A6}
	MOVE	#25,(A6)	* {add parameters}
	MOVE	#6,2(A6)	
	LEA	RES(A5),A0	
	MOVE	A0,4(A6)	

```
          JSR       HCF                      *   hcf (25, 6, res);
          ADDA      #8,SP                    *   {remove parameter block}
          MOVEM     (SP) + , D0-D7/A0-A7     *   {restore main program registers}
          STOP
STSIZ     EQU       200                      *   Stack
STACK     DS.B      STSIZ
M         EQU       0                        *procedure hcf (m, n:integer;
N         EQU       2                        *                var r:integer);
R         EQU       4                        *
T         EQU       0                        *var t:integer
                                             *begin
HCF       SUBA.L    #4, SP
          MOVEA.L   SP,A5
REPEAT    CLR.L     D0                       *   repeat
          MOVE      M(A6), D0                *     t := m mod n;
          DIVS      N(A6), D0
          MOVE.L    D0,T(A5)
          MOVE      N(A6),M(A6)              *     m := n;
          MOVE      T(A5),N(A6)              *     n := t;
          CMPI      #0,N(A6)                 *   until n = 0;
          BNE       REPEAT
          MOVEA.L   R(A6),A4                 *   r := m
          MOVE      M(A6),(A4)
          ADDA.L    #4,SP
          RTS
          END                               *end
```

Appendix 3
Summary of the Intel 8086 processor and high-level templates

This appendix follows a similar pattern to Appendix 2. The key features of the Intel 8086 are described so that equivalent templates to those developed in Chapters 6 and 7 can be presented. The architecture is irregular when compared with that of the MC68000. Hence this Appendix will not attempt to summarize the detailed mapping of assembler mnemonic to precise instruction formats. The view is a partial one and the reader is referred to the manufacturer's documentation (*Intel Microprocessor and Peripheral Handbook* (1988) and the *IBM PC Macro Assembler Manual*) for more information. Only a selection of instructions are described that allow the encoding of the HLL templates. The principal omissions include the manipulation of system registers, logical instructions and bit-manipulation instructions.

A3.1 Processor

The processor contains five principal elements: a set of four general registers, a total of four pointer and index registers, four segment registers, an instruction pointer (program counter) and a set of nine one-bit flags (status bits/register). All the registers are 16 bits long.

AX	*AH*	*AL*	Accumulator
BX	*BH*	*BL*	Base
CX	*CH*	*CL*	Count
DX	*DH*	*DL*	Data

SP		Stack pointer
BP		Base pointer
SI		Source index
DI		Destination index

CS		Code segment
DS		Data segment
SS		Stack segment
ES		Extra segment
IP		Instruction pointer
		Status flags

The general registers are denoted by *AX, BX, CX, DX*. The most significant and least significant bytes can be used separately when the names *AH, AL, BH, BL, CH, CL, DH, DL* are used. The pointer and index registers are denoted by *SP, BP, SI* and *DI*.

The 8086 can address up to 2^{20} bytes (1 Mbyte) of memory, but the processor can manipulate only 16-bit address objects. An additional mechanism is required to build a 20-bit address. The memory is divided into 65 536 byte *segments*. The base address of a segment is a multiple of 16, that is the address has the form $hhhh\,0_{16}$ where h is an arbitrary hexadecimal digit. At any instant the program can access four such segments: *current code segment, current data segment, current stack segment* and *current extra segment*. The last segment is usually used as an extra data segment. The most significant 16 bits of a segment base address are contained in the segment registers. Bytes and words are specified by a 16-bit *offset* address. The processor forms a 20-bit address by performing the following addition:

$$hhhh\,0_{16} \text{ plus } offset_{16}.$$

The organization of words in the memory is different to SRM and the MC68000. The least and most significant words are reversed.

least significant byte	most significant byte

Thus the least significant byte has the lower memory address.

The IP register contains the offset address of the next instruction within the current code segment. The nine individual bits or flags are used to record the processor status and to control the operation of the processor.

	11	10	9	8	7	6		4		2		0
	OF	*DF*	*IF*	*TF*	*SF*	*ZF*		*AF*		*PF*		*CF*

Flag name	Function
CF	set if carry generated, reset otherwise
AF	set if carry generated out of least significant four bits, reset otherwise
OF	set if overflow occurs in signed arithmetic, reset otherwise
ZF	set if result of operation is zero, reset otherwise
SF	set if result of operation is negative, reset otherwise
PF	set if result has an even number of bits, reset otherwise
DF	controls the direction of string manipulation instructions

IF	interrupt enable bit
TF	set for single-step execution

A3.2   Addressing modes and instructions

The instructions involving two operands are composed from the familiar elements:

$$\langle operation \rangle \; \langle specification\ of\ operand \rangle \; \langle specification\ of\ operand \rangle,$$

but the fields in the machine code instruction corresponding to the various elements are interleaved, i.e. the specification of one operand separates the two parts of the second. The detailed format will not be presented here. In describing the addressing modes the following notation will be used:

R	a general, pointer and index register
S	a segment register
$disp_8$	8-bit signed displacement
$disp_{16}$	16-bit signed displacement
$disp$	8- or 16-bit displacement
$offset_{16}$	16-bit offset address

The addressing modes are summarized in the following table:

Mode	Offset address	Segment register	Operand value	Assembler syntax
Immediate			d_8 or d_{16}	$\langle constant \rangle$
Register	R		(R)	R
Direct	$offset_{16}$	DS	$(offset_{16} + (DS))$	$\langle label \rangle$
Register indirect	(BX)	DS	$((BX) + (DS))$	$[BX]$
	(BP)	SS	$((BP) + (SS))$	$[BP]$
	(DI)	DS	$((DI) + (DS))$	$[DI]$
	(SI)	DS	$((SI) + (DS))$	$[SI]$
Base relative	$(BX) + disp$	DS	$((BX) + disp + (DS))$	$disp[BX]$
	$(BP) + disp$	SS	$((BP) + disp + (SS))$	$disp[BP]$
Direct indexed	$(DI) + disp$	DS	$((DI) + disp + (DS))$	$disp[DI]$
	$(SI) + disp$	DS	$((SI) + disp + (DS))$	$disp[SI]$
Base indexed	$(BX) + (SI) + disp$	DS	$((BX) + (SI) + disp + (DS))$	$disp[BX][SI]$
	$(BX) + (DI) + disp$	DS	$((BX) + (DI) + disp + (DS))$	$disp[BX][DI]$
	$(BP) + (SI) + disp$	SS	$((BP) + (SI) + disp + (SS))$	$disp[BP][SI]$
	$(BP) + (DI) + disp$	SS	$((BP) + (DI) + disp + (SS))$	$disp[BP][DI]$

The specification of the operand address is termed the *effective address* or *ea* for short. This term is used to cover the variety of ways in which the operand address is computed from more primitive elements that appear in the instruction itself.

The sub-set of instructions required for the high-level language templates is summarized in the following table:

Name	Assembler syntax	Operation	Illegal $\langle ea \rangle$
Add	$ADD\ R, \langle ea \rangle$	$(R) := (R) + (\langle ea \rangle)$	
	$ADD\ \langle ea \rangle, R$	$(\langle ea \rangle) := (\langle ea \rangle) + (R)$	$\langle data \rangle$
	$ADD\ \langle ea \rangle, \langle data \rangle$	$(\langle ea \rangle) := (\langle ea \rangle) + \langle data \rangle$	$\langle data \rangle$
Call a procedure	$CALL\ \langle label \rangle$	$(SP) := (SP) - 2;$	
		$((SP)) := (IP); (IP) := (IP) + disp;$	
Compare	$CMP\ R, \langle ea \rangle$	$(R) - (\langle ea \rangle)$	

	$CMP \langle ea \rangle, R$	$(\langle ea \rangle) - (R)$	$\langle data \rangle$
	$CMP \langle ea \rangle, \langle data \rangle$	$(\langle ea \rangle) - \langle data \rangle$	$\langle data \rangle$
Decrement	$DEC\ R$	$(R) := (R) - 1$	
	$DEC \langle ea \rangle$	$(\langle ea \rangle) := (\langle ea \rangle) - 1$	
Halt	HLT	Halt the processor	
Divide signed	$IDIV\ R$	$(AX) := (DX,AX)\ \textbf{div}\ (R);$	
		$(DX) := (DX,AX)\ \textbf{mod}\ (R)$	
	$IDIV \langle ea \rangle$	$(AX) := (DX, AX)\ \textbf{div}\ (\langle ea \rangle)$	$\langle data \rangle$
		$(DX) := (DX,AX)\ \textbf{mod}\ (\langle ea \rangle)$	
Multiply signed	$IMUL\ R$	$(DX,AX) := (AX)*(R)$	
	$IMUL \langle ea \rangle$	$(DX,AX) := (AX)*(\langle ea \rangle)$	$\langle data \rangle$
Increment	$INC\ R$	$(R) := (R) + 1$	
	$INC \langle ea \rangle$	$(\langle ea \rangle) := (\langle ea \rangle) + 1$	
Conditional jump	$Jcc \langle label \rangle$	**if** jump condition is true	
		then	
		$\quad (IP) := (IP) + disp_8$	
Unconditional jump	$JMP \langle label \rangle$	$(IP) := (IP) + disp_{16}$	
Load effective address	$LEA\ R, \langle ea \rangle$	$(R) := \langle ea \rangle$	
Move	$MOV\ R, \langle ea \rangle$	$(R) := (\langle ea \rangle)$	
	$MOV \langle ea \rangle, R$	$(\langle ea \rangle) := (R)$	$\langle data \rangle$
	$MOV\ S, \langle ea \rangle$	$(S) := (\langle ea \rangle)$	
	$MOV \langle ea \rangle, S$	$(\langle ea \rangle) := (S)$	$\langle data \rangle$
	$MOV \langle ea \rangle, \langle data \rangle$	$(\langle ea \rangle) := \langle data \rangle$	$\langle data \rangle$
Pop word of stack	$POP\ R$	$(R) := ((SP)); (SP) := (SP) + 2$	
	$POP\ S$	$(S) := ((SP)); (SP) := (SP) + 2$	
	$POP \langle ea \rangle$	$(\langle ea \rangle) := ((SP)); (SP) := (SP) + 2$	
Push word onto stack	$PUSH\ R$	$(SP) := (SP) - 2; ((SP)) := (R)$	
	$PUSH\ S$	$(SP) := (SP) - 2; ((SP)) := (S)$	
	$PUSH \langle ea \rangle$	$(SP) := (SP) - 2; ((SP)) := (\langle ea \rangle)$	
Return from call	RET	$(IP) := ((SP)); (SP) := (SP) + 2;$	
Subtract	$SUB\ R, \langle ea \rangle$	$(R) := (R) - (\langle ea \rangle)$	
	$SUB \langle ea \rangle, R$	$(\langle ea \rangle) := (\langle ea \rangle) - (R)$	$\langle data \rangle$
	$SUB \langle ea \rangle, \langle data \rangle$	$(\langle ea \rangle) := (\langle ea \rangle) - \langle data \rangle$	$\langle data \rangle$

The 16/32-bit multiply and divide instructions have been presented; 8/16-bit forms also exist. The mnemonic *Jcc* represents a set of conditional jump instructions where the *cc* is one or more letters representing the condition. Also the jumps, procedure call and return instructions have been given in their simplest intrasegment forms. Indirect and intersegment forms are possible.

A3.3   High-level language templates

The assembler directive statements have the fixed format:

$$\{\langle name \rangle\}\ \langle directive \rangle\ \{\langle address \rangle\}\ \{;\langle comment \rangle\}$$

whereas instruction statements have the form:

$$\{\langle label \rangle:\}\ \langle mnemonic \rangle\ \{\langle address \rangle\}\ \{;\langle comment \rangle\}$$

Note the presence of a colon (:) after a $\langle label \rangle$ in instruction statements and the use of the semi-colon (;) as a comment character. The braces { } indicate that a field is optional.

The *EQU* directive has the same effect as for SRM. Memory space is declared by the *DB*, *DW* and *DD* directives.

```
UBYTE     DB    ?              ; reserve one byte
UWORD     DW    ?              ; reserve one word
UDWORD    DD    ?              ; reserve one longword
UTABLE    DW    100 DUP (?)    ; reserve 100 words
```

The ? character is used to declare uninitialized workspace. The *DUP* operator repeats operands without having to enter them individually. Initialized variables are declared by replacing the ? character with a constant.

```
IBYTE    DB    31
IWORD    DW    2054
TABLE    DW    2, 4, 7, 456, 67, − 2, 0
```

The size of operands in an instruction can be determined implicitly, if a byte register or variable is used in the instruction. Only word data will be used in this Appendix.

All data variables must be declared in a data segment as follows:

```
DSEG     SEGMENT
I        DW          ?
J        DW          ?
TABLE    DW          2, 3, 67, 92, 0
DSEG     ENDS
```

The *SEGMENT* and *ENDS* directives simply mark the beginning and the end of a segment. The segment name is used to initialize the DS register. Stack and code segments are declared in a similar way. The full segment declaration will be given only for programs and not for code fragments.

A3.3.1 SIMPLE ASSIGNMENT TEMPLATES

The *MOV* instruction supports the assignment function. Suppose *P*, *Q* and *R* are memory variables, the following instruction sequence shows what is possible:

```
MOV    AX,Q     ; P := Q;
MOV    P,AX     ;
MOV    R,256    ; R := 256;
MOV    DX,BX    ; DX := Bx;
```

Memory-to-memory transfers are not possible. The immediate addressing mode is invoked implicitly by using a constant. The assignment of the memory offset of a variable is most easily implemented using the *LEA* (load effective address) mnemonic:

```
LEA    SI,P    ; SI := ⟨address of P⟩
```

A3.3.2   INTEGER ARITHMETIC

The recoding of the simple arithmetic expression $t := i + j - 6$ in Intel 8086 assembler is as follows:

```
MOV   AX,I    ;t := i + j - 6;
ADD   AX,J
SUB   AX,6
MOV   T,AX
```

The data registers are 16-bit and so the result of a word multiply is assigned to two registers. The most significant word of the result is assigned to the DX register and the least significant word to AX. The first operand must reside in the AX register. The encoding of $C := A * B$, where all the variables are in memory, is:

```
MOV   AX,A   ;C := A * B
IMUL  B
MOV   C,AX
```

The result is assumed to be a 16-bit value.

A3.3.3   HARDWARE SUPPORT FOR DECISIONS

The branching or jumping mechanism of the Intel 8086 is based on adding a *displacement* to the *IP* register. This discussion is limited to intrasegment jumps, that is to destinations within the same segment. Unconditional jumps (JMP) have a 16-bit signed displacement, whereas conditional jumps are restricted to an 8-bit signed displacement. Conditional jumps operate by testing one or more of the status flags (OF, SF, ZF, CF). The mnemonics and corresponding tests are given in the following table:

Mnemonic	Description	OF	SF	ZF	CF
JA	Jump on above	x	x	0	0
JB	Jump on below	x	x	x	1
JE	Jump on equal	x	x	1	x
JG	Jump on greater than	1	1	0	x
		0	0	0	x
JL	Jump on less than	0	1	x	x
		1	0	x	x
JNA	Jump on not above	x	x	1	0
		0	1	1	1
JNB	Jump not below	x	x	x	0
JNE	Jump on not equal	x	x	0	x
JNG	Jump on not greater than	x	x	0	x
		0	1	x	x
JNL	Jump on not less than	1	1	x	x
		0	0	x	x
JNO	Jump on not overflow	0	x	x	x
JNS	Jump on not sign	x	0	x	x

JO	Jump on overflow	1	x	x	x
JS	Jump on sign	x	1	x	x

The value of the condition code that results in a branch is indicated. The letter x denotes a 'don't care' value. The *Jcc* group of conditional branches and the *JMP* instruction form the basis for selection and sequencing constructs of a high-level language.

A3.3.4 **IF** ... **THEN** ... **ELSE** TEMPLATE

The encoding of the model Pascal **if** statement

if *A* = *B* **then** *S1* **else** *S2*;

is as follows:

```
        MOV   AX,A    ; if a = b
        CMP   AX,B    ; then
        JNE   ELSE
          .
        S1            ;S1
          .
        JMP   NEXT
ELSE:     .           ; else
        S2            ;S2
          .
NEXT:
```

If the difference in memory offsets between the label *ELSE* and the *JNE* instruction is greater than 127 bytes, then the **if** test would have to be recoded as:

```
        MOV   AX,A    ; if a = b
        CMP   AX,B
        JE    THEN
        JMP   ELSE
THEN:                 ; then
```

A3.3.5 **WHILE** AND **REPEAT** LOOP TEMPLATES

An example of each type of loop will be given: the variables *a* and *b* are assumed to be located in memory:

(a) **while** *a* ≠ 0 **do** *S*;

```
WHILE:  CMP   A,0     ; while a ≠ 0
        JE    NEXT    ; do
        S             ;   S;
        JMP   WHILE
NEXT:
```

(b) **repeat** *S* **until** *a* > *b*;

```
         REPEAT:                              ; repeat
                        .
                      S              ;   S;
         UNTIL:    MOV   AX,A        ; until a > b;
                   CMP   AX,B
                   JLE   REPEAT
```

A *JMP* will have to be inserted if the loop is too large. The *hcf* algorithm used in Chapter 6 will be recoded in Intel 8086 assembler to show a complete program with **repeat**, **while** and **if** constructs:

```
HCFDAT      SEGMENT                              ; {declare data segment}

M           DW          258
N           DW          9
T           DW          ?
RES         DW          ?
HCFDAT      ENDS
HCFCOD      SEGMENT
            ASSUME      CS:HCFCOD
            ASSUME      DS:HCFDAT
START:      MOV         AX,HCFDAT        ; {initialize DS}
            MOV         DS,AX
REPEAT:     MOV         AX,M             ; repeat
            CMP         AX,N             ;   if m < n
            JNL         WHILE            ;   then begin
            MOV         BX,M             ;       t := m;
            MOV         T,BX
            MOV         BX,N             ;       m := n;
            MOV         M,BX
            MOV         BX,T             ;       n := t;
            MOV         N,BX             ;     end
WHILE:      MOV         AX,M             ;   while m > = n
            CMP         AX,N             ;   do
            JL          UNTIL
            MOV         AX,N             ;       m := m − n;
            SUB         M,AX
            JMP         WHILE
UNTIL:      CMP         M,0              ; until m = 0;
            JNE         REPEAT
            MOV         AX,N             ; res := n;
            MOV         RES,AX
            HLT
HCFCOD      ENDS
            END         START
```

A3.3.6 FOR LOOP TEMPLATE

A typical form of this loop is

for *i* := *j* **to** *n* **do** *S*;

and its template encoding is as follows:

```
           MOV   AX,J      ; for i := j to n
           MOV   I,AX      ; do
   FOR:    MOV   AX,I
           CMP   AX,N
           JG    NEXT
            .
            .
            .
           S               ;   S;
            .
            .
           INC   I
           JMP   FOR
   NEXT:
```

The variables are assumed to be in memory. If a data register is available, it makes sense to use it for the control variable.

A3.3.7 ARRAYS AND RECORDS

Array variables can be declared in the same manner as for SRM.

```
   VECLB   EQU   1              ; type
   VECUB   EQU   20             ;   vec = array [1 .. 20] of integer;
   VECES   EQU   2
                                ; var
   V       DW    20 DUP(?)      ;   v:vec;
```

The encoding of the simple assignment

$$v[i] := 42;$$

is easily implemented by exploiting base relative and register indirect addressing modes. The offset calculation $(i - LB) * ES$, is developed in BX and memory offset of the ith element in DI.

```
           MOV   AX,I         ; v[i] := 42;
           SUB   AX,VECLB
           MOV   CX,VECES
           IMUL  CX
           MOV   BX, AX
           LEA   DI,V[BX]
           MOV   [DI],42
```

The declaration of records follows the same pattern as with SRM:

```
                                                ; type
                                                ;   time = record
          HOURS   EQU   0                       ;      hours:integer
          MINS    EQU   2                       ;      mins:integer
                                                  end;
                                                ; var
          T1      DW    2 DUP(?)   ;   t1, t2:time
          T2      DW    2 DUP (?)
```

The accessing of individual fields of records can normally use the direct indexed addressing mode. The *DI* or *SI* register contains the base address of the record and the relative address of the field maps onto the displacement. The encoding of the assignment

$$t1 := t2;$$

is as follows:

```
          LEA   DI,T1              ; t1 := t2;
          LEA   SI,T2
          MOV   AX,HOURS[SI]
          MOV   HOURS[DI],AX
          MOV   AX,MINS[SI]
          MOV   MINS[DI],AX
```

If the base type of an array is a record, then the same addressing mode can be used with *DI* or *SI* containing a pointer to the array element. The encoding of the weekly times example from Chapter 7 follows:

```
                                        ; type
TIMDAT   SEGMENT                        ;   time = record
HOURS    EQU      0                     ;      hours:integer;
MINS     EQU      2                     ;      mins:integer;
                                        ;   end;
DAYLB    EQU      1                     ; var
DAYUB    EQU      7                     ;   daytot:array[1 .. 7] of time;
DAYES    EQU      4                     ;
DAYTOT   DW       14 DUP (?)
I        DW       ?                     ;   i, sumhr, sumin:integer;
SUMHR    DW       ?
SUMIN    DW       ?
WTOT     DW       2 DUP (?)             ;wtot:time
TIMDAT   ENDS
TIMCOD   SEGMENT
         ASSUME   CS:TIMCOD
         ASSUME   DS:TIMDAT
START:   MOV      AX,TIMDAT
         MOV      DS,AX
         MOV      SUMHR,0               ; sumhr := 0;
         MOV      SUMIN,0               ; sumin := 0;
         LEA      DI,DAYTOT             ; {initialize DI to point to daytot[1]}
```

```
          MOV       I,1
FOR:      CMP       I,7                 ;for i := 1 to 7
          JG        OUT                 ;do begin
          MOV       AX,SUMHR            ;   sumhr := sumhr + daytot[i].hours
          ADD       AX,HOURS[DI]
          MOV       SUMHR,AX
          MOV       BX,SUMIN            ;   sumin := sumin + daytot[i].mins
          ADD       BX,MINS[DI]
          MOV       SUMIN,BX
          CMP       BX,60               ;   if sumin > = 60
          JL        NEXT                ;   then begin
          SUB       BX,60               ;       sumin := sumin - 60;
          MOV       SUMIN,BX
          INC       SUMHR               ;       sumhr := sumhr + 1
NEXT:     INC       I                   ;   end
          ADD       DI,DAYES            ;end;
          JMP       FOR
OUT:      LEA       SI,WTOT             ;wtot.hours := sumhr;
          MOV       AX,SUMHR
          MOV       HOURS[SI],AX
          MOV       AX,SUMIN            ;wtot.mins := sumin;
          MOV       MINS[SI],AX
          HLT
TIMCOD    ENDS
          END       START
```

A3.3.8 PROCEDURES AND FUNCTIONS

A procedure support is built around the use of a stack, which is used for saving registers and the dynamic allocation of parameter blocks and local variables. The template encoding for the Intel 8086 will be built around three dedicated registers: the stack pointer SP, the base pointer register BP and the source index register SI. The pointer SP contains the offset of the current top of the stack. The offset of the base address of the parameter block will be assigned to BP and the offset of the base address of the local variable area on the stack is assigned to SI.

The instructions to implement the procedure call and return are $CALL$ (call a procedure) and RET (return from call), which make explicit use of the stack:

CALL ⟨label⟩ $(SP) := (SP) - 2; ((SP)) := (IP); (IP) := (IP) + disp;$
RET $(IP) := ((SP)); (SP) := (SP) + 2;$

The $CALL$ instruction first adds the return address to the stack and then transfers control to the ⟨label⟩ specified in the instruction. The RET instruction uses the entry on the top of the stack and assigns it to the IP register.

Registers are saved and restored using the $PUSH$ and POP instructions. The assembler instruction

PUSH   AX

saves the AX register on the stack, automatically updating the stack pointer.

Provided the *SP* register points to the correct memory offset, the instruction

$$POP \quad AX$$

restores the original value from the stack. Registers have to be saved one by one on the stack and are restored in the reverse order to the saving.

Formal parameters are declared using the *EQU* directive and the encoding of the *hcf* example used in Chapter 7:

procedure *hcf* (*m*, *n*:**integer**; **var** *r*:**integer**);

is

$$
\begin{array}{lll}
M & EQU & 0 \\
N & EQU & 2 \\
R & EQU & 4 \\
\end{array}
$$

The allocation of $\langle p \rangle$ bytes of space on the stack for the parameter block and updating *BP* is achieved by the instructions:

$$
\begin{array}{ll}
SUB & SP,\langle p \rangle \\
MOV & BP,SP \\
\end{array}
$$

The base relative addressing mode is suitable for accessing actual parameters, for example the assignment $m := n$ can be encoded as

$$
\begin{array}{lll}
MOV & AX,N[BP] & ;m := n; \\
MOV & M[BP],AX & \\
\end{array}
$$

The assignment $r := m$ encodes as:

$$
\begin{array}{lll}
MOV & DI,R[BP] & ;r := m; \\
MOV & AX,M[BP] & \\
MOV & SS:[DI],AX & \\
\end{array}
$$

The operator *SS*: is required to override the default mapping between the *DI* register and the *DS* segment register, and use the *SS* (stack segment) register instead. All the default mappings between index and pointer registers and the segment registers can be overcome in this way. The declaration of local variables and allocation of space on the stack is done in a similar way, except *BX* is used as a base register.

The template for constructing a procedure is

⟨declare formal parameters⟩

⟨declare local variables⟩

```
⟨procname⟩   PROC
             SUB     SP, ⟨l⟩    ; allocate space for local variables
             MOV     BX,SP
                             .
                             .
                             .
                   ⟨procedure code body⟩
                             .
                             .
                             .
             ADD     SP, ⟨l⟩    ; remove local variables from the stack
             RET
⟨procname⟩   ENDP
```

The template for calling the procedure is

```
      PUSH    AX              ; save registers
      PUSH    BX
      PUSH    CX
      PUSH    DX
      PUSH    BP
      PUSH    DI
      PUSH    SI
      SUB     SP, ⟨p⟩          ; allocate space for parameters
      MOV     BP,SP            ; set BP to offset of parameter block
                   ⟨add parameters⟩
      CALL    ⟨procname⟩        ; activate procedure
      ADD     SP, ⟨p⟩          ; remove parameters from the stack
      POP     SI               ; restore registers of calling routine
      POP     DI
      POP     BP
      POP     DX
      POP     CX
      POP     BX
      POP     AX
```

If registers are not used in the calling routine, then they need not be saved on the stack. The *hcf* example given in Figs. 7.10 and 7.11 is recoded in Intel 8086 assembly language below:

HCFSTA	*SEGMENT*		
STACK	*DB*	200 *DUP* (?)	
HCFSTA	*ENDS*		
HCFCOD	*SEGMENT*		; **program** *ex 7–3*;
	ASSUME	*CS:HCFCOD*	
	ASSUME	*SS:HCFSTA*	
RES	*EQU*	0	; **var** *res*:**integer**;
HCF	*PROC*		; **procedure** *hcf* (*m*, *n*:**integer**;
M	*EQU*	0	; **var** *r*:**integer**)
N	*EQU*	2	
R	*EQU*	4	
T	*EQU*	0	; **var** *t*:**integer**;
	SUB	*SP*,2	; {allocate space for local variables}
	MOV	*SI,SP*	
REPEAT:	*MOV*	*DX*,0	; **repeat**
	MOV	*AX,M*[*BP*]	; *t* := *m* **mod** *n*;
	MOV	*BX,N*[*BP*]	
	IDIV	*BX*	
	MOV	*SS:T*[*SI*],*DX*	
	MOV	*AX,N*[*BP*]	; *m* := *n*;
	MOV	*M*[*BP*],*AX*	
	MOV	*AX,SS:T*[*SI*]	; *n* := *t*;
	MOV	*N*[*BP*],*AX*	
	CMP	*N*[*BP*],0	; **until** *n* = 0
	JNE	*REPEAT*	
	MOV	*DI,R*[*BP*]	; *r* := *m*;
	MOV	*AX,M*[*BP*]	
	MOV	*SS:*[*DI*],*AX*	
	ADD	*SP*,2	
	RET		; **end**
HCF	*ENDP*		
START:	*MOV*	*AX,HCFSTA*	; {*initialize stack & SP*}
	MOV	*SS,AX*	
	ADD	*AX,200*	
	MOV	*SP,AX*	
	SUB	*SP*,2	; {*allocate space for local variables*
	MOV	*SI,SP*	; *and initialize SI*}
	PUSH	*SI*	; {*save only register used*}
	SUB	*SP*,6	; {*allocate parameter block and*
	MOV	*BP,SP*	; *initialize BP*}
	MOV	*AX,25*	; {*add parameters*}
	MOV	*[BP]*,AX	
	MOV	*AX,6*	
	MOV	*2[BP]*,AX	
	LEA	*AX,S-*	
		S:RES [SI]	
	MOV	*4[BP]*,AX	
	CALL	*HCF*	; *hcf (25,6,*res*)*;
	ADD	*SP*,6	; {*remove parameter block*}
	POP	*SI*	; {*restore SI*}
	ADD	*SP*,2	
	HLT		
HCFCO-	*ENDS*		
D			
	END	*START*	

Index

Account, 162, 171, 174
ACIA (asynchronous communications adaptor), 63
Acknowledge, 50, 51, 66, 73–75, 78
Activation, 148, 150, 152, 154, 155
Algorithm, 24–25, 32, 34, 53, 134–135, 137, 143, 146, 150, 171–172, 176
Amplitude, 70
Analogue, 15, 69, 70
Application layer, 67
Arithmetic, 2, 4, 25, 31–33, 36, 46, 113, 123–124
Array, 140–146, 150, 158
ASCII (American Standards Committee for Information Interchange), 20–23, 59–60, 63, 73, 82–83, 92–94, 108–109
Assembler, 110–111, 114–115, 119–124, 132–138, 140, 143, 145–149, 155, 157–158
Asynchronous, 62–63, 75, 78

Backplane, 43
Band printer, 86
Bandwidth, 69, 71–72, 77–78, 95
Base of number, 17, 19, 24–27, 29, 34–35
BCD (binary coded decimal), 23
Binary, 17–20, 23–30, 33–37, 41–42, 61, 70, 121
Bit, 17–20, 23, 28, 30–37, 39–40, 44, 53, 61–63, 65–66, 73, 76–78, 81, 85, 91–92, 94–96
Block, 53–57, 66, 73, 78, 86, 102–104, 106–108
Borrow, 25–27, 113

Branch, 119, 121, 129, 131–132, 149
Bridge, 74
Broadcast network, 76
Buffer, 13–14, 53, 55, 57,73, 91, 103, 107
Bus of computer, 39, 42–44, 47–57, 59–61, 63, 71–72, 76–77, 99, 102

Cable, 2, 43, 61, 65, 67–70, 76, 78
Cambridge Ring, 10, 77–78
CC (condition code of SRM), 32
CCITT (Consultative Committee of the International Telegraph and Telephone), 60, 63, 74
Channel, 71
Character, 7, 9, 17, 20, 23, 50–53, 55, 59–63, 65–67, 69, 71, 73, 75, 78, 80–87, 89, 92–94, 96, 99, 162, 165–167, 172
Checksum, 74, 78
Circuit, electronic, 2, 41–44, 49, 63, 73–75, 78, 93
Clock, 9, 42, 48, 61–62, 77, 167, 169
Coaxial cable, 67, 69, 76, 78
Collision, 76
Communication, 10, 12, 14, 16–17, 20, 23, 39, 57, 59, 63, 65, 67, 69, 71–75, 77–78, 94, 96
Compiler, 1, 13, 110, 119, 149, 160–161
Complement, 27–31
Conversion of numbers, 17, 19, 24–25, 29–30, 34–36
Counter, 2, 4, 44, 46, 50, 51, 53–55, 63, 112, 122–123, 127, 129, 161, 169, 170
CRT (cathode ray tube), 89–90, 92, 94

Cursor, 92–93, 96
Cycle, 48, 51–52, 54–57

Daisy-chain, 51, 57
Datagram, 74
DCE (data circuit-terminating
    equipment), 75
Decision, 32, 129
Decode, 4, 44, 47, 63
Demodulate, 61
Descender, 81, 85
Device, 7, 13, 48, 51–54, 56–57, 63, 80,
    83, 85–87, 89, 94–97, 99, 107–108,
    167
Difference, 26–27
Digit, 15–19, 23–29, 33–37
Digital, 15, 17, 20, 25, 39, 65, 69–70
Directory, 163, 173–176
Disk, 1, 2, 9, 12, 15, 53–57, 80, 99,
    101–104, 107–109, 162, 167, 172,
    175–176
Dispatcher, 169–172, 176
Distributed, 84, 86
Division, 126
DMA (direct memory access), 54–57, 86,
    102–103, 107
Dot matrix, 81, 85–87, 91–92, 96, 99, 108
Drum printer, 86
DTE (data terminal equipment), 74–75
Duplex, 89, 94

Echo, 94
Enable interrupts, 51, 166
Encode, 16, 62–63, 110–111, 122, 142
Error, 17, 23, 36–37, 43, 52, 54, 57,
    61–62, 66, 73–78, 169, 175
Ethernet, 10, 75–78
Exchange information, 15, 17, 39–40, 42,
    48, 57, 59, 61, 63, 65, 67, 71, 73,
    75, 77–78, 80
Execute instruction, 44, 47, 53, 111–114,
    116, 118–119, 121, 127, 131–132,
    136, 148, 174
Exponent, 33–34, 36, 37

Fetch instruction, 2, 4, 44, 47, 51, 112,
    118–119, 121, 127
Fibre optic, 44, 59, 65, 67, 69–71, 76–78
File, 78, 99, 103, 161, 163, 169, 172–176
Floating-point, 33–34, 36–37, 118
Floppy disk, 101, 103
Font, 80–82, 85, 87, 92, 108–109
Format, 31, 33, 36, 73, 76, 115–116,

118–121, 123–124, 128–129, 131,
    142, 146, 148, 150, 153
Fraction, 33–37
Frame, 66, 75, 90–92
Frequency, 48, 61–62, 67, 69–71
Function, 135, 140, 155–158

Gateway, 12, 74
Graph plotter, 96–98
Graphics, 9, 87, 94, 96–98, 109
Gun of CRT, 89, 95

Hardware, 1, 2, 7, 14, 54, 129, 161, 169,
    175–176
hcf (highest common factor), 135,
    146–150, 155
HDLC (high-level data link control), 75
Header, 78
Hexadecimal, 17, 19–20, 24–27, 34–35,
    37, 119, 121
Hierarchical, 65

IEEE (American Institute of Electrical
    and Electronic Engineers), 33, 37,
    76
Immediate instruction, 113, 116–119,
    123–124, 129, 131
Impact printer, 83, 86
Index register, 114–118, 128–129, 131,
    140, 142, 151–152, 155
Indirect address, 117–118
Input, 2, 7, 14, 49, 59, 87, 89, 94, 96,
    161–163, 164–166, 168–170, 173
Integrated (see Circuit)
Interaction, 67, 161–162
Interconnection, 40–41, 60, 65
Interface, 43, 51, 60, 63, 74–76, 84, 86,
    97, 102, 107
Interrupt, 50–57, 63, 112, 166–170
ISO (International Standards
    Organization), 65

Keyboard, 9, 23, 50, 59, 63, 87, 89,
    93–94, 96

LAN (local area network), 10, 12, 59, 75
Laser, 44, 69–71, 86–87
Latency of disk, 103
Letter of alphabet, 15–16, 20, 23, 62,
    80–81, 84–85
Line printer, 86
Link layer, 66, 75
Link register, 149, 153

Literal, 124
Local area network (see LAN)
Local variables, 148–150, 152, 154–155,
    158–159
Logic of computer, 41–42, 46, 48, 51,
    53–54, 57
Longword, 19, 111, 113
Loop of program, 46, 131, 134–137
lsb (least significant bit), 17, 30

Magnetic recording media, 9, 99,
    103–104, 106–108, 173, 175–176
Magnitude of number, 18, 27–30, 33–34,
    37, 103
Mantissa, 33–35
Master, 42, 48, 57
Matrix, 81–82, 84–86, 91–93, 96
Message, 15–17, 40–41, 66–67, 70–73,
    75–76
Microprocessor, 94, 110
Minipacket, 77–78
Minuend, 29–30
Mnemonic, 114–115, 117–124, 131–132,
    137, 148, 153
Modulation, 59, 61, 63, 70–71
Monitor, 77
Monomode, 69
Morse, 15–17, 20
Mouse, 96
Multiaccess, 7, 9, 162, 163, 167, 170–172,
    174–175
Multimode, 69
Multiplexor, 75
Multiplication, 124, 126, 142–143

Negative number, 27–32, 36, 61, 113, 128
Networks, 10, 14, 60, 63, 65–67, 70–76,
    78
Node, 65–66, 71–77

Octal, 17, 19, 20, 24–27
Offset, 142
Operand, 113–119, 124–129, 131–132,
    155
Operating system, 1, 9, 12, 14, 161–169,
    175–176
Operation of instruction, 46–47,
    113–124, 127–129, 131, 142, 148
Optical, 69
os (see Operating system)
OSI (reference model for open systems
    interconnection), 65, 67, 74
Output, 7, 9, 14, 49, 82, 87, 89, 94, 96,

    161–163, 164–166, 169–170, 172
Overflow arithmetic, 30–32, 113
Overlap processes, 162, 165

Packet, 10, 66–67, 73–78
PAD (packet assembler-disassembler),
    12, 75
Parallel, 39, 42–43, 57, 59–61, 165–166
Parameter, 148–152, 154–156, 158–159
Parity, 23, 62–63, 77, 104
Pascal, 1, 14, 110, 114, 119, 121–124,
    127, 129, 131, 135, 137, 140–144,
    146, 149–150, 155, 158, 160
PC (program counter of SRM), 4, 44,
    46–47, 112, 118–119, 127–129,
    131, 148
Peripheral, 7, 9, 12, 14, 49–61, 63, 75, 80,
    82, 84, 86, 99, 108–109, 162,
    166–167
Phase of signal, 62, 70
Physical layer, 65–66, 74–75
Pixel, 90–92, 94–96
Plotter, 96–99
Pointer, 143, 149–150, 155, 168, 174–175
Positive number, 27–32, 36, 61, 129
Power, 17
Preamble, 76–77
Presentation layer, 67
Printer, 13, 80–87, 109, 162, 173
Printing, 80–87
Priority, 169–170
Procedure, 140, 146–150, 152–159
Protection, 163
Protocol, 65, 67, 73–78

Queue, 167–172

Radio, 67, 69
Raster, 90, 94, 96
Real number, 33, 36
Receiver, 17, 40, 42, 44, 61–63, 66,
    68–69, 73–74, 77–78
Record, 53, 140, 144–146, 150–152
Register, 2, 4, 44, 46–47, 50–55, 112–118,
    122–124, 126–129, 131–132,
    134–136, 142–143, 149–155, 157,
    159
Relative address, 96, 142, 145–146,
    151–152, 154
Reliability, 71–72, 175–176
Repeater, 69, 76–77
Response bit, 77

Return from subroutine, 148–149, 153,
    155–157
Ribbon, 43, 83–86
Ring (*see* Cambridge Ring)
Round-robin, 171
Rounding error, 35–37
Routine program, 148–150, 152, 155, 160
RS-232-C (American Electrical Industries
    Association standard VDU), 60,
    63, 66, 75
Runnable process, 167–170

Scheduler, 162, 170–172, 176
Sector of disk, 99, 102–103
Seek disk, 103
Sender of information, 42, 44, 61–62, 66
Serial communication, 59–63, 66, 76, 84,
    86
Serial system, 162, 165
Session layer, 67, 75
Sign of number, 27–33, 36–37
Simplex, 60
Slot, 77
Software, 1–2, 164, 169, 175
SR (status register of SRM), 52–56,
    111–112, 119, 127–129, 131–132
SRM (simple register machine), 14, 31,
    39, 46, 48–51, 53–54, 56, 110–113,
    117–118, 122–123, 138, 140,
    153–154, 157, 160
SRM-and (*see* Appendix 1)
Stack, 149–150, 152–153, 155, 158–159
Standardize number, 33, 35
Star network, 71
Start bit, 62, 66, 73, 77
Status (*see* SR)
Stop bit, 62–63, 66
Stream protocol, 78
Subtraction, 2, 23, 25–30, 32, 37, 124,
    129, 131, 135
Subtrahend, 29–30

Synchronous, 61–63, 75, 78

Tape, 80, 99, 103–104, 106–109, 172, 175
Task, 9, 13–14, 163–166, 167–173
Telephone, 12, 40, 57, 60–61, 63, 65,
    69–71, 73–75
Television, 9, 69, 90, 94–95
Template, 110, 123, 131–137, 140, 142,
    146, 148–149, 153–155, 157–158
Tens complement, 28–29
Terminal of computer, 1, 7, 9–10, 14,
    59–61, 63, 74–76, 80, 90, 92, 94,
    96, 161, 163, 172
Terminal-and (*see* VDU)
Thermal printing, 86
Timeout, 78, 169
Topology of network, 71–72, 75–77
Track of disk, 99, 103–104, 108
Transceiver, 76
Transmission of data, 16–17, 41, 43, 53,
    57, 61–63, 65–71, 74–78
Transport, 66–67, 75
Twisted pair cable, 67–69, 77–78
Twos complement, 28–29, 30–31
Typewriter, 84, 93
Typographic, 81–82

UART (universal asynchronous receiver
    transmitter), 63
Unrunnable process, 169

VDU (visual display unit), 9, 20, 49–53,
    59–60, 63, 66, 87–92, 164
Vector, 141–142
Virtual circuit, 74

Winchester disk, 99, 107
Window manager, 9–10
Word 16 bit, 19, 31, 52–54, 111–115,
    118, 122–124, 126–127, 131, 150,
    154